THE ASSUMPTIONS
ECONOMISTS MAKE

The Assumptions
Economists Make

JONATHAN SCHLEFER

THE BELKNAP PRESS OF
HARVARD UNIVERSITY PRESS

Cambridge, Massachusetts, and London, England
2012

Library of Congress Cataloging-in-Publication Data

Schlefer, Jonathan, 1949–
  The assumptions economists make / Jonathan Schlefer.
    p. cm.
  Includes bibliographical references and index.
  ISBN 978-0-674-05226-0 (alk. paper)
  1. Economics.   2. Economists.   I. Title.
  HB171.S376   2012
  330—dc23   2011042363

To Jane
with love and gratitude

Contents

A Personal Note

The germ of this book was planted more than two decades ago in my efforts to explain economic theory to myself. But why write a book, for myself or anyone else, trying to explain economic theory rather than proposing a concrete solution to one of the world's many urgent problems, such as how to alleviate income inequality or do something about global warming? Because I had grown tired of listening to heated arguments that always seemed to disagree for reasons I could never quite identify. Economics textbooks usually suggested doing nothing. For example, take the 2006 edition of the well-regarded graduate text *Advanced Macroeconomics*, by the relatively liberal economist David Romer. Of course, it wasn't available two decades ago, but I cite it so as not to be guilty of flogging some out-of-date caricature. Based on a standard macroeconomic model, Romer estimated that global warming between 1990 and 2050 might lower global growth by 0.03 percent a year.* That's 0.03

---

* Romer 2006, 43–44. Romer bases his estimate on two earlier efforts by William D. Nordhaus of Yale. I cite Romer because in 2006 he was still suggesting that these results constituted a reasonable scenario.

percent, not 3 percent. To be absolutely clear, if global growth would otherwise have been 3 percent annually, global warming would slow it to 2.97 percent annually. Trivial if you believe the model, and silly if you don't. I wanted some better framework to understand how such disputes arise and what underlies them.

In the 1980s and early 1990s, I was an editor, the managing editor, and the editor-in-chief of MIT's *Technology Review*, a magazine that discussed both promising advances in and important questions about technology. Among other things, we covered the environment (one article featured a photo of a bulldozer burying cardboard boxes labeled "RADIO-ACTIVE" at a nuclear weapons facility), artificial intelligence (Marvin Minsky, a pioneer in the field, argued that it wasn't half bad compared with human intelligence), and the arms race (after crescendoing amid Star Wars rhetoric, it mercifully began to subside as a result of meetings between President Ronald Reagan and Soviet leader Mikhail Gorbachev).

One area we covered regularly was productivity. At the time, practically every U.S. economic problem—from childhood poverty to the Japanese purchase of Rockefeller Center—was being blamed on our faltering productivity. For lack of another author who would produce a piece on a short deadline, I wrote an essay on *Made in America*, the report of the MIT Commission on Industrial Productivity. I asked a dumb question that the flurry of other press coverage about the report never even raised: Does productivity growth really matter, and if so why? I could see why it would matter in a poor nation that produced too little food, housing, transportation, and other essentials for its people. But why in such a rich nation as the United States? Hardship and poverty here principally result not from inadequate production but from maldistribution—a problem evident then and worse today. Economic textbooks declared that any attempt to remedy maldistribution (say, via trade unions or minimum wages) would just worsen unemployment or inflation.* They

* Samuelson and Nordhaus 1989, 440, 711–712.

painted productivity growth as the lodestar of prosperity but suggested no means to improve it. I wasn't convinced, and discovered several opposing conceptions. A "stagnationist" view saw economic problems resulting from weak demand for the plethora of goods that U.S. industry had the capacity to produce if only it could be assured of selling them. "Supply side" economics called for tax cuts and other stimulation for investment to create good jobs. An "institutional" approach (essentially the one adopted in most *Technology Review* articles, as well as by the MIT commission's report) sought specific strategies, such a Japanese just-in-time methods, to correct productivity problems. I wasn't sure how to judge among them. The question continued to trouble me.

Situated partway between journalism and academia at *Technology Review*, I could glimpse the intellectual landscape of political economy but couldn't locate even some of the largest boulders, much less turn them over. I audited a course called "Political Economy I" at MIT. (Where the roman numeral came from I'm not sure; there was no "Political Economy II.") Taught by Suzanne Berger, a political scientist, and Michael Piore, an economist, it examined alternative paradigms for understanding relationships among the economy, state, and society, providing important elements of the framework I sought but also raising more questions. I finally left my job to get a Ph.D. in political science—not anything I would advise sensible people to do in mid-career, but that's another story.

My major areas were international political economy and Latin American politics. Latin America interested me because, as an Argentine friend says, "More happens here in ten years than happens in Switzerland in five hundred." He's surely being unfair to Switzerland, but interesting things were indeed looming large in Latin America, not so unlike things that recently have loomed large across the developed nations. I did field work for my thesis as a visiting researcher at the Economics Institute of the National University of Mexico (Universidad Nacional Autónoma de México, or UNAM).

My thesis, published as *Palace Politics: How the Ruling Party Brought Crisis to Mexico,* examined Mexican politics in the twentieth century. U.S. politics is coming sadly close to resembling its worst features. The Mexican politics that mattered in those days played out between competing groups of political elites. A cooperative arrangement in the 1950s and 1960s ensured that all groups survived politically. If the leader of your group became the next president, your career would progress better than mine; but I would stay in government, and my boss might be president next time. This assurance of survival allowed competing groups to defend the political system's broader interests, not just narrow factional interests. In part as a result (though this fact is often forgotten), Mexico was the South Korea of the day, growing rapidly and steadily as workers' lives progressed. The International Monetary Fund even used the Mexican peso in a basket of currencies to support the French franc and the British pound when currency crises threatened them. But beginning in the 1970s, increasingly life-or-death struggles between political factions tore politics apart and erupted in economic crises, as the factions spent extravagantly and wagered other economic gambles to curry support at any cost in order to win power.

Be warned: as a card-carrying political scientist, I may entertain a certain smoldering envy toward the imperialistic powers of the social sciences—namely, university economics departments. But my outsider's perspective has its uses, since I am duly startled by features of the economics landscape that economists barely notice, so inured have they become to them. Moreover, I'm curious about economics. You need curiosity to write about anything you might criticize, because otherwise you never spend the energy and thought to figure out what it says in the first place. And sometimes when you figure out what it says, criticisms you thought you had evaporate, strengthen, or otherwise change.

During the Ph.D. program, I took several graduate-level economics courses at MIT and Harvard, multivariate calculus and all. Among them was a course in international economics taught by Paul Krugman, before he gained fame as a *New York Times* columnist and Nobel Prize winner but when he was still plying his not-so-humble trade as professor. On the first day of class, apparently to scare away business-school students, he warned, "If you want to learn about international trade, take my undergraduate class. If you want to learn how to be a professor of economics, take this class." I wanted to learn how professors of economics think, so I took his graduate-level class. Krugman was an excellent teacher, stripping complex models to their core, explaining the intuitions behind them, and weighing when they might or might not apply in practice.

I also studied with Lance Taylor. In the 1980s, few economists put much stock in the importance of demand. The first time I met Lance, I asked him why a course he had taught on alternative approaches to macroeconomics, which seemed to be just the thing I was looking for when I wrote the essay on productivity for *Technology Review,* had disappeared from the catalog. "Dropped for lack of demand," he quipped. I stayed in touch with Lance after he left MIT to become director of the Bernard Schwartz Center for Economic Policy Analysis and professor of economics at the New School. I also studied with Murray Milgate, who taught a course at Harvard on the history of economic thought—a vast panorama that I will trace in small part, as a way of understanding what contemporary theory is all about—before he was packed off to Cambridge University.

In researching this book and the economists I discuss, I made my way through their writings in glorious mathematical detail. Let me be direct. This book is not a tirade against mathematics. Math is fun and occasionally useful. I also read recaps in graduate-level texts or review articles that sometimes set out models more clearly. When I had trouble understanding an article, I found that my problem was usually with some twist of economic logic. I worked my way through the math line by line, returned to it, and usually began to see that twist of economic logic, whether or not I was persuaded. I despair of the articles I would have liked to read and couldn't. I had to stop or would have never have written this book at all. Even so, the book has turned out to be more ambitious than I ever imagined.

There are no mathematical requirements for *Assumptions,* but there are thinking requirements. The book is about what economists do in their secret lives as economists, when they aren't dashing off op-eds to tell everybody else what to believe, pulling the wool over undergraduates' eyes in textbooks, or otherwise engaging in public relations. What economists otherwise do is make simplified assumptions about our world, build imaginary economies based on those assumptions—otherwise known as models—and use them to draw practical lessons. In fact, we all do much the same thing less formally when we think about economies, since the real world is way too complicated to understand in all its multitudinous detail. I explain the structure of models in words because nobody disputes the math, and readers of this book don't need to be dragged through it. But grasping the intuitions that good models capture still demands thought. And the real disputes arise about assumptions that underlie a model, how to interpret it (what might this abstraction legitimately be interpreted as implying?), and whether it is at least not wildly inconsistent with experience. Where these disputes arise, my approach, as it was at *Technology Review,* is not to simplify but to roll up my sleeves and explain.

As well as reading extensively, I interviewed a few economists informally and haphazardly. I made some effort to be ecumenical but none to be systematic. For example, one interviewee was Michael Mandel, chief economist of *BusinessWeek.* The most theoretical economics graduate student you ever saw when I first met him at Harvard years back, he has since moved to the far pragmatic end of the spectrum. Another interviewee with a similar-sounding name but who couldn't differ more is Michael Mandler, professor at the University of London, an astonishingly clear thinker about the foundations of economic theory. Thomas Sargent was a principal founder of the "rational-expectations" movement, which took economics by storm in the 1970s. It breathtakingly assumes, as Sargent says, a "communism of beliefs": the true model of the economy that God has decreed is the model that individuals in the economy believe and just happens to be the model that the economist has built. Lance Taylor rejects the very idea of any such unique economic model, believing that one model works pretty well for one economy, another for another, and that the way we think about an economy depends in part on social custom and class. I am obliged to all these and other economists. I hope I haven't distorted what they mean to say, but please don't implicate them in my arguments.

Lance showed sustained interest in and support for my on-again, off-again notion of writing this book. The late Bennett Harrison, an economist who (among many other things) wrote a column for *Technology Review*, helped in early stages of my project. Michael Aronson, social-sciences editor at Harvard University Press, provided unflagging interest and thoughtful comments throughout. My agent Esmond Harmsworth offered critical (in the best sense of the word) comments at key moments. Rawi Abdelal, head of the Business, Government, and International Economy course at Harvard Business School, where I worked while researching and writing the book, provided an enormously supportive environment. Among other things, his observations on the initial draft helped me to frame *Assumptions* far more adequately. The comments of two anonymous reviewers, aside from correcting some details, significantly strengthened the book. Mark Schlefer, my father, offered helpful comments as a noneconomist who follows the economy. Both of my parents, Mark and Marion; my sisters, Kate and Ellen; and my significant other, Jane, provided more support than perhaps any of them realizes.

THE ASSUMPTIONS
ECONOMISTS MAKE

ONE

The Metaphor of
the Invisible Hand

Adam Smith's remark that individuals seeking their own self-interest in markets are led "as if by an invisible hand" to promote the good of society has received mixed reviews—beginning with Adam Smith. His most important work, *An Inquiry into the Nature and Causes of the Wealth of Nations* (1776), paints markets as powerful engines of growth but also of harm. If British banks in his day were allowed to charge exorbitant interest rates of 8 to 10 percent, he warned, they would lend only to "prodigals and projectors."[1] The ensuing speculation would end in financial crashes, like the one caused by the 1772 collapse of the Scottish Bank of Ayr. He therefore urged that regulation limit interest rates to 5 percent, so banks would seek only "sober" clients who made sound investments: "The obligation of building party walls, in order to prevent the communication of fire, is a violation of natural liberty, exactly of the same kind with the regulations of the banking trade which are here proposed."[2]

Unlike Smith, most economists in the 1990s and 2000s seemed blithely unaware of even the possibility that banking deregulation might lead to financial crisis. Barry Eichengreen, an economic historian at the University of California, Berkeley, who has written extensively about the dismal history of financial crises and who was not himself nearly as naïve as he makes out, sums up the consensus view of the profession: "We thought that because changes in central-bank policies had delivered low and stable inflation, the volatility of the pre-1985 years had been consigned to the dustbin of history; they had given way to the quaintly dubbed 'Great Moderation.' We thought that financial institutions and markets had come to be self-regulating—that investors could be left largely if not wholly to their own devices."[3]

"Finance economics"—formal financial models developed since the 1960s that won their authors half a dozen Nobel Prizes—contributed directly to this complacent thinking. In 2003 the editors of the standard encyclopedic volume on the field crowed that it had "influenced public policy throughout the world in a major way, played a crucial role in the growth of a new $100 trillion derivatives industry"—the industry that would generate so many toxic assets by 2008—"and affected how firms are managed everywhere."[4] That's $100 trillion, not a mere $100 billion. And the encyclopedia editors didn't present this accomplishment as a possibly mixed blessing, but as an unalloyed good.

Economists in government weakened financial regulations. Treasury secretary Lawrence Summers, Federal Reserve chairman Alan Greenspan, and Republican senator Phil Gramm championed, among other things, the Commodity Futures Modernization Act of 2000, deregulating financial instruments that often turned toxic.[5] All hold Ph.D.'s in economics. Gramm isn't a serious economist, and Greenspan is a practitioner, not an economist's economist. But Summers, one of the youngest professors ever tenured at Harvard, is a bellwether of the economic mainstream.[6] It was left to Brooksley Born, head of the Commodity Futures Trading Commission—and not coincidentally a lawyer—to try to head off disaster. For her efforts, she was muscled out of the administration.[7]

At the January 2009 meeting of the American Economic Association, I attended a panel of five luminary economists discussing the global financial crisis that was then raging. They had discovered instant explanations blaming greedy Wall Street bankers, inept Washington regulators, and clueless American debtors. So what else is new? Were they born yesterday? But they didn't even ask whether their own thinking might have contributed. In talks by economists to economists, that question was not on the agenda. I would have hoped for a little more reflection about their own thinking.

In this book I discuss how we think about economies, why we often disagree about them, and ways we might understand them better, but I focus particularly on the thinking of economists. As John Maynard Keynes wrote in 1936, "Practical men, who believe themselves to be quite exempt from any intellectual influences, are usually the slaves of some defunct economist."[8] It is dangerous to be slaves of economists (or anybody else), but it is useful to know what they have said. Economists living and dead have espoused an extraordinary range of ideas, clashing head-on across decades and ideologies, and have often developed the clearest formulations for disputing economic ideas, right or wrong. In this account of how we think about economies, I therefore turn back two centuries to Adam Smith and bring the discussion, sometimes leaping forward, sometimes backward again, toward the present.

Before turning back, in this chapter I examine the metaphor of the invisible hand: the notion that decentralized market trading leads, as if by an invisible hand, to a stable and optimal economy. It is a mere metaphor because, weird as it might sound to some readers, economists have never developed a rigorous model—a model that theorists themselves would accept according to their own criteria—showing how decentralized markets could lead to any stable economy at all, let alone an optimal one. The invisible-hand metaphor is hardly the alpha and omega of economic thinking. There have been generations of economists who did not believe in it; there are cutting-edge theorists who have decisively rejected it. But the invisible-hand metaphor seems a useful focus for the first chapter because it has shaped many central economic claims.

This metaphor underlay the misguided thinking that helped to cause the 2008 financial crisis, but I am interested less in the specific causes of this crisis, or its viral spread across other nations, or the sovereign debt crises threatening Greece, Ireland, and Portugal as I write, than in the ways economists think. Until invisible-hand thinking changes, we cannot devise workable ideas to solve a range of problems. One obvious problem is that of re-regulating financial industries. But even if the authorities manage the intellectual reversal of expunging the invisible-hand metaphor from their minds and do bring some stability to the global economy, other problems that this metaphor has helped to create are only now emerging for all to see, like rocky shores as the tide recedes.

For example, the notion that markets best determine the distribution of income—who earns how much—depends on the invisible-hand metaphor because, absent this metaphor, markets alone cannot determine *any* wage at all, let alone an optimal one. In the mid-1980s, Paul A. Samuelson, one of the world's most influential economists, declared that unions and minimum-wage laws cause unemployment, while "a labor market characterized by perfectly flexible wages cannot underproduce or have involuntary unemployment."[9] How such a prominent and often thoughtful economist could have fallen so decisively for a mere metaphor is a puzzle I will take up shortly. But with Democratic economists like Samuelson, the Reagan revolution met little opposition as it attacked unions, minimum wages, and the very concept of a living wage that might help to equalize workers' power in bargaining with multinational corporations. This attack on labor impelled decades of worsening income inequality, as economists such as Frank Levy and Peter Temin of MIT have recently agreed.[10] Stagnant earnings, prompting members of the middle class to borrow against the supposed equity of their homes, arguably contributed to the 2008 crisis. In any event, ever since the crisis deflated that borrowing, income inequality has loomed as a continuing social threat.

The Financial-Deregulation Fad

Financial deregulation was part of a broader deregulatory wave—of airlines, communications, energy, and other industries—that emerged in the 1970s. This innovation was bipartisan. It was not the Republicans but a Democratic economist, Alfred E. Kahn, director of the Civil Aeronautics Board under President Jimmy Carter, who principally launched deregulation in the United States. "I really don't know one plane from the other," he famously declared. "To me, they're all marginal costs with wings."[11]

Some deregulation proved useful, but the most intrepid gamble was surely in finance. In the 1989 edition of the best-selling textbook *Economics*, Paul A. Samuelson and his co-author William D. Nordhaus showed none of Adam Smith's qualms about deregulating interest rates. "In earlier times, lending at interest was a crime," they announce, referring to medieval usury laws.[12] They lament the idea of imposing any legal maximum on interest rates: "While 18 percent a year might seem high for a credit-card or a car loan, this high rate might barely cover administrative costs and the risk of default. What is the result of too low a ceiling on interest rates? Funds dry up." A decade after the fact, they didn't even consider the possible downsides of a 1978 Supreme Court ruling that knocked down those medieval restrictions on credit card rates. After the ruling, credit card companies pushed up interest rates, and as a result, a study by the Federal Deposit Insurance Corporation concluded, the rate of bankruptcy filings quadrupled.[13] In line with Samuelson's view, President Carter signed a law lifting interest rate ceilings on bank accounts and prohibiting states from capping mortgage interest rates.[14] President Ronald Reagan signed the Garn–St. Germain Act deregulating savings-and-loan banks. Both laws helped to lay the ground for the savings-and-loan crisis of the late 1980s and for the 2008 financial crisis.

The developing world proved fertile ground for financial experiment. After General Augusto Pinochet grabbed dictatorial power in Chile in 1973, for lack of any idea what to do about the economy, he turned to "los Chicago boys," Latin Americans' nickname for the famously free-market economists from the University of Chicago.[15] (They like the English word "boys" in the phrase, as it rolls off the tongue better than the Spanish equivalent.) Los Chicago boys deregulated finance, inflating a financial bubble. Business conglomerates known by epithets such as the "Piranhas" and the "Crocodiles" used loans from banks they owned to buy stock in firms they owned, luring in foreign speculators.[16] When this financial house of cards collapsed in 1982, leaving Chile an "economic disaster," as the *Economist* categorized it, the government declared that the foreign speculators had gambled and lost.[17] Not so fast: the International Monetary Fund (IMF) and New York banks forced Chile to bail the foreigners out. While Socialist president Salvador Allende had left Chile with $7 billion of debt in 1973, los Chicago boys saddled it with three times that much by 1982.[18] After firing four finance ministers in a row, Pinochet finally found one who seemed to know what he was doing.[19] Chile kept proclaiming its free-market credentials—and preserved some useful free-market reforms alongside some useful state industrial policies—but quietly instituted controls on international financial flows. The economy did splendidly.

An unsobered IMF, staffed by Ph.D. economists (albeit tarred as third-rate graduates of top schools), along with rest of the "Washington Consensus" and enthusiastic politicians in developing countries, set about "liberalizing" finance.[20] Economists spoke of "liberalizing" rather than "deregulating," since, in their fanciful world, developing countries weren't just supposed to lift interest-rate ceilings and free global financial flows, but were to institute "prudential" supervision. The idea was that they would ensure banks complied with frameworks to limit exposure to risk.[21] Of course, most developing countries did no such thing. But then, neither did the United States, which economists supposed had already instituted state-of-the-art prudential supervision. Carlos Díaz Alejandro, an unorthodox economist, wrote a prescient article in 1985 titled, "Goodbye Financial Repression, Hello Financial Crash." Just to mention some highlights, the 1994 Mexico crisis, the 1997 Asia crisis, the 1998 Russian crisis, and the 2001 Argentine crisis were the worst such events that had struck those economies since the 1930s.

Financial liberalization was an important cause of these crises. In 1998—the first time economists seem to have done a comprehensive study of the results of the financial-liberalization wave—John Williamson and Molly Mahar found that there was "ample reason to believe that the process can spawn financial crisis."[22] Williamson is none other than the economist who coined the term "Washington Consensus."[23] The World Bank, itself a sometime promoter of financial liberalization, found that this policy had helped to exacerbate crises by fueling "rapid growth in credit to weak public and private enterprises and the government, as well as real estate."[24]

Undaunted by failures of poor countries that obviously didn't get "prudential" supervision, the Clinton administration passed two seminal pieces of financial deregulation. I've mentioned the sorry tale of the Commodity Futures Modernization Act of 2000. Prominent economists also championed the repeal of the major Depression-era law intended to safeguard the banking industry, the 1933 Glass-Steagall Act. "At the end of the 20th century, we will at last be replacing an archaic set of restrictions with a legislative foundation for a 21st-century financial system," Lawrence Summers proclaimed.[25] Glass-Steagall had separated commercial banks (the kind we used to deposit our savings in) from investment banks (the kind that used to trade financial instruments). The repeal allowed commercial banks, as well as insurance companies such as the suicidal American International Group (AIG), to go into high-profit, high-risk speculative adventures.

Economists broadly supported the repeal of Glass-Steagall, the *Washington Post* and the *New York Times* reported. Economists ridiculed the

old canard, going back to Adam Smith, that letting banks charge whatever interest rates they chose might lure them into making bad loans.[26]
And they insisted that banks' financial speculation had not caused the
11,000 bank failures that occurred during the Great Depression.[27] In *A
Monetary History of the United States,* the Nobel laureate Milton Friedman and the economist Anna J. Schwartz had argued that the Federal Reserve's inept policies, not unregulated private finance, caused the
Great Depression.[28] This view had swept the profession.[29] For example,
in 2002, a financial economist by the name of Ben Bernanke, on the
Federal Reserve Board though not yet its chairman, lauded Friedman at
a conference honoring his ninetieth birthday: "I would like to say to Milton and Anna: Regarding the Great Depression. You're right, we did it.
We're very sorry. But thanks to you, we won't do it again."[30] Imagine
Bernanke's surprise in 2008, when Friedman's theory blamed him, as
chairman of the Fed, for doing just what he had promised not to and
causing the financial crisis. In the wake of the crisis, governments made
some effort to re-regulate finance, though the results have been criticized
as insufficient. In any event, conventional thinking will trump what's
written on paper. If conventional thinking fails to reject the invisible-
hand metaphor, it will prepare the way for future crises.

The Invisible Hand That Couldn't Be Found

As a few members of the profession have charged, including the *New
York Times* columnist Paul Krugman and the New York University professor Nouriel Roubini, some bad models led economists astray. But the
problem goes deeper. The really strange thing is that economists had
developed some useful models that should have warned of the danger of
crisis. These were not obscure models. They belonged to a prominent
line of research—"general-equilibrium theory"—about the fundamental
nature of markets. It concluded decades ago that the invisible hand is
just a metaphor. Even perfect markets do *not* lead an economy to equi-

librium. They are unstable. This conclusion is as decisive as any in economics has ever been.

I am not voicing my own opinion here but just reporting consensus conclusions. To be sure, economists always hoped to reach the opposite conclusion. Beginning in the 1870s, theorists sought to build a model of the invisible hand. They wanted to show how market trading among individuals, pursuing self-interest, and firms, maximizing profit, would lead an economy to a stable and optimal equilibrium. Those theorists never succeeded. Quite the contrary: in the early 1970s, after a century of work, they concluded that no mechanism can be shown to lead decentralized markets toward equilibrium, unless you make assumptions that they themselves regarded as utterly implausible.

The canonical effort along these lines is the general-equilibrium model published in 1954 by the Nobel laureates Kenneth Arrow of Stanford University and Gerard Debreu of the University of California. It is called a *general*-equilibrium model because it seeks to understand the interaction of all markets across an economy. Arrow and Debreu did prove that, if you make assumptions intended to characterize competitive markets and rational actors, there is always a set of prices at which supply would equal demand. However, no one was ever able to demonstrate that some invisible hand would actually move market prices toward this level. It is just a set of prices that might balance supply and demand if by some chance it happened to occur. Since there is an infinite number of possible sets of prices in the model, the probability that such a special set of prices would occur is zero.

Frank Hahn, a general-equilibrium theorist at Cambridge University, sums up efforts to model the invisible hand: "We have no good reason to suppose that there are forces which lead the economy to equilibrium."[31] Of course, economists tell a story about the "law of supply and demand," Hahn hastens to add. "Here the invisible hand is actually set in motion. When demand of anything exceeds its supply the price will go up, and vice versa when supply exceeds demand." But the story is not credible:

"In taking this account seriously, one finds oneself studying a rather complex dynamic system. It is a fact that this study has not led to the conclusion that this behavior of prices must guide the economy to its tranquil equilibrium. Indeed, almost the converse is true: only very special assumptions seem to ensure this happy outcome."[32] By "very special" assumptions, Hahn means assumptions that are not generally credible.

An engineering analogy may help to illustrate the point. The invisible hand sees market economies as being like passenger planes, which, for all the miseries of air travel, are at least aerodynamically stable. Buffeted by turbulence, they just settle back into a slightly different flight path. General-equilibrium theory showed that economies are more like military jets. Buffeted by the slightest gust, they wouldn't just settle into a slightly different path but would spin out of control and break asunder if "fly-by-wire" computer guidance systems did not continually redirect their flight paths to avert disaster.

Stranger and Stranger

A closer look at general-equilibrium theory and the metaphor of the invisible hand is useful. Any serious economics theory text, such as Hal Varian's *Microeconomic Analysis*, includes several chapters on general equilibrium, but the noneconomist could be excused for having heard little about it. While physicists incessantly debate the foundations of their field in the press, even if at a simplified level that the rest of us can pretend to understand, economists just issue pronouncements. My search of the *New York Times* index since 1981 turned up 199 hits for "string theory" but only 11 for "general equilibrium," most of which were just book titles or other passing mentions. Twice the phrase was used as a synonym for geeky and incomprehensible, and only one reporter tried to explain it—in two sentences. Why hasn't general-equilibrium theory trickled down? I expect because it failed to develop the coherent basis for the invisible-hand metaphor that economists wanted.

General-equilibrium theorists assumed perfect markets, but not because they believed that markets actually are perfect.[33] Rather, they hoped to build an idealized invisible-hand model that would provide a framework for more realistic models incorporating observable "imperfections" such as monopolies, trade unions, protectionism, or what-have-you. Kenneth Arrow has said that his Ph.D. exams were focused largely on imperfect competition, and he believed that "competitive equilibrium was not a good description of the economy."[34] Rather, in building a general-equilibrium model, he "wanted to clear up what the theory was." Precisely what did you have to assume to get a perfect-market economy to work?

Arrow and Debreu made about a dozen assumptions aimed at characterizing what economists mean by "competitive markets" and "rational actors." There are many different individuals, firms, and goods.[35] "Rational" individuals can have almost any preferences they want, no matter how whimsical. I might like to eat at McDonald's, and religion might dictate your diet. But if we're "rational" actors, we must be consistent—if I prefer A to B, and B to C, I cannot turn around and prefer C to A. Firms can have a variety of production technologies. But if one assumes "competitive markets," then increasing returns to scale, important in any actual economy, are ruled out. Increasing returns occur, for example, when automakers can produce 100,000 cars at a lower per-unit cost than they can if they produce only 10,000. Increasing returns allow a few firms to capture a market and charge monopolistic prices, so they are assumed away to create the theoretical conditions for competitive markets.

According to Arrow and Debreu's assumptions, goods are distinguished by place and date. For example, toothpaste delivered in Boston on January 1, 2020, is a different commodity from toothpaste delivered in the Australian outback on the same date—it would presumably cost more in the outback. Goods also are distinguished by the "state of nature." An umbrella delivered when it's raining is a different commodity from the umbrella delivered when the weather is clear. You can agree to purchase goods depending on the state of nature. You can even contract for payments at a future date if you are unemployed: your job status is treated as an aspect of the state of nature. In other words, you can insure against anything.[36]

How does the Arrow-Debreu model economy based on these assumptions operate? There is actually no trade between individuals, but, rather, an imaginary auction at the beginning of time. Before any production or consumption occurs, an "auctioneer" calls out proposed prices for every good. All "agents" report back how much they would freely produce or consume at those prices. The auctioneer might raise the price of a good if the demand for it exceeds supply, and might lower the price if the supply of it exceeds demand.

Given their assumptions about individuals, firms, and markets, and using the auctioneer mechanism, Arrow and Debreu prove that there always exists at least one set of prices for all goods that the auctioneer need not change. At those prices, the amount of each good that consumers report they will freely demand, given their preferences, exactly equals the amount that firms report they will freely supply, given their efforts to maximize profits. This is an "equilibrium."

The proof involves applying a remarkable piece of mathematics: the "fixed-point theorem" of topology. To give a physical example, the fixed-point theorem says that if you pour coffee into a cup, swirl it around, and let it settle down again, at least one infinitesimal point in the coffee must end up in exactly the same spot where it started. It is a fixed point. When I first saw the application of this theorem to economics, it struck me as somehow both fascinating and appalling. How could a type of geometry be twisted into implying this central proposition about economies? But mathematics is the ultimate abstraction: the same theorem can describe utterly different phenomena.

Arrow and Debreu invented an imaginary shape—a sort of multi-dimensional coffee cup—representing an economy. Each point in the shape corresponds to some set of prices. Moving a point, say, one unit to the right corresponds to raising the price of some good by one unit. In effect, if agents tell the auctioneer they would demand more of that good than firms say they would produce at a given price, the auctioneer might move the point to the right to increase its price. In response to reports from firms and consumers, the auctioneer thus keeps stirring points around. At least one point must remain fixed. If the auctioneer calls out the set of prices corresponding to that point, consumers demand exactly as much of each good as producers supply. This is an economic equilibrium. Q.E.D.

The equilibrium is "Pareto optimal," a concept invented by the nineteenth-century Italian economic and political theorist Vilfredo Pareto. Suppose everyone owns some goods. The situation is Pareto optimal if no individual can be made better off by acquiring goods that he or she considers preferable without another individual's being forced to accept goods that he or she considers worse. Given the Arrow-Debreu free-trade setup, the conclusion about optimality seems little more than a fancy way to restate the obvious: If you have something I want, and I have something you want, we can gain from free exchange. When no one can gain from free exchange, the economy is optimal.

So powerful is the invisible-hand metaphor, that economists supposed that the auction process would lead to a stable economy: they thought that as the auctioneer cried out prices, agents responded, and the auctioneer adjusted prices, the economy would inexorably move toward a tranquil equilibrium.[37] Indeed, the model makes assumptions that seem calculated to help markets lead toward an equilibrium. Among other things, it prohibits destabilizing speculation. In the real world, you can buy pork belly futures as a bet that the price will go up, but in Arrow-Debreu if you buy pork belly futures, you're going to get a truckload on your doorstep. And you can't even sell it because all sales were final at the auction at the beginning of time. There is no second auction.

However, not long after Arrow and Debreu published their model, theorists began to suspect that the auctioneer's process—and by implication competitive markets—might not drive an economy to equilibrium. In 1960 Herbert Scarf of Yale invented an Arrow-Debreu economy that was unstable, cycling among different sets of prices.[38] The prospects for carving out some plausible assumption that could make an Arrow-Debreu economy stable steadily dimmed, until, in the early 1970s, three seminal papers, one by none other than Gerard Debreu, eliminated "any last forlorn hope" of proving stability, as the MIT theorist Franklin Fisher says.[39] "The extremely relevant 'stability problem' has never been solved either rigorously or sloppily," agrees the economic historian Mark Blaug.[40] "Cycles of any length, chaos, or anything else you can describe" could disrupt the economy, says the Tufts University economist Frank Ackerman, a critic of general-equilibrium theory: "Not only does general equilibrium fail to be reliably stable; its dynamics can be as bad as you want them to be."[41]

It's worth noting *why* the single-point theorem does not imply that the auction process should lead, as if by an invisible hand, toward equilibrium. The theorem merely says that, among the infinite number of points in the multidimensional coffee cup representing the economy, there happens to exist one that is fixed—at which the supply of each good would balance the demand for it. If by sheer accident the auctioneer happened to call out that set of prices, he, she, or it would find that supply would perfectly balance demand. But the fixed-point theorem does *not* say that the auctioneer's rules for adjusting prices would ever lead prices to that magic level. As the auctioneer pushes prices of multitudinous goods up or down, the economy might just keep swirling forever. Choosing the right prices to balance supply and demand for all goods would be comparable to divining, before the cup was stirred, which infinitesimal point in the coffee would wind up exactly where it started.

Assumptions can be invented to ensure that the Arrow-Debreu model is stable. One possibility is to assume that all goods are "gross substitutes."[42] For example, butter and margarine are plausibly gross substitutes, in that if the price of butter increases, people are likely to demand more margarine as a substitute. An Arrow-Debreu economy is stable if *every* good is a gross substitute for *every other* good—for example, if the price of gasoline quadruples, people will demand more SUVs as a substitute. But no one believes that idea. The assumption that all goods are gross substitutes, Fisher told me, is known in the field as the "Santa Claus" condition.[43]

Some economists might call the fighter-jet analogy I suggested a polemic, or might object to Ackerman's tone, but no knowledgeable theorist would claim that Arrow-Debreu is stable. Thus, economists have misappropriated the very word "equilibrium" to describe a situation that is not an equilibrium, either in plain English or in engineering. This is more than a semantic quibble. Economic equilibrium—a stable state toward which an economy would move—reveals a hope on the part of economists, not a mechanism that they have captured in a credible model. Continuing to speak of "equilibrium" allowed them to fool themselves—and others—into thinking they had shown that perfect-market economies were stable.

What Were Economists Thinking?

How did macroeconomists, who study the operation of economies as a whole, manage to ignore general-equilibrium theorists' negative conclusions about the invisible hand? To begin with, macroeconomics established a foothold in the 1950s and 1960s, while most economists still assumed that some invisible hand was at work in the economy. So-called Keynesian economists constituted the mainstream. (Whether their models had much to do with what Keynes actually said is a debate I will avoid for the moment.) They held that markets are self-regulating but that various impediments prevent them from moving toward an optimal equilibrium. Among other things, wages and prices are "sticky"—they do not adjust as rapidly as a strong invisible hand might ensure. As a result, economies can badly underperform. Governments could play an important role in "fine-tuning" economies, speeding their otherwise halting course toward optimal equilibrium.

It was never quite clear why sticky prices and wages should cause such outsized trouble. As James Galbraith of the University of Texas puts it, in the fall semester "microeconomics" class about optimizing agents, you learned how prices and wages automatically adjust to balance supply and demand. Over winter break, those lessons sank into oblivion. In the spring semester "macroeconomics" class, you learned that sticky prices and wages cause serious recessions.[44]

Robert Lucas won the Nobel Prize in economics for noticing winter break. He challenged the idea of sticky prices. If there is some shortfall in demand for widgets, and widget makers aren't selling their product, why don't they just cut prices? He couldn't understand sticky wages either. Why would workers refuse pay cuts that would lower production costs, boost sales, and save their jobs? There must be a reason that business cycles occur even if people respond sensibly to the forces of supply and demand. In 1972 Lucas published a model that assumes the invisible hand is at work. Firms instantaneously adjust prices to balance supply and demand as they perceive it. They try to push markets to instantaneous equilibrium. But the central bank messes things up. It fools firms by tampering with the money supply and inflation, so they misjudge real prices. To the extent that firms are fooled, they adjust prices suboptimally, causing booms and busts. Thus, inept government efforts to smooth business cycles actually cause them. Lucas's model supports Friedman's argument that the Fed caused the Great Depression.

Macroeconomists began to build models attempting to show how the "microeconomics" of firms and consumers making optimal decisions in an invisible-hand economy might be reconciled with the "macroeconomics" of business-cycle booms and busts that hardly look optimal. So long as markets are competitive, these models depict perfect invisible-hand economies. However, various factors can impinge on the invisible hand. External shocks—moments of technological dynamism followed by moments of stagnation—can drive cycles of growth and decline. Alternatively, market imperfections, such as a central bank that ineptly manages the money supply or monopolistic firms that refuse to cut prices, can cause business cycles.

If general-equilibrium theorists were unable to model an invisible-hand economy, how did macroeconomists manage to build models with an underlying invisible hand? Unlike the Arrow-Debreu model, their models do not depict distinct consumers, firms, and commodities, but rather aggregate—or homogenize—them. For example, they aggregate corn seed, machine tools, software, and all other productive inputs into one uniform quantity of stuff that they call "capital" and label "K." Most important, they homogenize diverse individuals into one "representative agent," or perhaps two or three agents, such as one worker and one retiree. Thus, although macroeconomists claimed to base their models on the "microfoundations" of optimizing individuals—the very label sounds like a Good Housekeeping seal of approval—it was less than truth-in-advertising. If you homogenize all individuals and commodities in aggregate models, it is mathematically easy to build stability into the defining equations as a pure assumption. But it is a pure assumption. If you want, you can just as easily build instability into the model's defining equations.

Economists boasted of their new "dynamic stochastic general-equilibrium" models—truly a phrase to inspire shock and awe.[45] The dynamic and stochastic aspects don't really matter here, but I hasten to allay the reader's curiosity. The models are "dynamic" in that they attempt to capture not a static picture of an economy, but a movie progressing frame by frame over time. They are "stochastic" in that they suppose economies are hit by random shocks, such as technological dynamism and stagnation. The term "stochastic" comes from *stokhos*, Greek for "target." A stochastic process throws metaphorical darts at a target and misses by random amounts. Thus, a "dynamic stochastic general-equilibrium" model depicts an economy that changes frame-by-frame over time, is hit by random shocks, and treats all markets as instantaneously and eternally in equilibrium. It's called a "DSGE model," for short. For once, the acronym is less painful than the term itself. But although general equilibrium is woven into the very name, such models starkly ignore key general-equilibrium instability results. Instead—and perhaps this is the weirdest part of a supposedly scientific theory—they are founded on pure faith in an invisible hand.

These models are mathematically elaborate, despite simplifying assumptions. Perhaps the mathematics lured economists into forgetting that, at a fundamental level, the models are just a tautology: the model economy is stable because it is assumed to be stable. Just looking at results, economists grew ever more optimistic that markets are self-regulating.[46] Central bankers such as Bernanke used DSGE models, and economists saw the models as anchoring an era of "Great Moderation." They elaborated the study of the Great Moderation into a whole subfield. Robert Lucas declared in his 2003 presidential address to the American Economic Association that the "central problem of depression-prevention has been solved, for all practical purposes."[47]

Failure to warn of the impending crisis rested on nothing more or less than faith in the invisible-hand metaphor. Alan Greenspan—more cautious about formal economics than some of his colleagues, since he was already a prominent financial consultant before he received his Ph.D. in economics—concedes that not a model but "ideology" led him to believe that "free competitive markets are by far the unrivaled way to organize economies."[48] Many economists thought the same way without even realizing it.

How Did Economists Forget?

How could macroeconomists in the 1970s incorporate the invisible-hand story ever more tightly into their models, even as general-equilibrium theorists abandoned it? The sociology of the profession is part of the reason. Macroeconomics constitutes one kingdom of the discipline; microeconomics, another. General-equilibrium theory is only a fiefdom within microeconomics. Even though general-equilibrium theory investigates the operation of an entire economy, it is considered part of microeconomics because it does not aggregate individual consumers, firms, and commodities. Thus, Hal Varian covers general equilibrium in *Microeconomic Analysis*. It is a big step away from macroeconomics.

Furthermore, stability is only one topic within general equilibrium. Varian runs through some mathematical-instability results on pages 398 to 400, but without serious discussion of their significance. And after slogging through 398 pages of calculus, you can easily miss the formal results. I did. In talking with Duncan Foley, a wide-ranging theorist at the New School, I mentioned that I didn't recall anything in Varian about general-equilibrium instability. He assured me it was there, but added, "You would miss it."[49] Sure enough, I found it on reviewing Varian.

Varian's three forgettable pages on the instability results are about all the typical graduate student who plans to be a macroeconomist will likely encounter. Michael Mandler, a theorist at the University of London, notes that practical economists have very limited knowledge of general-equilibrium theory: "They had three weeks of it in one course in grad school and regarded it as too mathematical and for geeks." As well, academia is not set up to encourage individuals in one subdiscipline to worry about what goes on in another: "There is no professional reward for doing so," as Mandler says. Thoughtful attention to general-equilibrium theory would only get in the way of macroeconomists' ability to publish models in journals and get tenure.

Still, the best macroeconomists are not ignorant of the instability results. How do they respond? "The mathematical failure of general equilibrium is such a shock to established theory that it is hard for many economists to absorb its full impact," suggests Frank Ackerman.[50] They simply practice several "styles of denial." Sophisticated researchers agree sotto voce, but do not set down in writing, that "no one" believes general-equilibrium stability anymore. Ackerman adds: "The profession has moved on to game theory, complexity theory, evolutionary frameworks, and other techniques." Someone should tell those innocents who build general-equilibrium models for the Federal Reserve that the cognoscenti have long since gone on to bigger and better things.

Milton Friedman once told Franklin Fisher that he saw no point in studying the stability of general equilibrium because the economy is obviously stable—and if it isn't, "we are all wasting our time."[51] Fisher quips that the point about economists' wasting their time was rather perceptive. The point about economies being obviously stable was *not* perceptive. Properly speaking, economies are never stable, since prices of goods such as gold or oil are perpetually changing in ways that cannot be anticipated even a moment ahead.

True, economies mostly avoid catastrophic fluctuations—except, of course, when they don't. But what mostly saves them? Theorists' failure to model an invisible hand, even if markets were perfectly competitive, is ironically powerful. If economists since the late nineteenth century have failed to model how some invisible hand might move perfect markets toward equilibrium, why should we believe that any such mechanism exists? Something outside markets—such as social norms, financial regulation, or Ben Bernanke in his happier moments—perhaps averts disaster. Friedman's claim that markets are self-regulating and that only inept government monetary policy caused the Great Depression is not only wrong in practice, but wrong in theory as well.

The Rational Speculator

The Arrow-Debreu model is so abstract that it leaves an important question unanswered: Just why is an imagined perfect-market economy unstable? Franklin Fisher, who does practical as well as theoretical economics—he served as chief economist for the Justice Department's antitrust suit against Microsoft—developed a more realistic general-equilibrium model that suggests an answer. In short, the answer is speculation. When published twenty-five years ago, Fisher's *Disequilibrium Foundations of Equilibrium Economics* was received favorably but with little fanfare. Why didn't it get more attention? He is a well-respected professor in a top university department. I suppose economists just didn't want to hear more about the problems of so-called general equilibrium.

Fisher makes more realistic assumptions than Arrow-Debreu. Dispensing with the auctioneer, that grand central computer cranking out prices at the beginning of time, he allows people to continue to trade as they produce and consume. He allows for the possibility of monopolistic pricing. He incorporates money, where Arrow-Debreu has only barter. He hoped to show how markets would lead an economy to equilibrium, now in a real sense. His imagined economy is initially out of equilibrium, and he asks whether decentralized trading can lead it, as if by an invisible hand, toward an equilibrium where prices stop changing. He didn't manage to prove that an economy will reach equilibrium, but he missed in a fascinating way.

To think about whether an economy might reach an equilibrium, first consider what might drive it out of equilibrium—why prices might change. For one thing, external shocks to markets can make prices change. The discovery of vast North Sea oil reserves around 1970 and the loss of oil production after the 1979 Iranian Revolution drove changes in oil prices, hence in many other prices. Another possibility is technological innovation. Improvements in the design and production of integrated circuits dramatically lowered computing prices over the course of decades. The dot-coms built a whole new range of Internet services, creating goods and demand for them that had never existed before. The Harvard economist Joseph Schumpeter famously argued that innovation, interrupting what he called the "circular flow" of markets in equilibrium, drives development.

If such external shocks were the only mechanisms that interrupted the circular flow, they would not undermine the idea of the invisible hand. That idea only needs to suppose that trading in markets drives economies *toward* equilibrium. If innovation or resource discoveries strike from outside markets, and markets themselves move to restore the circular flow of equilibrium, then it would be a good enough invisible hand.

The problem is that, rather than restoring the circular flow, markets may disrupt it further. Consider the dot-coms. One entrepreneur had an innovative idea, persuaded investors, hired workers, and made money. Another entrepreneur had an idea that would flop, but its ultimate fate was not immediately known. This entrepreneur went through the same initial steps, generating activity and helping to inflate the dot-com bubble. There was no clear line showing where innovation stopped and the bubble started. As Greenspan noted in January 2000, imagining what people might say from the vantage point of 2010:

> We may conceivably conclude that, at the turn of the millennium, the American economy was experiencing a once-in-a-century acceleration of innovation, which propelled forward productivity, output, corporate profits, and stock prices at a pace not seen in generations, if ever. . . . Alternatively, that 2010 retrospective might well conclude that a good deal of what we are currently experiencing was just one of the many euphoric speculative bubbles that have dotted human history. And, of course, we cannot rule out that we may look back and conclude that elements from both scenarios have been in play in recent years.[52]

Pure perceptions, right or wrong, operating through markets, can disrupt equilibrium. Suppose a major wheat trader suddenly concludes that a blight will strike the harvest next year, raising prices. The trader buys wheat futures, moving the market. Other owners of wheat futures reap unexpected gains, which they may use to make additional investments. Prices keeps moving, rather than settling toward equilibrium.

Looking at the problem from another perspective, consider how the rational individuals of economic theory might act to move an economy toward equilibrium. They must realize that it is out of equilibrium—that supply and demand are not balanced at current prices—and try to benefit from price changes they expect.[53] If Macintosh apples are piling up on shelves, but Cortlands are disappearing, speculators grab Cortlands to sell at a profit. They may drive the price higher than consumers who just want to eat Cortlands would pay. Such a process happened in the U.S. housing market in the early 2000s, and happens all the time in commodity markets. Financial institutions employ sophisticated techniques to project where prices are heading, and act on these perceptions, right or wrong. These techniques are often developed by Ph.D. mathematicians not notably preoccupied with general equilibrium. The very actions that rational individuals take to move prices out of disequilibrium may inflate bubbles, rather than moving an economy toward equilibrium.

The invisible-hand metaphor was only one factor leading the way to the financial crisis. But if supposedly practical economists had admitted to the rest of us—and to themselves—that it was merely a metaphor, policymakers might not have knocked out all the props that held things somewhat steady. How economists think is an issue that matters. They should clearly say what they don't know, not just broadcast what they think they know. And they should explain the assumptions underlying what they think they know. In the following chapters, I underline at least some of the key assumptions that give rise to disputes over economic ideas.

TWO

What Do Economists Do?

In his well-known textbook *Economics,* Paul Samuelson depicts our economic world as being like the universe of Newtonian physics. Though he concedes that deciding on policies may involve value judgments—eliminating rent control may hurt individuals, even though it benefits the economy—he promises to focus on the economic science of cause-and-effect. "*Positive economics* describes the facts and behavior in the economy," he insists.[1] The emphasis is his. Questions in this realm may be "easy or tough," but they "can be resolved only by reference to facts." In another popular text, Walter Nicholson similarly tells students: "'Positive' economists believe that one reason for the success of economics as a discipline is that it has been able to emulate successfully the positive approach taken by the physical sciences rather than becoming involved in the value-laden normative approach taken by some of the other social sciences."[2]

Economists' insistence that their discipline is like physics sounds a little nervous. Did you ever hear a physicist boast to the world that that physics is like economics? More important, when they talk about economics this way, Samuelson, Nicholson, and other economists are misrepresenting what they do and what economics is. From Adam Smith to Karl Marx, from John Maynard Keynes to Milton Friedman, economists have sought to gain insight into economies by building models of them. They make simplified assumptions about the economic world we inhabit and construct imaginary economies—in other words, models—based on those assumptions. They use these imaginary economies to draw practical conclusions about the actual economies we inhabit.

Nearly everything economists do is based on some model. For example, the famous story that prices are determined by supply and demand is a model. Consider the price of oil. On the one hand, there is supposed to be an upward-sloping "supply curve": the higher the price of oil rises, the more oil producers want to pump. This curve is an imaginary construct intended to describe the different amounts of oil that producers *would* pump at any given time, if oil prices *were* at different levels. On the other hand, there is supposed to be a downward-sloping "demand curve": the lower the price of oil falls, the more businesses and consumers want to buy. This curve is likewise an imaginary construct intended to describe the different amounts of oil that consumers and businesses *would* buy at any given time if prices *were* at different levels. The point where the imaginary curves intersect—where the price is such that the amount of oil producers would pump just equals the amount of oil businesses and consumers would buy—is supposed to determine the actual price of crude oil and the amount of oil that is pumped.

All we ever see is the point where the imaginary curves are supposed to intersect: the actual oil price. Nobody has ever seen supply or demand curves; they are models. They can be useful, but should not be mistaken for a literal picture of reality. If you trace, over time, the movement of actual gasoline prices versus consumption, you see loops and zigs and zags that don't look anything like imagined supply and demand curves.[3]

Moreover, some factors that affect oil prices are inconsistent with the model. For example, energy-intensive industries such as aluminum smelters may hedge against possible oil price increases by entering into contracts to buy oil at some fixed price at a given date in the future. Oil producers sell such contracts. They also speculate by buying such contracts. They have insider information about oil prices—if a platform explodes, the firm that owns it knows before the public gets the news—but are exempt from laws against insider trading. Alexander Elder, a commodities trader, describes visiting a friend at the trading desk of a multinational oil company: "After passing through security that was tighter than at Kennedy International Airport, I walked through glass-enclosed corridors. Clusters of men huddled around monitors trading oil products. When I asked my host whether his traders were hedging or speculating, he looked me straight in the eye and said, 'Yes.' I asked him again and received the same answer."[4] When oil companies speculate on oil prices, they move prices, but there is no supply or demand curve. Sophisticated tests of the supply-and-demand model can be framed, but they depend on other models, some of them statistical, that can in turn be challenged.

Textbooks make economics sound like physics by blurring the distinction between the idealized world of models, which does behave like a physics, and the messy real economic world, which does not. To make sense of economics, you can never ignore the distinction. Not only does Samuelson fail to make this clear in his textbook; he doesn't even explain what an economic model is. Oh, let me not exaggerate! In the thirteenth edition—the one I happen to have read—Samuelson and his coauthor, William Nordhaus, provide a brief definition of a model in an appendix, on page 977.

Blurring the ideal world of model economies with the complex world of real economies deeply confuses students. Some feel cheated, as if they were watching a magician put on a stage show, the workings of which are hidden from sight. Others like the stage show better than the messy everyday world. As students thus encounter economics, David Colander of Middlebury College laments, "They either love it and think economists have something to say that they aren't saying, or they hate it and think economists have something to say that they aren't saying."[5]

A model is never a full-dimensional hologram of real economies, but at best a partial two-dimensional perspective. Much that I say will be controversial, but this point should not be. Robert Lucas, one of the most creative model-builders, tells a story about his undergraduate encounter with Gregor Mendel's model of genetic inheritance.[6] He liked the Mendelian model—"you could work out predictions that would surprise you"—though not the lab work breeding fruit flies to test it. (Economists are not big on mucking around in the real world.) Over the weekend, he enjoyed writing a paper comparing the model's predictions with the class's experimental results. When a friend returned from a weekend away without having written the required paper, Lucas agreed to let the friend borrow from his. The friend remarked that Lucas had forgotten to discuss how "crossing-over" could explain the substantial discrepancies between the model and experimental results. "Crossing-over is b—s—," Lucas told his friend, a "label for our ignorance." He kept his paper's focus on the unadorned Mendelian model, and added a section arguing that experimental errors could explain the discrepancies. His friend instead appended a section on crossing-over. His friend got an A. Lucas got a C-minus, with a comment: "This is a good report, but you forgot about crossing-over." Crossing-over is actually a fact; it occurs when a portion of one parent gene is incorporated in the other parent gene. But Lucas's anecdote brilliantly illustrates the powerful temptation to model-builders—across the ideological spectrum—of ignoring inconvenient facts that don't fit their models.

As Lucas says, "The construction of theoretical models is our way to bring order to the way we think about the world, but the process necessarily involves ignoring some evidence or alternative theories—setting them aside. That can be hard to do—facts are facts—and sometimes my unconscious mind carries out the abstraction for me: I simply fail to see some of the data or some alternative theory." Often I disagree with Lucas, but I like the transparency with which he discusses models. He has said that a model is a "mechanical imitation economy," a "robot imitation of people," a "thought experiment."[7] It must be distinguished from reality because "in practice all axioms for models we can actually solve will be crude approximations at best, and determining which axioms produce reliable models will involve judgment, testing, and luck."[8]

Why Use Models At All?

A popular line of criticism lambastes economists for their use of abstract models. For example, Richard Parker, lecturer in public policy at the Kennedy School of Government, takes economists to task for "their deductive method, their formalism, their over-reliance on arcane algebra, their imperviousness to complex evidence."[9] The economic columnist Robert Kuttner attacks economists for blithe ignorance of the real world: "Economics, especially macroeconomics, tends to attract mathematical theorists, many of whom are astonishingly innocent of actual economic institutions. These whiz kids, often tenured before age 30, thrill each other with arcane manipulations of models, many of which depend on assumptions not rooted in economic reality."[10]

Some of what Kuttner and Parker say is just. But there are good reasons to consider models. For one thing, if you want to get to the heart of what economists say, whether you agree or disagree, you must look at their models. "Facts can only dent a theorist's hide," Samuelson said, now talking to fellow economists in a tone very different from the one he uses when talking down to students.[11] "In economics it takes a theory to kill a theory"—and by "theory" he meant a model. Economists' opinion pieces, textbooks, and clamorous advice are exercises in public relations. What they do as economists is to build models. Their models profoundly influence policy debates, as well as other social sciences.

More important, we all think in models, even if—like Molière's bour-

geois gentleman, who spoke prose his whole life without knowing it—
we are unaware of the fact. Unfiltered reality is too complicated to understand. It is littered with irrelevant details. To make sense of it, we
ignore countless facts that we deem unimportant to a question we want
to answer, focus on features of reality that we deem central to that question, and try to figure out how they fit into a coherent picture that suggests an answer. In short, we think about a model. And we *should* think
about a model.

Common sense isn't an alternative to models. What we call "common
sense," singling out some salient aspects of our world and ignoring myriad others, is just a collection of implicit and sometimes fuzzy models,
each with as much *prima facie* claim to be right or wrong as any formal
model. The problem with common sense is that it fails as a guide when
your common sense disagrees with mine. We disagree because we make
conflicting assumptions that we may not have quite articulated—or that
may not even be internally consistent—and use them to spin conflicting
arguments. If we try to express our common-sense ideas in clear models,
we are more likely to find ourselves stating assumptions explicitly and
reasoning consistently. We might, at least, see what we disagree about.

To put the same point differently, everyone knows how important assumptions are: the conclusions we reach depend on the assumptions we
make. Models may sound stranger and more dubious, but they are what
get us from assumptions to conclusions. Without models, assumptions
would just be assumptions. It is true that you can usually build a model
to reach almost any preconceived conclusion, and you can usually build a
model *based on* almost any preconceived assumptions. But you *cannot* at
the same time have any assumptions you want and reach any conclusions
you want. A model provides a check on thinking: it restricts us at least to
consistent economic worlds, however imaginary they might be.

The catch is that models can be treacherous. While some assumptions made by economists capture important insights, others are insane.
All you have to do is decide which capture insights, which are insane,

and in which situations. Unfortunately, this turns out not to be such an easy challenge. It always and inevitably involves some difficult mixture of logic, judgment, and ideology. There is an element of ideology because models involve simplification, highlighting some elements of reality and ignoring others, and such simplification is inherently ideological. Yet despite ideological differences, there remain grounds for reasoned debate about explicit assumptions and models. In the course of this book, I will take up some central debates about assumptions and models—and about what criteria we can sensibly use to judge assumptions and models, good or bad.

Those Who Forget the Past

Most discussions of economics treat it as a self-contained set of theories that moves ever forward and need hardly glance back at what Olivier Blanchard, of MIT, distressingly calls "the trash bin of history of thought."[12] Undergraduate texts, which I will often complain about, reduce economics to a one-dimensional present, and a 2007 survey found that history of economic thought had "all but vanished" from graduate programs.[13] Mark Blaug, a historian of economic thought at the University of Amsterdam, sums up the profession's prejudice: "No History of Ideas, Please, We're Economists."[14] The history of economic thought is not a trash bin, but a living museum of ideas, challenges to those ideas, and responses to the challenges.

I take the somewhat unusual, but hardly unique, approach of revisiting this living museum as I discuss economic ideas. I weigh rival assumptions and models, starting with Adam Smith and proceeding in a loosely chronological fashion—though jumping backward and forward as I find the theme demands it—to cutting-edge work.

Yet *Assumptions* is not a history of economic thought, nor am I a historian. I care about whether the assumptions, models, and ideas of pioneering economists, as I interpret them after reading their work (but little of historians' debates about it), shed light on today's economic questions. I treat assumptions and models that are two hundred years old essentially the same way I treat those that are two years old. I ask if the assumptions seem plausible and if the models shed convincing light on economies or aspects of economies.

Why take this loosely chronological approach to discussing economic ideas? For one thing, I find it a more appealing way to talk about those ideas. For example, while I cannot ignore contemporary textbook economics, I rarely sympathize with it. If I tried to explain it straight, as disembodied theory, I would write some colossally boring chapters. But I can sympathize with the struggles of earlier thinkers to forge ideas that were borrowed, smoothed over, and (I will argue) often distorted into contemporary textbook theory. Sometimes those earlier thinkers arrived at striking insights; sometimes they ran into impenetrable troubles. How could I describe—or even see—some timeless dictum, rather than a series of reactions and borrowings, discoveries and troubles?

More important, I discuss pioneering thinkers going back two centuries because they raise fundamental questions and engage in powerful debates that the contemporary mainstream has largely forgotten. Indeed, after reading a good deal of contemporary economics and seeing some criticisms of some key elements, I discovered that many of those criticisms had already been more clearly and fully articulated in the past— and then practically relegated to Blanchard's trash bin. Perhaps if economics were a "positive" science like physics—or at least like economists' envious notion of physics, because I'm not sure physicists would necessarily concur—it might be treated with nary a backward glance. But economics is not that kind of enterprise. It is more like political philosophy, inextricably combining theoretical and moral dimensions. If you discuss liberalism, you go back at least to John Locke, and if you discuss conservatism, you go back at least to Edmund Burke. Political thinking cannot usefully be distilled into a pure timeless theory—and the same is true for economic thinking.

THREE

In Search of a Model

You can't help liking Adam Smith, and you can't help arguing with him. His *Wealth of Nations* reveals an enormous intelligence struggling to incorporate incredibly thoughtful and varied observations into a theory. He made a start toward what's now called classical political economy, or classical economics—the approach sharpened by his successor David Ricardo into a coherent model and, I will argue, muddled by Ricardo's successor Karl Marx. Classical political economy assumes that the division of income between profits and wages is not determined by supply and demand in markets, but rather by society—social custom for Smith and Ricardo, class struggle for Marx. Either way, classical political economy sees this major economic fact as socially decided outside of markets. Markets then enter to determine the prices of goods, how much capitalists invest, how many workers are employed, and how fast the economy grows. The classical model, though crude, remains useful today, and I will have far more to say about it. I will also discuss more sophisticated recent models based in part on it.

Yet Smith gets lost along the way. In subsequent chapters I will discuss assumptions and models that I find good, bad, or indifferent. In this chapter I look at the problems of not having a model at all. Smith makes conflicting assumptions, and no matter which of his conflicting assumptions you grant him, he fails to build a model. For lack of consistent assumptions or a model, his driving argument for a system of "natural liberty" and against "mercantilism"—government favors and subsidies granted to large merchants, manufacturers, and medieval guilds—runs into hopeless trouble. Had he made coherent assumptions and built a consistent model, he might have been more effective.

The Evils of Mercantilism

Professor of moral philosophy at the University of Glasgow and later commissioner of His Majesty's Customs for Scotland, as he duly notes on the title page of *The Wealth of Nations* (evidently he could make peace with tariffs), Smith describes a vast drama of social conflict, both hopeful and fearsome, stretching from the ancient world to the future.[1] Though he barely traveled beyond Glasgow, Edinburgh, and London— he did spend two years in France tutoring a young duke—he investigates economies from the Byzantine Empire to the American colonies, from China to Peru. Writing on the eve of the American Revolution, he essentially imagines the coming Industrial Revolution. Except in a few trades, his society remained one of handcraft production. The latest invention in textile industry, which would soon power industrialization, was the spinning wheel.[2] Smith's famous description of how the division of labor in a pin factory boosts output sounds like something out of Jules Verne. In what must have been a flight of fancy, he estimates that, while a single worker might make at most twenty pins a day, ten workers specializing in aspects of the process might make 48,000.[3]

Like nearly all important economists, Smith was preoccupied with both promoting policies to solve social problems and developing a theory to support those policies. The realms of abstract theory and concrete policy merge. His policy concerns are the clearer element. *The Wealth of*

Nations asserts his claim for a system of "natural liberty." How could you disagree with his moral impulse? He stands with yeoman farmers, craftsmen, and spinners—"poor people, women commonly, scattered about in all different parts of the country, without support or protection"—as well as natives of colonies brutalized by Europeans.[4] He stands against powerful monopolists and policies that support them, famously warning that "people of the same trade seldom meet together, even for merriment and diversion, but the conversation ends in a conspiracy against the public, or in some contrivance to raise prices."[5]

Some of the regulations that Smith paints as affronts to natural liberty and obstacles to progress were medieval. Each trade was legally incorporated, and anyone who would enter it had to apprentice for seven years. Master cutlers in Sheffield could have only one apprentice; weavers in Norfolk, two.[6] "Poor laws"—here "poor" means "common people"— required each parish to provide for its unemployed, infirm, and elderly.[7] To prevent invasion by paupers, "settlement laws" blocked common people from seeking work in a parish where they did not reside. Smith calls for the repeal of these practices "so that a poor workingman, when thrown out of employment either in one trade or in one place, may seek for it in another trade or in another place, without the fear either of a prosecution or of a removal."[8]

Smith directs his greatest ire against mercantilism, which he describes as an economic system promoted by and for merchants.[9] It equated a nation's wealth to its store of gold and silver. "A rich country, in the same manner as a rich man, is supposed to be a country abounding in money," he laments.[10] The principal means of amassing precious metals was through foreign trade. Thomas Mun's mercantilist tract, *England's Treasure by Foreign Trade,* had become "a fundamental maxim in the political œconomy, not of England only, but of all other commercial countries."[11]

Spain and Portugal took the direct path to heaping up gold and silver:

"Folly and injustice seem to have been the principles which presided over and directed the first project of establishing [their] colonies; the folly of hunting after gold and silver mines, and the injustice of coveting the possession of a country whose harmless natives, far from having ever injured the people of Europe, had received the first adventurers with every mark of kindness and hospitality."[12]

Since Britain had few precious metals to dig up, it set about accumulating them by exporting other goods, which its trading partners paid for in gold and silver. A notable example was the famous treaty with Portugal requiring it to freely import British manufactured textiles and, in return, allowing free imports of port wine into Britain. In the fairy tale of modern economics texts, this treaty was supposed to benefit both nations. In fact, as Smith relates, the British saw it as a "masterpiece" of mercantilist policy to accumulate gold.[13] Portugal paid for its lopsided imports of manufactured goods not by exporting port wine—the British would have had to be terrible lushes to balance that sort of two-way trade—but by sending a reputed £50,000 in gold on the weekly packet boat to London.[14]

Britain deployed trade policies—promotion of exports and protection from competing imports—to support industries that could dominate foreign markets. These policies favored "the industry which is carried on for the benefit of the rich and the powerful," says Smith. "That which is carried on for the benefit of the poor and the indigent, is too often, either neglected, or oppressed."[15] Imports of linen yarn were encouraged, in order to drive down the price of yarn spun at home by women of limited means. Meanwhile, the "great master manufacturers" who wove yarn into cloth kept cloth prices high by "extorting" tariffs to block imports and by obtaining subsidies for exports.[16]

Then Britain established its famous trading companies to hunt for foreign wealth, granting the South Sea Company, the Hamburgh Company, the Russia Company, the Turkey Company, the Africa Company, and other firms exclusive franchises to trade with their particular corners of the world.[17] Monopoly was the "sole engine" that succeeded in promoting these mercantilist ventures, Smith charges.[18]

For example, Smith tells the saga, starting in 1600 under Elizabeth, of the series of brutal and wasteful corporate entities known as the East India Company. The company secured the franchise to trade products such as silk, indigo, tea, and opium with India, but ended up garnering more treasure by ruling, or rather plundering, that nation. In the late 1600s it was saddled with minor competition, which had the "miserable effects," in its view, of raising production in India and lowering the prices of its exports to England. It nearly went bankrupt in 1702, but the crown bailed it out.[19] With its exclusive franchise renewed, it again began making a profit but wanted more. Allowed to build forts in India, it arrogated to itself the right of making war and conquered the rich areas of Madras, Pondicherry, and Calcutta.[20] By 1769 its annual revenue from looting India and, in lesser measure, carrying on trade came to nearly £3 million sterling a year—on a capital of £3.2 million.[21] Not bad profits. Alas, they only provided company officers "a pretext for greater profusion, and a cover for greater malversation." In 1773, again on the edge of bankruptcy, the company threw itself on "the mercy of the government" for a £1.4 million loan.[22] Parliament granted it but imposed—yes—a reorganization plan. To make a long story short, by 1784, when Smith published his third edition, the company had fallen into "greater distress than ever; and, in order to prevent immediate bankruptcy [was] once more reduced to supplicate the assistance of government."[23]

What most angers Smith is the company's appalling government of India: "No other sovereigns ever were, or from the nature of things ever could be, so perfectly indifferent about the happiness or misery of their subjects, the improvement or waste of their dominions, the glory or disgrace of their administration, as, from irresistible moral causes, the greater part of the proprietors of such a mercantile company are; and necessarily must be."[24]

The System of "Natural Liberty"

Smith attacks policies that confer monopolies on trading companies, grant protection and subsidies to manufacturers, and restrict entry into medieval guilds as unnatural, on the one hand, and inefficient, on the other. Let's start with his view of what is natural. Capital might be invested in agriculture, manufacturing, or trade. In the natural course of things, Smith says, "the greater part of the capital of every growing society is, first, directed to agriculture, next manufactures, and last to foreign commerce."[25] He claims that this is not only the natural course of things, but also the most efficient way to allocate capital. Capital invested in agriculture provides jobs for the greatest number of workers and adds the greatest value to a nation's annual produce. "After agriculture, the capital employed in manufactures puts into motion the greatest quantity of productive labour, and adds the greatest value to the annual produce. That which is employed in the trade of exportation, has the least effect of any of the three."[26] Thus, not only is the system of natural liberty morally superior. By allowing the natural order of things to prevail, Smith claims, it increases economic efficiency.

Smith's famous quote about the invisible hand expresses this idea, though focusing only on the supposed superiority of domestic industry over foreign trade and omitting agriculture. It's worth giving in full, including portions usually excised that express Smith's dim view of foreign trade:

> As every individual . . . endeavours as much as he can both to employ his capital in the support of domestic industry, and so to direct that industry that its produce may be of the greatest value; every individual necessarily labours to render the annual revenue of the society as great as he can. He generally, indeed, neither intends to promote the public interest, nor knows how much he is promoting it. By preferring the support of domestic to that of foreign industry, he intends only his own security; and by directing that industry in such a manner as its

produce may be of the greatest value, he intends only his own gain, and he is in this, as in many other cases, led by an invisible hand to promote an end which was no part of his intention. Nor is it always the worse for the society that it was no part of it.[27]

What Is Value?

To combat mercantilism, Smith must discredit the idea that gold is the ultimate measure of value. And he must replace it with another theory of value and distribution. That is, he needs a theory about how the value, or price, of goods is determined, and how total revenue is distributed among capitalists who receive profits, workers who receive wages, and landlords who receive rent on land or natural resources.

He starts out by distinguishing "value in use" from "value in exchange."[28] "Nothing is more useful than water," he notes—we would die without it—"but it will purchase scarce any thing; scarce any thing can be had in exchange for it. A diamond, on the contrary, has scarce any value in use; but a very great quantity of other goods may frequently be had in exchange for it." Setting use value aside, he sets out to explain exchange value. Why does a diamond exchange for a large quantity of other goods, while water exchanges for a small quantity of other goods (if, indeed, for any at all)?

The supply-and-demand story was already conventional wisdom in Smith's day. "The market price of every particular commodity is regulated by the proportion between the quantity which is actually brought to market, and the demand of those who are willing to pay" its production costs, as Smith puts it.[29] He agrees that supply and demand affect prices in the short run: "A public mourning [such as the one following the king's death] raises the price of black cloth . . . and augments the profits of the merchants who possess any considerable quantity of it."[30] But Smith argues that the supply-and-demand mechanism does not govern prices over the longer run. It ensures only that market prices gravitate toward their "natural," or normal, price: "Whatever may be the obstacles which hinder them from settling in this center of repose and continuance, they are constantly tending towards it."[31]

What determines a good's natural price? In an idea reaching back at least to John Locke's *Second Treatise of Government*, the philosophic foundation of the American Declaration of Independence, Smith posits a labor theory of value. It applies in the "early and rude state of society," before anyone owns natural resources or accumulates capital. In that situation, he says, "The proportion between the quantities of labour necessary for acquiring different objects seems to be the only circumstance which can afford any rule for exchanging them one for another."[32] If it takes twice as much time to hunt and kill a beaver as a deer, a beaver is worth two deer.[33]

Under capitalism, production requires not only labor but also, precisely, capital: factories, ships, tools. Moreover, natural resources such as farm land or coal seams, all of which Smith lumps together under the rubric "land," are claimed as property and can no longer be used free of charge. Thus, the "natural" price of each good must be the sum of its component parts—the natural wages of labor that go to workers, the profits of stock that go to capitalists, and the rent of land that goes to landlords.[34] This accounting seems sensible. The price paid for a good has to go for labor, capital, or land.

The question is: What determines "natural" wages, profits, and rents? Smith makes a start toward the classical theory that Ricardo would articulate. He argues that each society establishes a wage allowing workers to acquire "necessaries." Necessaries are defined by a socially accepted minimum, not a biological minimum: "By necessaries I understand not only the commodities which are indispensably necessary for the support of life, but whatever the custom of the country renders it indecent for creditable people, even of the lowest order, to be without."[35] In England in his day, the custom of the country deemed leather shoes necessary: "The poorest creditable person of either sex would be ashamed to appear in public without them." In France they were not thought necessary; one could appear in public, without discredit, in wooden shoes or barefoot.

The term "natural" is confusing here. It suggests what countless popular and academic interpreters of Smith, Ricardo, and Marx have taken it to mean, but what in fact they did *not* mean: that the wage is set by a biological minimum. I keep the term "natural," since changing unfortunate conventions often causes more confusion than accepting them. But the so-called natural wage is socially determined.

Of course, different occupations are paid at different rates. Smith assumes, as do modern macroeconomic models, that wages for special types of work are roughly adjusted as multiples of a standard or natural wage.[36] For example, coal miners earn two or three times as much as common laborers because they face unusual hardships, Smith says. Lawyers charge enough to compensate for the time and expense of their education. This adjustment occurs completely only when there is "perfect freedom" to practice trades; impediments such as apprenticeship interfere with it.[37] But since it's just an approximation used for understanding the operations of the economy, Smith ignores those imperfections.

Smith turns next to profits and rents. Profits on capital, like wages for labor, can vary from the norm, he argues. For example, when a business puts capital at greater risk than usual, it earns a higher rate of profit than normal.[38] If a high crime rate makes innkeeping unusually risky, that occupation will earn extra-high profits. Monopolistic franchises, such as those that the trading companies enjoyed, also earn outsized profits. Absent such special circumstances, firms earn the natural profit rate. Somehow, society establishes this "ordinary or average rate."[39] But Smith gives no clear account of how.

His story about rent is worse. In his day, landlords commonly owned estates and rented them to farmers to till. Smith says the landlord must leave the tenant farmer enough to cover the natural wages of labor and the natural profit on invested capital—farm equipment, seed, and other inputs. "Whatever part of the produce, or, what is the same thing, whatever part of its price, is over and above this share, [the landlord] naturally endeavours to reserve to himself as the rent of his land."⁴⁰ In other words, Smith says that rent is the sale price, whatever it might be, minus wage-and-profit costs. But he has also said that the sale price is the rent plus wage-and-profit costs. The logic is circular. For specific wage-and-profit costs, pick any rent you want, and the rent determines the sale price; pick any price you want, and the price determines the rent. This is no theory at all.

And Now Another Story

Smith then recalls the project posed in his book's full title: *An Inquiry into the Nature and Causes of the Wealth of Nations.*⁴¹ The very term "political economy," he notes, refers to the study of "the nature and causes of the wealth of nations."⁴² His policy prescription to increase national wealth calls for a system of natural liberty and an end to mercantilist franchises for trading companies, to protection and subsidies for manufacturers, and to guild restrictions. Such special privileges, he believes, raise profits for chosen industries but undermine wages and make the nation itself poor: "No society can surely be flourishing and happy, of which the far greater part of the members are poor and miserable."⁴³

The British colonies in India, says Smith, exemplify how special privileges produce a high-profit, low-wage nation—that is, a poor nation: "The great fortunes so suddenly and so easily acquired in Bengal and the other British settlements in the East Indies, may satisfy us that, as the wages of labour are very low, so the profits of stock are very high in those ruined countries. The interest of money is proportionably so. In Bengal, money is frequently lent to the farmers at forty, fifty, and sixty per cent. and the succeeding crop is mortgaged for the payment."⁴⁴

Smith seems at a loss when it comes to deriving his policy prescription for a system of natural liberty from his original assumption about distribution—namely, that social custom determines the natural wage-

and-profit rate. So he posits alternate assumptions about distribution—inconsistent with his original assumptions—that he bases on a supply-and-demand story. One alternate assumption supposes that the more rapid the accumulation of stock—the higher the level of investment, as we would say—the greater the demand for labor and hence the higher the wages:

> The demand for those who live by wages . . . necessarily increases with the increase of the revenue and stock of every country, and cannot possibly increase without it. . . . It is not the actual greatness of national wealth, but its continual increase, which occasions a rise in the wages of labour. It is not, accordingly, in the richest countries, but in the most thriving, or in those which are growing rich the fastest, that the wages of labour are highest. England is certainly, in the present times, a much richer country than any part of North America. The wages of labour, however, are much higher in North America than in any part of England.[45]

In his alternate assumptions, Smith also supposes that investment supply and demand determine profits, but they move the opposite way from wages: "The rise and fall of the profits of stock depend on the same causes with the rise and fall in the wages of labour, . . . but these causes affect the one and the other differently. The increase of stock, which raises wages, tends to lower profit."[46] He motivates this notion with an argument about monopolistic industries: "When the stocks of many rich merchants are turned into the same trade, their mutual competition naturally tends to lower its profit; and when there is a like increase of stock in all the different trades carried on in the same society, the same competition must produce the same effect in them all."

If America exemplifies high investment and prosperity, China, for Smith, exemplifies stagnant investment and misery. Accounts of all travelers concur that it had "been long stationary," or, in other words, was investing little.[47] The "monopoly of the rich" let them garner outsized profits: "Twelve per cent. accordingly is said to be the common interest of money in China, and the ordinary profits of stock must be sufficient to afford this large interest" while still leaving a surplus.[48] Meanwhile, "The poverty of the lower ranks of people in China far surpasses that of the most beggarly nations in Europe."[49]

The Wealth of Nations

Smith's alternate assumption that investment supply and demand determine the division of income between profits and wages does not square with his original assumption that social custom determines that division. Conceivably, Smith might argue, social custom operates over some very long run, while investment supply and demand operate over some shorter run. But he claims that stagnant investment has ensured high profits and low wages in China for as long as anyone can remember. Once such a division of income has been so durably enforced, how could social custom do anything but ratify the status quo? The carefully constructed story about social determination has no possible force.

It gets worse. Let Smith drop his story about social determination, and keep his assumption about investment supply and demand. He still lacks a model based on this assumption to argue for his system of "natural liberty." Except for short-run models of the business cycle, a time frame that Smith was certainly not thinking about, no models I know of relate investment—or the *growth* of the capital stock—to the *level* of wages or profits. And there certainly is no such model in *The Wealth of Nations*.

To see the implausibility of any such model, consider an example. During the first decade of the 2000s (in stark contrast to Smith's day), Chinese investment averaged well over twice the U.S. level (39 percent of GDP versus 16 percent, respectively), and Chinese wages grew a lot faster than U.S. wages, but the *level* of Chinese wages averaged a tenth of the U.S. level ($4,333 dollars per year versus $41,463).[50] There is simply no plausible reason to believe that a poor country such as China, no matter how rapidly it invests, can have wage levels higher than those in a rich country such as the United States.

Smith's claim about the natural order of investment and the efficiency of different sectors is also doubtful. Is agriculture really more productive than manufacturing, or manufacturing more productive than trade? In what sense? Would Europe have emerged from the Middle Ages if nobles had continued to use serf labor to cultivate estates—if long-distance trade had not begun to break down that traditional order?

A more serious problem is that Smith wants to drive profit rates down. Only capitalists saved and invested in Smith's day; he never even suggests that workers might. Regardless of that particular situation, if profits fall, how will capitalists continue to save and invest at a high rate?[51] Really, Smith has tied his argument into knots.

Historically, moral objections notwithstanding, it is not clear that monopolies, protectionism, and subsidies must undermine growth. Virtually all of today's developed nations achieved that status by deploying such industrial policies.[52] Exhibit A would be the United Kingdom in the decades after Smith published *The Wealth of Nations*. Was it just an accident that Britain forced Portugal into providing a market for its manufactured textiles? Of course not. Nor was it just an accident that Britain prohibited all but the smallest-scale manufacturing in its colonies. It thereby forced them to import the mother country's manufactured goods. In effect, Britain established "a great empire," as Smith quips, "for the sole purpose of raising up a nation of customers who should be obliged to buy from the shops of our different producers."[53]

The very industries that Smith charges with enjoying the most protection and subsidy would, in fact, prove to lead England's industrialization. For example: "Our woollen manufacturers . . . have not only obtained a monopoly against the consumers by an absolute prohibition of importing woollen cloths from any foreign country; but they have likewise obtained another monopoly against the sheep farmers and growers of wool, by a similar prohibition of the exportation of live sheep and wool."[54] At one point any exporter of English sheep, apparently a superior breed, "was for the first offense to forfeit all his goods for ever, to suffer a year's imprisonment, and then to have his left hand cut off in a market town upon a market day, to be there nailed up."[55] The second offense was punished by death. Those penalties had been somewhat softened by Smith's day. But to prevent foreigners from copying British textile machinery or tools, both the person who exported them and the master of any ship that conveyed them were fined £200 sterling, a small fortune at the time.[56]

Exhibit B in the case against Smith's economic policy of natural liberty is the United States, which did not fail to learn from its former colonial master. In the late nineteenth and early twentieth centuries, it rose to become the world's leading industrial power, behind prohibitive trade barriers against manufactured imports.[57] When the U.S. government, over time, gave away a land area as large as New England to the railroads, they led industrialization not only by building a transport and communication network (via telegraph) to support industry, but also by providing a vast market for steel, glass, engines, electrical equipment, and other manufactured goods.

Smith famously accords consumption priority over production: "Consumption is the sole end and purpose of all production; and the interest of the producer ought to be attended to, only so far as it may be necessary for promoting that of the consumer. The maxim is so perfectly self-evident, that it would be absurd to attempt to prove it. But in the mercantile system, the interest of the consumer is almost constantly sacrificed to that of the producer; and it seems to consider production, and not consumption, as the ultimate end and object of all industry and commerce."[58] Many modern economists share this perspective. Dissenters—from Alexander Hamilton to Karl Marx to John Maynard Keynes—have, for very different reasons, accorded more priority to production.

FOUR

Economics When Society Matters

In the half-century after Adam Smith published *The Wealth of Nations,* the shock of industrial revolution, as well as the American and French political revolutions, struck Britain close to home. Not surprisingly, conservatism launched a counter-revolution. Just as Gothic revival sought to recreate a disappearing architecture, political conservatism sought to restore an eroding social order. The restored order would be guided not by individualism and the market but by what the Romantic poet and political Tory Samuel Taylor Coleridge called "the spirit of State."[1] Amid revolutions and counter-revolutions, David Ricardo published *The Principles of Political Economy and Taxation* (1817), seeking to defend and improve Smith's liberal political economy. A look at Ricardo's policy concerns seems useful before I discuss the model he developed to support them.

Historians no longer much like the term "industrial revolution," because it conjures up exaggerated scenarios of steam power and mass production inexorably obliterating a quaint past. In fact, steam power did not become a major factor in the weaving industry until the 1810s or in the spinning industry until the 1840s.[2] Even in the mid-nineteenth century, London, the hub of manufacturing, produced clothing, chemicals, paper, and other goods by handcraft methods.

Yet there *was* an industrial revolution. It started in the country, as the rural gentry claimed and fenced off common lands that small farmers had used to graze sheep, grow crops, and collect firewood. In Smith's era, some 60,000 acres were enclosed per decade, according to Arnold Toynbee, the nineteenth-century historian of the industrial revolution, but by Ricardo's day the rate of enclosure had risen more than tenfold.[3] Toynbee quotes a contemporary of Ricardo as saying that, in one parish, a certain Lord Carnarvon had amalgamated a single estate from lands "that those now living remember to have formed fourteen farms, bringing up in a respectable way fourteen families."[4]

You can see the industrial revolution in the roaring furnaces and smoke-billowing factories that light up J. M. W. Turner's industrial landscapes. Alluding to a myth that Jesus had once come to England to found a new Israel, William Blake asked, "And was Jerusalem builded here,/Among these dark Satanic Mills?" From 1780 to 1850, English pig iron output increased by a factor of thirty-five; cotton exports, by a factor of thirty-two.[5] Farmers displaced by enclosures migrated to industrial towns such as Liverpool and Manchester. Boyd Hilton, a historian not given to overplaying social change, writes, "All large industrial towns had brothels, gins shops, alehouses, thieves' dens, filthy courts, rookeries, communal privies, cesspools, middens, dung heaps, and dangerous ill-paved streets crawling with wild dogs, wolves, and rats."[6] In industrial parishes, those decades "may have been the worst ever . . . for life expectancy since the Black Death."[7]

The reaction against industrialization dominated politics and letters. Coleridge, the high Tory, and Blake, the radical, were equally dismayed about the exercise of Smith's "natural rights"—workers' rights to leave their parishes and labor in the mill town of their choice. The mad-hat conservative essayist Thomas Carlyle, who used more exclamation marks on a page than anyone should use in a whole book, famously dubbed political economy the "dismal science." He used the phrase in an essay arguing that laissez-faire would "give birth to progenies and prodigies; dark extensive moon-calves, unnamable abortions, wide-coiled monstrosities, such as the world has not seen hitherto!" Whatever he meant by that list of horribles, his essay provides an unfortunate context for the famous phrase. He was not arguing for a restoration of some misty old England that could at least be defended on sentimental grounds. His essay, titled "The Nigger Question," defended that most brutal—and not at all traditional—of social institutions: Caribbean slave labor.

A supporter of liberalism who sympathized with workers, Ricardo fought two sets of laws passed by the conservative Parliament. The Corn Laws, enacted in 1815, blocked wheat imports. ("Corn" properly refers to a region's principal grain; in England in Ricardo's day it meant wheat, not American maize.) Ricardo saw those laws as giveaways to rich landowners. The impetus for the Corn Laws goes back to 1793, when Britain entered the Napoleonic Wars, wheat imports were cut off, and landlords found that they could demand soaring rents for their estates from the farmers who actually worked the land and sold the produce. Toynbee reports a case in which an estate in Essex rented for 10 shillings an acre in 1793 and for 50 shillings an acre in 1812.[8] The effect on the hired farmworker, Toynbee laments, was "most disastrous." The worker "felt all the burden of high prices, while his wages were steadily falling, and he lost his common-rights."[9] The Corn Laws, passed after the war, locked in landlords' gains.

Whereas Smith fought merchants and manufacturers who wrested advantage from the state, Ricardo took aim at landlords for their protectionist Corn Laws. Today free trade, or what's tendentiously called free trade (you need only a sentence to specify free trade, not thousand-page treatises), is often seen as benefiting multinationals. Ricardo saw the protectionist Corn Laws as benefiting landlords and harming workers. Landlords are "never so prosperous, as when food is scarce and dear," he wrote, "whereas, all other persons are greatly benefitted by procuring cheap food."[10]

Ricardo also opposed the Poor Laws. Traditional poor laws had required parishes to provide relief to the infirm, the elderly, and those who accepted make-work in the poorhouse. The ranks of the poor swelled as enclosure of common land and the decline of subsistence farming created a rural proletariat, and gave rise to industrial unemployment as we know it. After wheat prices soared during the Napoleonic Wars, villages in southern England began to subsidize wages to assure families of subsistence.[11] This may well have been a reasonable anti-poverty measure, but at the time intellectuals and politicians saw it as a monstrosity.[12] Employers might cut pay, relying on subsidies to make up the shortfall, and subsidies that leveled pay could weaken incentives to work.[13] Families supported by subsidies, it was supposed, often landed in the poorhouse and stayed there. There has never been a more incisive or eloquent defender of social protection than Karl Polanyi, but in his book *The Great Transformation,* having based his research on commentaries by intellectuals and politicians of Ricardo's day, he captures their dim view of the Poor Laws: "The decencies and self-respect of centuries of settled life wore off quickly in the promiscuity of the poorhouse." From Blake to Carlyle, from the market apologist Harriet Martineau to the Marxist Friedrich Engels, everyone believed that "the very image of man had been defiled by some terrible catastrophe."[14]

Ricardo's friend Thomas Malthus essentially argued that humans' irrepressible sex drive would cause unmanageable population growth, which would outpace society's ability to provide food. Ricardo saw the poorhouse, which he believed promoted "early and improvident marriages," as aggravating these concerns. But he showed far more sympathy for inhabitants of the poorhouse than for landlords. Since the poorhouse had become an entrenched institution, he warned that its "abolition should be effected by the most gradual steps."[15]

Scion of a Sephardic Jewish family, Ricardo married a Quaker and gained fabulous wealth as a stock "jobber"—a trader and market maker. He managed to move effortlessly into London's intellectual circles.[16] His essay for the *Morning Chronicle* on the inflation of paper money drew the attention of James Mill, a political economist and the father of John Stuart Mill. James Mill later encouraged Ricardo to write his *Principles of Political Economy*. Ricardo apparently met Malthus, his eternal friend and critic, through a London club. But Piero Sraffa and Maurice Dobb, editors of the definitive edition of Ricardo's collected works, suggest that the most important influence on his political economy was his self-education in mathematics, chemistry, and geology.

Along with his practical concerns—such as ending the Corn Laws and gradually disbanding the poorhouses—Ricardo conceived an intellectual problem: to straighten out Adam Smith's incoherent meanderings and produce a consistent model, although he never used that term. His *Principles of Political Economy* formulated the clearest articulation of what has come to be known as classical political economy. *Principles* could hardly have been a more different kind of book from *The Wealth of Nations*. Smith's fertile vision drew a panorama of world economies laced with acute perceptions and contradictions. Ricardo's writing is not so elegant, but is focused, sharp, rigorous.

Ricardo never described his economic model in equations, but he presented such clear numerical examples that you can almost visualize the underlying algebra. Piero Sraffa spelled out the algebra in a short, important book in 1960. Unlike Smith's brilliant but often contradictory perceptions, Ricardo's model of classical economics led him robustly toward his conclusions.

Ricardo's Assumptions

It helps to compare the assumptions Ricardo uses to build his classical economics model with standard contemporary assumptions used to build the so-called neoclassical model. First, a word about the term "neoclassical." Neoclassical theory, as it's known, initially shaped by late nineteenth-century academics in Britain and on the Continent, evolved into today's textbook economics. A more appropriate name would have been "anticlassical" economics, because the theory constituted a reaction against Ricardo. But the term used is "neoclassical"—and on this point, as elsewhere, I prefer to avoid confusion by following standard usage, rather than reinventing it. I should add that, as a rigorous theory, neoclassical economics underwent important changes in the twentieth century. But the simplified neoclassical models that have been taught in textbooks and mostly applied in practice changed far less. Unless I indicate otherwise, what I say about neoclassical economics refers to this textbook version.

One of Ricardo's key assumptions, also adopted in the neoclassical model, is called Say's "law," after the French economist Jean-Baptiste Say, who popularized it. (This is another misnomer since it's an assumption, not a law.) It assumes that all income, both capitalists' profits and workers' wages, is spent to purchase goods. A useful way to see the implications of Say's law is to consider what would happen if all income were *not* spent—in particular, if instead of spending all their profits to purchase investment goods, capitalists hoarded a portion of them, perhaps stashing pounds sterling in safe-deposit boxes. The result would be what classical economists called a "general glut" of goods. The amount of money spent in the economy would fall short of the value of goods produced. Because of the shortfall, goods would either sit on the shelves or would have to be sold at steep discounts. Businesses that weren't selling goods or that were forced to sell at steep discounts would reduce their investment and cut payrolls. The economy would contract.

A modern version of this scenario occurs when banks hoard cash by depositing it as reserves with the central bank, rather than lending it out. For example, the cash reserves that U.S. banks held at the Federal Reserve Bank, over and above legal requirements, soared from about a billion dollars in January 2008 to a trillion dollars in June 2010.[17] The banks hoarded cash out of fear that they might need it to stay solvent, or that borrowers were not creditworthy. When potential borrowers, both firms and consumers, spend a trillion dollars less than they would have spent in other circumstances, the economy contracts.

Say's law claims that no general glut of goods can occur. It concedes that there can be an oversupply of goods in one sector or another (demand for land-line telephones drops as consumers switch to cell phones), forcing businesses out of that sector and into another. But no general, economy-wide glut can occur.[18] Adam Smith, who posited Say's law well before Say, explains the idea well: "In all countries where there is tolerable security, every man of common understanding will endeavour to employ whatever stock he can command in procuring either present enjoyment or future profit." A rational man employs his "stock" for present enjoyment by buying consumer goods. He employs it for future profit by investing it directly in production or lending it to someone else who will do so. "A man must be perfectly crazy who, where there is tolerable security, does not employ all the stock which he commands, whether it be his own or borrowed of other people, in some one or other of those three ways."[19] Since all income is spent, everything that has been produced is sold at its normal, or "natural," price. The economy proceeds without a hitch, and no recessions or depressions occur.

Say's law does not seem realistic for any capitalist economy. The industrial revolution ushered in booms and depressions. The usual response to the evidently implausible assumption that all savings are necessarily invested, as well as the obvious fact of business-cycle booms and recessions, is that these are short-term phenomena and do not affect the economy's long-run trajectory. Say's law, this response maintains, holds, on average, over the business cycle. During booms, capitalists (and consumers in a modern economy) may borrow and spend more than their incomes; during recessions, they may increase saving and spend less than their incomes on investment and other goods; but the cycle averages out.

On average, Say's law is said to capture long-run economic performance. Let's leave this debate for the moment, and return to it later.

Ricardo's classical model departs from the neoclassical model in two principle assumptions. First, a key assumption he shares with Smith, which I think has some plausibility and which I will examine further in connection with recent models that adopt it, sees long-run, or "natural," wages as determined not by markets but by social custom. It bears repeating that this assumption is about social custom, not biological subsistence:[20]

> It is not to be understood that the natural price of labour, estimated even in food and necessaries, is absolutely fixed and constant. It varies at different times in the same country, and very materially differs in different countries. *It essentially depends on the habits and customs of the people.* An English labourer would consider his wages under their natural rate, and too scanty to support a family, if they enabled him to purchase no other food than potatoes, and to live in no better habitation than a mud cabin; yet these moderate demands of nature are often deemed sufficient in countries where "man's life is cheap," and his wants easily satisfied. Many of the conveniences now enjoyed in an English cottage, would have been thought luxuries at an earlier period of our history.[21]

The idea that wages are fixed by social convention is accepted by many noneconomists. For example, Senator Byron Dorgan, Democrat of North Dakota, argued in a Senate committee hearing in 1994 that U.S. wage levels had been determined by "enormous battles between labor and those who employ labor [regarding] the proper apportionment of the income streams that go to rents and profits and wages." The resulting "political equilibrium" had settled how to apportion national income.[22] Dorgan must have had some other theory about rents, but he agreed with Ricardo about profits and wages. Likewise, Louis Uchitelle, a *New York Times* economics reporter, suggested in 2003 that profits had risen as a percentage of GDP (gross domestic product) because labor had grown "too weak to prevent many companies from pocketing virtually all the gains from productivity."[23] Though most contemporary economists have long been reluctant to accept the idea that institutions such as unions, minimum-wage laws, and executive pay boards fundamentally determine wage levels, the extraordinary and persistent worsening of income inequality in the United States and several other countries since the 1970s has led some, such as economists Frank Levy and Peter Temin of MIT, to rethink views on the matter more along Ricardo's lines.[24]

Ricardo's assumption about the social determination of wages means that society and markets are inextricably intertwined in an economy. Markets play an important role, but there is no exclusive market sphere. An economy, however efficient or inefficient it might be, cannot even be imagined outside of a social framework. By contrast, neoclassical theory admits only individual preferences working through markets. Each individual knows what gives him or her more utility or less utility: which goods are preferable to which other goods. Not only may individuals disagree with one another, but their views about utility cannot be compared. Thus, neoclassical theory sees markets alone as creating an economy and does not even admit the concept of society.

Furthermore, Ricardo differs from the contemporary mainstream in his concept of technology. He assumes that, at any given "state of the art," essentially only one technique for producing goods is known. An accounting firm hires accountants, each equipped with a state-of-the-art computer and software embodying the latest accounting rules. One firm's techniques may differ somewhat from another's—perhaps they use different software—but the differences are assumed to be minor enough that the model can ignore them. By contrast, most neoclassical models assume that, even at a given state of the art, each firm has access to a wide range of techniques. A firm can employ more labor and less capital, or vice versa, to produce the same output. Presumably, an accounting firm could hire more accountants and employ less information technology, or vice versa, though I have no idea concretely how. The neoclassical assumption about technology, envisioning firms as shopping for more capital and less labor, or vice versa, supports the idea that supply and demand determine wages and profits. The classical assumption that firms have essentially one technique to produce goods at a given state of the art—and cannot simply shop for more labor and less capital, or vice versa—undermines the supply-and-demand story.[25] It supports the view that social custom must somehow determine how income is divided between profits and wages.

Ricardo's model also accepts two more assumptions common to neoclassical models. The wage of each worker—the day laborer, the lawyer, the miner—is supposed to be some known multiple of a standard wage. The model therefore needs to handle only that standard wage. The model also assumes away monopolistic industries, and investors are supposed to be able to move readily from one sector to another.[26] The implication is that there is one economy-wide profit rate. These assumptions are hardly unproblematic, but I'll postpone discussing them, as they do not lead to salient differences between Ricardo's classical model and neoclassical theory.

Ricardo's Model

Before laying out his model, Ricardo explains that he won't even try to explain the prices of unique goods, such as "rare statues and pictures, scarce books and coins," which cannot be produced. Since their supply is fixed, their value depends solely on the "varying wealth and inclinations"—in modern terms, views about "utility"—of the people who demand them.[27] Since Ricardo knows nothing about the wealth and inclinations of those people, and, moreover, since these types of goods constitute a tiny part of an economy, he ignores them and turns to commodities produced by ongoing industries.

Like Smith, Ricardo assumes that supply and demand drive short-run fluctuations, but they don't enter his long-run model. They only cause prices of commodities, wages of labor, and profits on capital to gravitate toward their "natural," or long-run, levels.[28] As with Smith, "natural" isn't quite the right word, since social custom determines wages. I will speak of "natural," "normal," "conventional," or "long-run" prices.

Unlike Smith, Ricardo uses his assumption of socially determined wages to build a model that coherently determines profits and rents. Start with rent for land or, more broadly, natural resources.[29] Ricardo treats land as fundamentally different from capital and labor. For one thing, capital and labor can continue growing forever, while land and resources were created once and for all. For another thing, capital and labor represent humans' participation in economic production; land contributes without any human intervention. In other words, "labor" is shorthand for workers who, with their minds and bodies, carry out production. "Capital" is shorthand for entrepreneurs whose investment in factories or ships is necessary to production. Land and other resources were merely granted by nature. Of course, people conventionally called "landlords" may build barns and improve the soil, but barns and improved soil constitute productive capital; to the extent that they make such investments, landlords are really acting as capitalists. Landlords per se just lay claim to resources. Whether English gentlemen in 1817 or Saudi princes in 2011, they merely inherited title to resources from ancestors who probably grabbed them in some brutal past. And maybe not a distant past, as landlords in Ricardo's day kept driving commoners off the land by enclosing it.

If the "original and indestructible powers" of the land were created by nature, why can landlords charge rent for the use of that land? So long as rich land is freely available, no one pays rent, just as no one today pays rent for air—an essential input for many chemical plants, not to mention life—because it is "inexhaustible and at every man's disposal."[30] When the population grows to the point where all the richest land is being farmed, second-rate land must be cultivated. Those who work second-rate land must receive normal wages for their labor and normal profits on capital such as barns; otherwise they would enter some other industry. Their wages and profits set the price of corn. Landlords who own richer land see that, with the same labor and capital, it produces, say, 10 percent more than second-rate land. They charge farmers who rent their land that extra 10 percent, still leaving them with normal profits and wages. After all of the second-rate land is farmed, third-rate land must be cultivated. Now the normal wages and profits for working this land—the poorest land that must be cultivated to feed everyone—set the price of corn. Landlords with second-rate land receive, say, an extra 10 percent in rent; those with first-rate land, an extra 20 percent. And so on.[31]

Is this just a quaint story from some fairy-tale world? I think not. In the twenty-first century, the most important natural resource is energy. Vast free-energy sources are available if entrepreneurs invest the capital and labor to tap them: the sun and wind. Of course, the solar panels, windmills, and other equipment needed to generate electricity from them are expensive. Since drilling for petroleum and refining it costs substantially less, oil companies must lease—pay rent on—oil fields to get access to this more cheaply exploited source. (Except in the United States, they typically lease oil fields from governments, who retain a claim on them.) Nor are sun and wind the only possibilities. Commercial processes exist to extract oil from formerly abandoned wells, as well as other minerals from abandoned mines. For example, chemicals are driven horizontally into old oil wells to extract large but dispersed deposits. These are today's zero-rent farms. Since exploiting them, like exploiting sun and wind, costs more capital and labor than exploiting richer deposits, owners of the richer deposits receive lease payments analogous to landlords' rent.

Ricardo thus explains rent as a sort of monopolistic supplement paid to those who own the richer supplies of natural resources. The price of corn—or petroleum or minerals—is determined by the normal wages of labor and the normal profits on capital required to produce these commodities from the poorest available natural resources.[32]

Having explained rents, Ricardo now needs to explain the returns to only two factors of production: labor and capital. How are they determined? The algebra starts to get complicated when there are many commodities in the model: all of workers' "food, necessaries, and conveniences," as Ricardo says, as well as luxury goods consumed by the wealthy and capital goods required by firms. Fixed capital—factories or barns that provide a return over period of years—introduce further complications. Sraffa showed that all of these complications can be handled in Ricardo's model; but to simplify matters, let's suppose (as Ricardo initially does) that there is only one commodity in the entire economy: wheat or, as he said, corn. Capitalists plant corn; they pay workers' wages in corn; they grow and harvest corn; and they put away enough corn to invest in next year's seed and wages. Any surplus corn they grow, over and above that amount, constitutes their profit. All value is measured in bushels of corn.

Does this model sound ridiculously oversimplified? As I mentioned in Chapter 1, contemporary "dynamic stochastic general-equilibrium" (DSGE) models have only one aggregate commodity. The fact that they are one-commodity models never seems to bother macroeconomists. They could even call the commodity "corn" without any substantive effect on the models. Ricardo at least worried that his one-commodity model was unrealistic and tried to incorporate diverse commodities— wheat, sheep, clothes, carriages, steel, steam engines, and what have you. He never quite worked out the algebra, but Sraffa did in 1960. For the sake of simplicity here, let's stick with a pure corn economy.

The economy's corn harvest is divided between profits and wages. No economic law dictates how the whole harvest must be divided, except that profits must be less than the whole, wages must be less than the whole, and together they must add up to the whole. Ricardo assumes that the normal wage is determined by social custom, so if you multiply the number of workers by the conventional wage—an amount of corn— you get total economy-wide wages. Capitalists advance workers these wages at the beginning of the year and also provide the seed corn. Their total investments are thus their outlays for corn wages, plus those for seed corn. The surplus harvest, over and above these investments, constitutes their profits. Divide total profits by total investments, and you get the profit rate.

The relationship between the profit rate and the wage rate couldn't be simpler. "If the corn is to be divided between the farmer and the labourer," says Ricardo, "the larger the proportion that is given to the latter, the less will remain for the former."[33] This inverse relationship is preserved in Sraffa's algebraic model with many commodities.

Say's law completes Ricardo's model. Workers spend all of their wages on consumption goods, while capitalists devote all of their profits to investment, either planting seed for the next crop or hiring workers to till the fields. (The extreme assumption that workers consume all of their wages is unrealistic for a modern economy, and, of course, capitalists cannot invest all of their profits—they must eat something—but this assumption does not affect the model's conclusions. So long as workers save a smaller portion out of wages than capitalists save out of profits, and so long as all income is spent on consumption or investment, the results come out essentially the same.)[34] Higher profits produce higher investment, faster growth, and more employment.

Ricardo does *not* believe that there will necessarily, or even likely, be full employment. In the neoclassical model—since capitalists can always use less capital and more labor to produce the same output—so long as wages fall sufficiently, it is to their advantage to hire all available workers. Not so in Ricardo's classical model. True, because Ricardo accepts Say's law, he assumes that investment proceeds without a hitch, as capitalists plow all their profits back into production and hire as many workers as they need. But there is essentially only one technique to produce goods. If it doesn't require hiring all available workers, the unemployed go to the poorhouse or starve. In practical terms, why would Ricardo assume full employment if he believed that the ranks of the poor were swelling by the year?[35] He makes it clear, in his chapter "On Machinery" (among other places), that unemployment can persist: increased productivity can leave workers permanently out of jobs. As always, Ricardo means in the long run, after short-term market fluctuations have been worked out.[36]

Was Ricardo Right?

Ricardo's great concern was the exhaustion of fertile land or, in modern terms, natural resources. As population and manufacturing expand, but the rich land bequeathed by nature does not, food prices soar. Landlords extract ever-rising rents for the use of their land. Or, in modern terms, as we reach peak oil production, energy prices soar. The Organization of Petroleum Exporting Countries (OPEC) and other resource owners extort monopolistic profits, or what Ricardo would call "escalating rents." In his model, workers' real purchasing power doesn't change, since social custom dictates how much wheat—or the basket of goods in a multi-commodity model—their wages should buy. Instead, rising rents deplete capitalists' profits, as occurred during the oil crises of the 1970s. Investment ultimately falters, reducing economic growth and employment.

Ricardo recognizes that technological advances can keep the Malthusian exhaustion of resources at bay. The tendency of profits to fall "is happily checked at repeated intervals . . . by discoveries in the science of agriculture which enable us to relinquish a portion of labour before required," and therefore to lower the price of corn.[37] Since Ricardo's day, technology has mostly stayed a step ahead of Malthus's ghost. Agricultural improvements have fed the growing population, and advances in tapping fossil fuels and other energy sources have fed industrialization. But the race continues as we seek sustainable energy sources in hopes of yet again outrunning Malthusian dangers.

A well-regarded estimate by William Nordhaus of Yale, based on a neoclassical model, downplays these dangers. Resource depletion might reduce growth rates by one quarter of a percent.[38] Why does Nordhaus conclude that the effects would be so small? The standard neoclassical model assumes that, at a given state of the art, firms have available a variety of techniques to substitute capital for labor, using more capital and less labor or vice versa. Nordhaus makes similar assumptions about natural resources. Firms are assumed to have knowledge of and the ability to switch to techniques using more or less capital, more or less labor, *and* more or less natural resources to produce the same output. In other words, the model assumes that technology makes it possible to substitute capital or labor to replace a substantial shortfall of natural resources. The model thus assumes precisely what we don't know. In a related article, Nordhaus estimates that global warming might lower growth through the year 2050 by an utterly trivial three-hundredths of a percent per year, and recommends against policies to cut greenhouse gases.[39] Ricardo does not assume that technology provides any known way to substitute other factors for natural resources. His model realistically warns that needed technological advances may or may not be developed in time.

Ricardo's opposition to the Corn Laws follows irrefutably from his model. If those laws block corn imports, they exacerbate the rise of rents, bleeding profits, investment, growth, and employment.[40] Conversely, free imports of corn, in effect extending the range of fertile territory from which corn can be supplied, hold down the price of corn. Capitalists can maintain workers' real purchasing power, as required by social custom, while retaining good profits and investing them. As Ricardo puts it, "Wealth increases most rapidly in those countries where the disposable land is most fertile, where importation [of corn] is least restricted, and where through agricultural improvements, productions can be multiplied without any increase in the proportional quantity of labour, and where consequently the progress of rent is slow."[41]

Did Ricardo have good advice for England in that day? He was certainly right to see England's future as workshop of the world. Poor, stony land that had not previously been farmed was in fact brought into cultivation during the Napoleonic Wars. Rents did soar, as the model predicts, and the Corn Laws ensured that rents stayed high after the wars.[42] It is hard to see how these rents significantly squeezed manufacturing investment, as Ricardo feared. Recall, for example, that from the late eighteenth to the mid-nineteenth century, English cotton exports rose by a factor of thirty-two. But as bread prices reached exorbitant levels, real wages did stagnate.[43] Not too bad a job for an economic model.

Ricardo's classical model has glaring omissions. For one, Say's law denies even the possibility that faltering aggregate demand might cause the periodic depressions that plagued the course of the industrial revolution. But the model captures important problems. It admits threats from exhaustion of natural resources that neoclassical models tend to trivialize. The classical model allows a shifting balance of power and social views about who deserves what—changing norms outside of markets—to skew income distribution. Ricardo famously explained the advantages of international trade. Those advantages must be qualified if aggregate demand can affect growth in the long term, but Ricardo's insight didn't make bad sense for the England of his day or for at least some economies today. In short, for an economic model, Ricardo's did rather well.

If There Are Many Commodities

I have slipped trade into what I presented as a one-commodity corn model: a tortured effort, since who would trade corn for corn? In his *Essay on the Influence of a Low Price of Corn on the Profits of Stock,* published in 1815, Ricardo argued along these lines, but he understood the one-commodity problem and sought to correct it in his *Principles.*

If I may depart slightly from the letter of Ricardo's argument, imagine a model with two commodities. At the beginning of each year, farmers invest by planting corn seed and paying their workers corn wages. Thus, corn continues to be the wage good. Of course, farmers also harvest corn at the end of each year. Manufacturers produce manufactured goods, which I'll call iron. At the beginning of each year, they invest in a quantity of iron, which they use to produce more iron. (Using iron to produce iron is a metaphor, but it avoids bringing in more commodities that would complicate matters.) Manufacturers also pay their workers corn wages, so they trade some of the iron they produce each year for corn. They save the rest of the iron to invest in making more iron.

Now cheap corn imports are allowed. First, what happens to manufacturers? They invest the same quantity of iron each year, pay workers the same quantity of corn wages (the wage is established by custom), and produce the same amount of iron (technology hasn't changed). But they can trade less of their iron for cheap imported corn to pay wages. The extra iron that they keep gives them higher profits, which they invest. What happens to landlords? Those who own the worst land are out of luck: it's no longer worth tilling because it doesn't produce enough corn to pay normal profits and wages and still compete with cheap corn imports. Landlords with richer soil can still charge rent it but are forced to lower it. Too bad for them. What happens to farmers? Those who were tilling the worst land are squeezed in the face of cheap imports. They sell their existing stock of corn and move into manufacturing. (Remember, this is a model; capital is supposed to move freely between sectors.) Other farmers benefit. Their production process remains the same: they invest the same amount of corn seed, pay workers the same amount of corn wages, and reap the same amount of corn harvest. But with rents pushed down, they keep a larger portion of the harvest, so they earn the same higher profit rate that manufacturers now do.

The classical model has interesting implications for trade and technological advance. If either trade or technological advance merely reduces the cost of luxury goods for the wealthy—if "wine, velvets, silks, and other expensive commodities should fall 50 per cent," as Ricardo says—the benefits are narrowly restricted to those particular goods. Only if a nation more efficiently obtains the "food, necessaries, and conveniences" consumed by workers do the effects matter broadly. Today, consumer products such as cars that require energy to produce or operate would be included. In this case workers can retain their purchasing power while profits and investment rise.[44]

To hold the Malthusian problem at bay, Ricardo also hopes society will support gradually rising wages: "The friends of humanity cannot but wish that in all countries the labouring classes should have a taste for comfort and enjoyments, and that they should be stimulated by all legal means in their exertions to procure them. There cannot be a better security against superabundant population."[45] In effect, if wretched conditions cause promiscuity and aggravate population growth, a higher standard of living must encourage workers to have fewer children and must lower population growth.[46]

Was this idea right? The theory of the demographic transition, generally accepted today, holds that as incomes rise during the height of the industrial revolution, people live longer, and population surges. After incomes approach the levels of today's middle-income countries such as Mexico, children become an expense—instead of earning income as laborers, they must be supported through school—so parents start having fewer offspring, and population growth levels off. Population has, in fact, been leveling off in Mexico, and in some European nations it has been declining. Ricardo's insight captures some real truth, but it was not applicable during the height of the industrial revolution.

Note that Ricardo made his sociological assumption—that a more prosperous working class would reduce population growth—in effect *outside* of his economic model. In other words, the economic model says nothing about the relationship between wages and population growth. It simply assumes that customary wages and other factors are given, and it plugs them in to determine profits, savings, investment, and growth. The sociological assumption that higher wages tend to reduce population growth is not part of the model itself. There is a lesson here. In applying a model, pay attention not only to the model itself, but also to external assumptions that you plug into it.

Suppose higher wages do reduce population growth, as they seem to in middle-income countries today. According to the model, will they result in faster or slower economic growth? It depends. On the one hand, higher wages claim a greater share of income, reducing profits, investment, and growth. On the other hand, since higher wages lower population growth, they diminish pressure on natural resources, reducing rents. Capitalists retain higher profits, raising investment and growth. Since higher wages reduce growth through one channel, while they raise it through another, the net effect is indeterminate, as economists say. ("Indeterminate" is a good term: it means the same thing in economics that it does in ordinary English.) To ascertain the net effect of higher wages in Ricardo's model, you would have to statistically compare the strength of the opposing mechanisms. Let's not go there. Ricardo might respond that, given the ambiguity of the situation, and given that he saw the Malthusian exhaustion of resources as a persistent threat, support for moderate wage increases seems both humanitarian and practical.

Before leaving Ricardo, I should mention his view about tax cuts. He claimed that "there are no taxes which have not a tendency to lessen the power to accumulate [capital]."[47] Taxing capitalists directly erodes profits and investment. Taxing workers has the same effect, since capitalists are obliged to raise their wages by the full amount of the tax, so as to maintain real wages as dictated by social custom. Not a tax-cut zealot, Ricardo plods through many tedious chapters seeking some tax source that will not erode profits. He finds it—surprise!—in a tax on rents. It would only reduce the rents that landlords extract for the use of land. The problem, Ricardo concedes, is practical. Landlords' charges that are nominally called "rent" in fact include both true rent on the land itself and profit on investments in barns or other capital improvements. Thus, in practice, a tax on what is called "rent" would affect farming investment, and it could be as bad as any other tax.

FIVE

Chasing a Chimera

In the 1820s British pamphleteers who were later dubbed "Ricardian socialists" drew on Ricardo's model to launch working-class critiques of capitalism.[1] Though Ricardo saw capitalists and workers as sharing progressive interests that backward landlords frustrate, the class-structure framework of his model certainly leaves room for conflict between capitalists and workers. In *Labour Defended against the Claims of Capital,* an effort to dissuade Parliament from passing anti-labor legislation in 1825, Thomas Hodgskin leaves no doubt that he sees such conflict: "Wages vary inversely as profits; or wages rise when profits fall, and profits rise when wages fall; and it is therefore profits, or the capitalist's share of the national produce, which is opposed to wages, or the share of the labourer."[2]

Hodgskin moves toward a Marxian labor theory of value: the idea that labor, and labor alone, creates value. He says that "the real price of a coat or a pair of shoes or a loaf of bread, all which nature demands from man in order that he may have either of these very useful articles, is a certain quantity of labour." Capitalists just extract unnecessary profits:

"For the labourer to have [a coat, shoes, or bread] he must give over and above the quantity of labour nature demands from him, a still large[r] quantity to the capitalist. Before he can have a coat, he must pay interest [that is, a profit rate] for the farmer's sheep, interest on the wool after it has got into the hands of the wool merchant, interest for this same wool as raw material, after it is in the hands of the manufacturer, interest on all buildings and tools he uses, and interest on all the wages he pays his men."[3] Since profit is an exploitive addition to real prices, Hodgskin denies capital "any just claim to the large share of the national produce now bestowed on it."

The Ricardian socialists did not confine their arguments to the polite halls of Oxford or Cambridge, but sought to educate workers about economics and mobilize them through "mechanics institutes" in industrial cities.[4] Working-class movements amplified the pamphleteers' ideas, and the ideas supplied impetus to the movements. After the Reform Act of 1832 extended the vote from landed and moneyed classes to the middle class but stopped there, the London Working Men's Association drew up its People's Charter demanding universal male suffrage, the secret ballot, and other reforms. Leaders rallied "workers," not "citizens," and attacked the exploitation of labor.[5] The Chartists launched a string of protests, foisted petitions on Parliament with as many as 3.2 million signatures, and unleashed a general strike that ended with 15,000 arrests. In April 1848, as revolts spread across continental Europe, some 150,000 Chartists who gathered in London to press demands for the vote were confronted by 4,000 police and a posse of 85,000.[6] The government rejected their petition and arrested the leaders.

Both British working-class movements and the Ricardian socialists were ultimately reformist, making essentially moral claims. Hodgskin wrote: "The contest is not only one of physical endurance, or who can stand out longest, but of argument and reason. It is possible for the workmen to force their masters into compliance, but they must convince the public of the justice of their demands." In concluding *Labour Defended,* he expresses his hope that "final success must be on the side of justice."

Karl Marx was inspired by the Ricardian socialists and leaned heavily on Ricardo.[7] While neoclassical economists see the distribution of income between profits and wages and the value of goods as determined by individuals' subjective preferences, Marx, like other classical economists, saw distribution and value as determined by social decisions. Workers' purchasing power includes a "historical and moral component," Marx agreed, and it is set at a conventional level, not at a subsistence level.[8]

Unlike Ricardo, however, Marx maintained the labor theory of value (Adam Smith's view is not quite clear).[9] Marx saw the values of commodities as depending only on the hours of labor required to produce them. Of course, value appears also to include capitalists' profits, but this appearance is superficial. As Maurice Dobb of Cambridge University puts it, the labor theory revealed for Marx "the 'hidden essence' and 'inner form' lying beneath the superficial 'outward disguises' or 'market appearance' of things."[10] Since capitalists own the means of production, they bargain with workers on unequal terms and can require workers to spend more hours on the job than are equivalent to the labor value of the goods they produce. Capitalists extract the difference as "surplus value."[11]

An Inconsistent Model

Marx's writings deal with issues ranging from philosophy to politics, and largely stand or fall on their own, quite apart from the labor theory. Moreover, the labor theory of value isn't a bad approximation. It is often taken as such, even in some neoclassical models. As the economic historian George Stigler titled one essay, in practical terms it might not be far wrong to accept the "93 Percent Labor Theory of Value."[12] Labor is surely a better gauge of value than gold, because it fluctuates far less erratically. But Marx doesn't want to be 93 percent right; he wants to be scientifically and philosophically right. He insists that the labor theory is the only "scientific" way to analyze an economy and charges that his critics are motivated by "their apologetic dread of a scientific analysis of value."[13]

The labor theory does not work. The problem is that producing two different goods may require the same number of labor hours, but shorter or longer periods of time. For both producers to earn the same profit rate—the same return on investment *per year*—the one whose production process takes longer must receive a higher value for that commodity.

For example, suppose the economy-wide profit rate is 10 percent.[14] (In the long-run classical model, profits are equalized across all industries.) A sheep farmer hires twenty hands for one year, advancing twenty labor-years of wages at the beginning of the year and selling the wool at the end of the year. A rancher hires ten cowboys for two years—also twenty years of labor—but advances ten labor-years of wages at the beginning of the first year, then another ten labor-years of wages at the beginning of the second year, and sells his cattle only at the end of the second year. The cattle must sell for 5 percent more than the wool. The reason is that the rancher had to advance half of the wages two years ahead rather than just one year ahead. In order to make a 10 percent profit rate on half of the wage bill that first year, the rancher must be paid 5 percent more than the sheep farmer.

A clever proponent of the labor theory might argue that Marx really isn't in trouble. Even though two commodities made with the same number of labor hours over different periods of time must have different values, their values can still be measured in labor-hours, just as they could be measured in pounds sterling.

If the profit rate changes, however, Marx *is* in trouble. In the case of the sheep farmer and the rancher, suppose the economy-wide profit rate is 20 percent. Now the cattle must be valued at 10 percent more than the sheep, rather than 5 percent more. As the profit rate increases, the value of the cattle must rise relative to that of the sheep.[15] The labor-year ruler of value has to stretch as if it were rubber. Labor hours cannot provide a fixed gauge of value because the profit element cannot be extracted from that gauge.

Marx himself understood this rubber-ruler problem, called the "transformation problem" by subsequent Marxists, though he expressed it in somewhat different form. It had sunk from sight until Paul Sweezy, a brilliant and personable Marxist whom I once had the opportunity to meet in his home in New Hampshire, resurrected it in 1946 in his *Theory of Capitalist Development*. He sparked a decades-long debate pitting Marxists versus anti-Marxists, including Paul Samuelson. The upshot is that the transformation problem cannot be solved in any sense that Marx himself would have accepted.[16] Proponents tried to rescue the labor theory by reinterpreting it. In *Economics and Ideology*, Ronald Meek concedes that the transformation cannot be solved in the way Marx wanted to, but argues that "the equilibrium prices of commodities can still be shown to be 'indirectly' and 'ultimately' determined by certain crucial ratios of aggregate quantities of embodied labour applicable to the economy as a whole."[17] Oh dear! I believe I once figured out what he meant, but let's not go there. Such a convoluted sentence does not capture what Marx meant by the labor theory—he always wrote clearly and, I might add, elegantly—nor do I find it a plausible reinterpretation of the labor theory.[18]

The problem with the labor theory I have been discussing has nothing to do with whether profits are or are not justified. The problem is theoretical. Values or prices, call them what you will, cannot be consistently measured in terms of labor-hours alone.[19] Marx deserves credit for taking the labor theory seriously enough, and trying hard enough to work it out within his classical model, to notice the transformation problem and recognize that he hadn't solved it, even though he hoped it could be solved. Adam Smith articulated the labor theory so vaguely, once he moved beyond his myth of an "early and rude state of society," that he never even realized what a mess he was in. But Marx insisted on a theoretical chimera that he failed to model. The labor theory became a religion that generations of Marxist politicians and theorists used as if it were a science. The power of such chimeras to overwhelm practical judgment is terrifying.

Oddly, the failure of the labor theory may also pose problems for John Locke's liberalism and the philosophical foundation of the Declaration of Independence. Since labor created all value in an early "state of nature," Locke argues, it created a natural right for individuals to own and bequeath property. Moreover, Locke seems to have supposed that some actual precapitalist state of nature existed, in which individuals produced and traded goods based on the labor content of those goods. This would be the weirdest reading of the church-and-manor economy of medieval Europe that anyone ever conceived. If such a labor-based economy never existed in practice, and if the labor theory cannot be justified in theory, what happens to the foundations of liberalism? Once profits contribute inextricably to prices, and rent on natural resources conquered by rapacious ancestors does so as well, the natural right to property no longer looks so secure. The question might require another book, so I leave it unanswered.

SIX

Utopia

As the so-called Ricardian socialists roused the British working class, academic economists and their politician allies—often the same individuals—worried.[1] Even Ricardo's close friend James Mill confided concerns about Hodgskin's lectures in a letter: "If they were to spread they would be subversive of civilized society."[2] By the 1830s, these economist-politicians were crafting proto-neoclassical ideas to extricate society from classical theory and replace it with individual-utility maximization.[3]

George Poulett Scrope, a member of Parliament whose countless pamphlets earned him the nickname "Pamphlet Scrope," asked if Ricardian political economy would reconcile workers to "the hardships of a condition of almost ceaseless toil for, in many cases, but a meager subsistence."[4] On consulting Ricardo, he could not find "any answer likely to satisfy the mind of a half-educated man of plain common-sense and honesty who should seek there some justification for the immense disparity of fortunes and circumstances that strike the eye on every side." Something had to be done.

Mountifort Longfield, professor of political economy at Trinity College, Dublin, and member of the Irish privy council, disputed Ricardo's view that society could collectively determine customary wage levels, declaring that the "wages of the labourer depend upon the value of his labour."[5] Legislation or labor union action to raise wages would only do "mischief," so right thinking was imperative to forestall such efforts. "It depends in some degree upon every person present," he warned in a lecture in 1833, "whether the labourer is told that his interest will be best promoted by prudence and industry, or by a violent demolition of the capital destined to his support."[6]

Nassau Senior, a professor of political economy at Oxford and a Whig Party advisor, was perhaps the most important of these economist-politicians. He proposed that value arises from the "pleasure" derived from a good, and defended capitalists as contributing to production through "abstinence," his morally tinged word for saving.[7] Abstinence, he argued, deserves remuneration, since it "stands in the same relation to profit as labour does to wages."[8] His political economy led him to oppose trade unions and draft the Poor Law Reform of 1834, an infamously harsh measure to end wage subsidies and force destitute families into the dreaded Poor House.[9]

The neoclassical theory that emerged in Britain over the course of the nineteenth century seemed to respond to these economist-politicians' concerns. It rejected the assumption that social custom determines the division of income between capital and labor, and replaced it with assumptions about atomistic individuals and firms. Consumers are supposed to buy more oranges and fewer apples at the market, or vice versa, to maximize utility. Firms are likewise supposed to chose between factors of production on the market, hiring more capital and less labor—more machinery and fewer workers—or vice versa, to minimize costs. These purely individualistic choices determine the division of income between capital and labor, as well as the prices of goods. The very concept of society is banished.

Political authority and neoclassical theory did not fit together so well in the rest of Europe. In 1848, as largely middle-class revolts spread across the Continent, and working-class movements hitched themselves to the cause, Karl Marx and Friedrich Engels proclaimed *The Communist Manifesto*. Conservative politicians put down the revolts, but the specter haunting Europe did not inspire them to espouse proto-neoclassical ideas. In Germany, the famous political coalition of iron and rye (industrialists and estate owners), forged by Chancellor Otto von Bismarck, provided trade protection for manufacturing and agriculture, while affording some social insurance for workers. It seems doubtful that Bismarck cared for even a moment about economists' ideas, and, in any event, most economic thinking was hardly neoclassical. It was dominated by the German historical school, best remembered for the industrial-policy advocate Georg Friedrich List.

However, a smattering of neoclassicals did spread across the Continent and did conceive a political mission of defeating Marx. The Austrian economist Eugen von Böhm-Bawerk, who launched an effective theoretical criticism of the labor theory of value, underlined its political implications. "In the war in which the issue is the system under which human society shall be organized," Böhm-Bawerk warned, the labor theory of value constituted "the focal point about which attack and defence rally."[10] Looking back from the year 1901, Knut Wicksell, professor at Lund University in Sweden, commented that socialists regarded capitalists "as parasites on production, and their rewards a robbery at the expense of labour, which is alone entitled to remuneration." He noted that for economists, "the establishment of a new and better-founded theory of exchange value was, therefore, not only of abstract theoretical importance, but also of eminent practical and social interest."[11]

The New Economics

Though neoclassical theory, like all economic theories, responded to its social and political situation, to see it as no more than such a response would profoundly miss its intellectual force. Professor William Stanley Jevons of University College London gathered the various strands of proto-neoclassical ideas into a powerful argument in 1871, in his neo-classical landmark, *The Theory of Political Economy*. He even introduced the word "economics" in its modern sense, in the second edition in 1879. He there proposed adopting an informal usage he had heard among his colleagues and replacing "the old troublesome double-worded name of our Science"—political economy—with "the single convenient term *Economics*."[12] He hoped that "*Economics* will become the recognised name of a science."[13] He meant a science like Newtonian physics. Though he adopted ideas from the anti-labor economist-politicians such as Nassau Senior (I lifted Senior's quotes, cited above, from Jevons), a reading of Jevons's book leaves little doubt that he cared more about new scientific ways of thinking than about a social agenda.

Jevons sought to distinguish economics from any historical discipline such as "Mr. Spencer's Sociology."[14] Instead, it should be a deductive science, proceeding from agreed-upon assumptions—those that any reasonable person can accept—to logical conclusions. He thought we can agree, for example, that "every person will choose the greater apparent good; that human wants are more or less quickly satiated; that prolonged labour becomes more and more painful." He argued that "from these axioms we can deduce the laws of supply and demand, the laws of that difficult conception, value, and all the intricate results of commerce, so far as data are available."[15]

Jevons had a good case for proceeding deductively. As John Stuart Mill had argued, economists run into trouble if they try to draw conclusions inductively from observations. One way to see the problem is to consider a situation such as drug trials, in which you *can* draw persuasive conclusions inductively. In a reliable drug test, individuals given the drug are compared with members of a control group—alike in age range, health, and other characteristics—who are given a placebo. In economics, Jevons argues, you would need one factor to vary—say, free trade versus protectionism—while everything else about the economy remained the same. But everything else about economies never does remain the same:

> Entirely to prove the good effects of Free Trade in England, for example, we ought to have the nation unaltered in every circumstance except the abolition of burdens and restrictions on trade. But it is obvious that while Free Trade was being introduced into England [with repeal of the Corn Laws in 1846], many other causes of prosperity were also coming into action—the progress of invention, the construction of railways, the profuse consumption of coal, the extension of the colonies, etc. etc. Although, then, the beneficent results of Free Trade are great and unquestionable, they could hardly be proved to exist a posteriori; they are to be believed because deductive reasoning from premises of almost certain truth leads us confidently to expect such results, and there is nothing in experience which in the least conflicts with our expectations.[16]

Ricardo also reasoned deductively, but Jevons rejected his specific assumptions: "The only hope of attaining a true system of Economics is to fling aside, once and for ever, the mazy and preposterous assumptions of the Ricardian School."[17] Assumptions about utility-maximizing individuals and firms—like bodies in physics obeying laws—would refashion the new science after what was then called mechanics: "As all the physical sciences have their basis more or less obviously in the general principles of mechanics, so all branches and divisions of economic science must be pervaded by certain general principles. It is to the investigation of such principles—to the tracing out of the mechanics of self-interest and utility, that this essay has been devoted."[18] In a century when Newtonian physics remained the model science, economics sought to emulate it. In the first paragraph of his canonical history of neoclassical theory—a history that itself shares the neoclassical ethos—George Stigler says the theory transformed economics "from an art, in many respects literary, to a science of growing rigor."[19]

The founders of neoclassical theory were professors. A triumvirate is credited with the pioneering works of the 1870s. Jevons was one. In 1874, Leon Walras, professor of political economy at the University of Lausanne in Switzerland, published *Elements of Pure Economics,* a mathematical tour de force that aimed to develop a model of general equilibrium. In 1871, Carl Menger, professor of political economy at the University of Vienna, published *Principles of Economics,* a less mathematical account of neoclassical ideas. Stigler singles out ten neoclassical innovators, all but one of whom he lists as primarily professors; the one exception was first a minister and second a professor.[20] As the "amateur of the past" thus gave way to the specialist, the historian Mark Blaug notes, "economics began to emerge as a professional discipline with its own network of associations and journals."[21] Economists settled into universities, which were themselves being transformed into something that might better have been called "multiversities," loose agglomerations of schools, each advancing its distinct disciplinary line of research.

I will first discuss neoclassical assumptions about utility, which economists developed first, and turn later to assumptions about production. I'll start with Jevons, partly for the parochial reason that he wrote in English, but partly because he struggled interestingly to lay the philosophical foundations of utility theory. I will sometimes skip forward to Knut Wicksell's *Lectures on Political Economy,* published in 1901. The early neoclassicals bollixed some things up that he did a clear and nuanced job of straightening out.[22] He is interesting, as well, because he thoughtfully weighed the claims of classical economics.

Strange New Ideas

The neoclassicals made profound contributions to economics. Before one questions them, it's useful to understand them—in particular, their assumptions about what "utility" means and how rational individuals seek to maximize it. These assumptions are widely misrepresented. For example, a supposedly "groundbreaking" work by the sociologist Alan Wolfe, quoted in the *New York Times,* argues that economists' view of "human beings as pure calculators of self-interest . . . ignores virtually all differences across time, space, temperament and culture."[23] Where exactly did Wolfe find this account of utility? Jevons emphasizes that there is no objective, universal gauge of utility. He says he never attempts "in any single instance . . . to compare the amount of feeling in one mind with that in another." On the contrary, he insists, "Every mind is . . . inscrutable to every other mind, and no common denominator of feeling seems to be possible."[24] Gary Becker, who won a Nobel Prize for work on economic rationality, declares that individuals "maximize welfare *as they conceive it,* whether they be selfish, altruistic, loyal, spiteful, or masochistic."[25] The italics are his. All economists fundamentally ask is consistency. If you prefer A over B and B over C, you cannot turn around and prefer C over A. I can prefer C over B and B over A, so long as I am consistent. Our preferences assuredly may vary according to our culture and personal temperament.[26]

Utilitarianism—the notion that we seek pleasure or happiness, and that public policies should provide the greatest happiness to the greatest number—was a century old before Jevons wrote his *Principles,* but it remained awfully vague. How can you gauge happiness, and what on earth is "the greatest happiness for the greatest number"? Jevons gave the concept meaning. He posited that each individual defines pleasure—or "utility," as he called it—for himself or herself, according to purely personal standards. Whatever the individual *says* gives him or her more utility in fact *does* so. We each judge our own utility; there is no external standard to tell us what it is. Adding different people's utilities then becomes impossible—but it turns out that you don't need to add utilities to determine consumer demand, even consumer demand across an entire economy.

Jevons ponders what we mean by the "utility" of, say, water. On the one hand, he notes, "A quart of water per day has the high utility of saving a person from dying in a most distressing manner." On the other hand, the low price we typically pay for water—often nothing—suggests that we value its utility hardly at all. He resolves this paradox, raised by Adam Smith a hundred years earlier, by arguing that utility is not a fixed quantity that can be attached to a commodity; it is impossible to say that water has more utility than a diamond or vice versa. A commodity's utility depends, in part, on how much of the commodity we already have. The first gallon of water has vast utility, but the more we have, the less utility each additional gallon provides:

> Several gallons a day may possess much utility for such purposes as cooking and washing; but after an adequate supply is secured for these uses, any additional quantity is a matter of comparative indifference. All that we can say, then, is, that water, up to a certain quantity, is indispensable; that further quantities will have various degrees of utility; but that beyond a certain quantity the utility sinks gradually to zero; it may even become negative, that is to say, further supplies of the same substance may become inconvenient and hurtful.[27]

To illustrate how the neoclassical model sees us as maximizing utility and determining our demand for goods, I adapt a parable from Wicksell.[28] It's silly, but its silliness underlines the fact that it is a model. A pioneer harvests two hundred bushels of corn and won't harvest more until next year. He puts aside the first forty bushels as seed. He saves the next forty bushels as the minimum he needs to eat next year to survive. He uses another forty bushels to raise forty chickens, because he considers those chickens as having more utility for him than that much additional corn to eat as grain. He uses forty more bushels of corn to distill ten barrels of whisky, and the last forty bushels to feed parrots. Again, he prefers devoting his corn to each of these uses—parrots provide him company—rather than keeping the additional corn to eat as grain. However, a different pioneer has different preferences. She also harvests two hundred bushels of corn, but after putting aside forty to sew next spring, she keeps sixty bushels to eat as grain, uses twenty to raise chickens, converts twenty to whisky, and feeds the final sixty bushels to her friendly parrots.

The pioneers both allocate corn so as to obtain, according to their own personal preferences, the most utility they can. If they felt they could derive more utility by using an additional bushel of corn to raise another chicken while sacrificing a quarter barrel of whisky, or vice versa, they would do so, and increase their utility. If they believed they could derive more utility by reallocating a bushel of corn among any of the feasible alternatives—eating it as grain, raising a chicken, distilling a quarter-barrel of whisky, or feeding parrots—they would do so, and thereby increase their utility.

Notice a few points here. The pioneers have different preferences, and there is no claim that the utility the first pioneer gets from drinking whisky or consuming any other good bears any relation to the utility that the second pioneer gets from consuming any good. "Every mind is . . . inscrutable to every other mind, and no common denominator of feeling seems to be possible," as Jevons says. Indeed, because of their different preferences—their different conceptions of utility—the pioneers have different demands for corn as grain, for chickens, for whisky, and for the company of parrots.

However, each pioneer does privately weigh alternative choices according to his or her own personal, internal gauge. As Jevons says, the motives in one mind are weighed against "other motives in the same mind."[29] The pioneers do not try to gauge the total utility derived from any use of corn. The total utility of the corn that provides a minimum of grain to survive equals life itself. But the utility of consuming an *additional* bushel of corn can be weighed against the utility of using an *additional* bushel to raise a chicken.

The pioneers try to get the same utility from the last bushel of corn that they devote to each alternative use. For example, the second pioneer should get the same utility from the sixtieth bushel of corn she uses to eat as grain, the twentieth used to raise chickens, the twentieth used to distill whisky, and the sixtieth used to feed parrots. If, say, she feels she will get less utility from the sixtieth bushel used to feed parrots than from the twentieth used to distill whisky, she can feed the parrots a bushel less, use that additional bushel to distill whisky, and thereby increase her overall utility.

The pioneer scenario is effectively identical to a model in which individuals maximize utility and determine their demand for chickens, whisky, or other goods when the prices of those goods have already been fixed in terms of corn.[30] That is, it's as if the same two farmers had grown two hundred bushels of corn, and instead of using the corn to raise chickens or distill whisky, they took the corn to market and traded a bushel of corn for a chicken or a quarter-barrel of whisky. Presumably, if their preferences remained unchanged, the individuals faced with those same exchange ratios would make the same choices.

Two explanatory remarks: First, so far we aren't trying to understand *why* goods trade at those ratios, such as one bushel of corn for one quarter-barrel of whisky; we're asking only how individuals would react *if* faced with those ratios. In effect, labels pricing goods in terms of corn have already been stamped on products at the market. Second, goods are priced in terms of bushels of corn because the model assumes that it doesn't matter if a bushel of corn costs £10 or $15 or 150 pesos; only the ratio at which other goods trade for corn matters. Microeconomic models are usually constructed this way in "real" terms. Money is usually treated later, as a sort of afterthought.

As individuals in our model maximize their utility, they want the "final degree of utility" they receive from each good, as Jevons put it—the utility received for exchanging the last bushel of corn for each good—to be equal. In terms of money, if in my estimation the last dollar's worth of spinach gives me less utility than the last dollar's worth of tomatoes, I buy the tomatoes. I seek to equalize my final degree of utility from each good without even knowing it.

Neoclassical usage today refers to "marginal utility" instead of "final degree of utility." As you acquire more of a good, the marginal utility you derive from an additional unit of it diminishes. *Homo economicus* wants the marginal utility derived from the last dollar, or the last bushel of corn, spent on each good to be equal.

Can You Count Utils?

Did we just fall for a slight-of-hand trick? Jevons concedes, "I hesitate to say that men will ever have the means of measuring directly the feelings of the human heart. A unit of pleasure or of pain is difficult even to conceive."[31] Then, later in the same paragraph, he insinuates: "We can no more know nor measure gravity in its own nature than we can measure a feeling; but, just as we measure gravity by its effects in the motion of a pendulum, so we may estimate the equality or inequality of feelings by the decisions of the human mind." Wait! We can very well measure gravity. It is a force usually measured in a unit called a newton. A kilogram, weighed on the earth's surface, exerts a downward force of about 10 newtons.

Can utility be measured in some unit that we might call "utils"? Nineteenth-century neoclassicals wrote as if there were such a unit, though they conceded that my measure of utils may differ from yours. In effect, I might measure utility in kilometers, and you might measure it in miles. The difficulty gets worse. Zero miles is still zero kilometers, but my zero-point of utility might not be yours. To switch analogies, I might measure utility in Centigrade, and you might measure it in Fahrenheit. What I call 0, you call 32, and we proceed from there at different rates. But even if the translation from Centigrade to Fahrenheit and back may tax our arithmetic abilities, it can be done. A thermometer-like gauge, more properly called a "cardinal gauge," is still a valid measure of quantity. It's hard to catch nineteenth-century neoclassicals baldly stating that utility is a cardinal quantity like temperature, but much of their math works only if utility is cardinal.[32]

By the 1930s, economists were rejecting the idea of cardinal utility. They developed the modern notion of utility in terms of preferences.

Offered bundles of goods labeled A, B, and C, I can rank them, saying I prefer A the most and C the least, but I can't say in any quantitative sense how much I prefer one bundle to the next. Alphabetical order is a common noncardinal ranking. "Aardvark" comes before "aardwolf," but you can't say how much before. This is the kind of merely "ordinal" ranking of goods that modern theorists assume our preferences allow us to make.

Not coincidentally, just about the time economists gave up assuming any cardinal unit of utility, they realized that no such concept is necessary, or even very useful, to model consumer behavior. Here a verbal account would get intricate, but—trust me—even though nineteenth-century neoclassicals did assume cardinal utility, they didn't need that assumption in order to model how we individually allocate our money among different goods, or even how economy-wide demand is determined.[33] Deny neoclassicals the right to conceive of utility as having cardinal units, and the theory of consumer behavior gets more intricate but still stands. I will sometimes speak of utility as if it were cardinal and could be gauged in utils, as economists routinely do, but this is only a manner of speaking. The same things could be said, more elaborately, without any such unit.

Supply, Demand, Equilibrium

I have been discussing neoclassicals' assumption about utility maximization. It describes how individuals react, given a set of prices already stamped on goods—for example, given how many bushels of corn you must exchange for a barrel of whisky. But how does the neoclassical model determine the price at which goods actually trade in a given market (the ratio of how many bushels of corn are exchanged for one barrel of whisky) and the total demand for the goods (how many barrels of whisky in all are traded for corn at that ratio)?

To model the neoclassical market, you need supply-and-demand curves. In an economics class I once audited, MIT economist Rudiger Dornbusch gave a useful piece of advice: "Whenever you have a curve going down, you need another curve going up." Or else he said the opposite; I can't remember. The price of a good is usually plotted on a vertical scale, and, for each price, the amount that people desire to buy or sell is plotted on a horizontal scale. As the price of a good falls, people are supposed to want to buy more of it, so you get a falling demand curve. As the price of a good rises, producers are supposed to want to sell more of it, so you get a rising supply curve.

Jevons never drew supply-and-demand curves. Alfred Marshall, Jevons's longer-lived contemporary who became the preeminent English Victorian economist, is often credited with developing them.[34] He tended to emphasize rough, practical applications of economics, shying away from sweeping statements and relegating math to notes at the end of the numerous editions of his *Principles of Economics*. There is much to be said in favor of his practical bent, but it led him to blur theory.[35] I adapt my accounts of supply-and-demand curves from Wicksell, a precise theorist. Incidentally, he, too, explained key points verbally and did the calculus in finer-print sections.[36]

If one person's utility can't be added to another's, how does neoclassical theory derive market demand for a good? And even nineteenth-century neoclassicals conceded that different individuals' utilities can't be added, since if I gauge utility in Centigrade and you gauge it in Fahrenheit, adding our utilities together gives a meaningless number. But the neoclassical model does *not* add utilities. It adds the amounts of *commodities*, such as whisky or chickens, that individuals demand at a given price, and it adds the amounts of commodities that they supply. Barrels of whisky and numbers of chickens are readily added.

To construct a market demand curve, start with one individual's demand for a good at different prices. Still gauging prices in terms of bushels of corn, imagine that a farmer who brings corn to market might be allowed to trade it for chickens at different rates. A chicken might cost one bushel, one and a half bushels, or two bushels of corn—and as it does, the farmer who is maximizing utility will buy different numbers of chickens. For example, at the exchange rate I posited earlier, when one bushel of corn traded for one chicken, the first farmer traded forty bushels of corn for forty chickens. If he discovers, instead, that two bushels of corn must be traded for one chicken, he would have to trade eighty bushels for forty chickens. The chickens are not worth that much corn to him, so he buys fewer. Depending on his preferences, he might decide to trade only twenty bushels for ten chickens to eat on special occasions; keep ten more bushels of corn to eat as grain, and spend ten more bushels of corn on whisky to console himself.

As the price of chickens in terms of bushels of corn rises, the farmer will buy fewer. Or as their price in terms of bushels of corn falls, the farmer will buy more. He has a falling demand curve for chickens. The second farmer also has a falling demand curve for chickens, though she may well have a different curve, depending on her preferences.

Economy-wide demand is now easy to determine. Given any price chickens might trade for in terms of bushels of corn, individuals maximizing utility will decide on their personal demands for chickens. And even though one person's *utility* cannot be added to another's, their *demands* for chickens, at any given price, can perfectly well be added: just count up the chickens. Adding together all individuals' demands gives the market demand, at any given price.[37] On this point, the theory works without a hitch even if individuals can express their preferences only in some alphabetical-like order, without cardinal utils. And since each individual's demand curve is falling, so is the market demand curve, or aggregate demand curve.

Now, as Dornbusch advised, we need a curve going up: the supply curve. I'm postponing the account of production, but you can get a supply curve even in a pure trading economy. Again, imagine that different individuals bring corn, chickens, or whisky to the market to trade. And to simplify matters, suppose that each one comes to the market bringing only one type of good to trade, whether corn, chickens, or whisky. The question is how these individuals trade the goods they bring to the market to obtain their preferred combination of goods to consume.

Suppose a chicken farmer brings twenty chickens. For any given chicken price, still gauged in bushels of corn, how many chickens will she supply, or trade, for corn? If the price is very low—say, she gets only a tenth of a bushel of corn for a chicken—she may not want to buy any corn at all and will instead take the chickens home to eat. If the price of chicken rises, so that she gets a half-bushel of corn for a chicken, she will consult her preferences and decide that she wants to supply, or trade, ten chickens for five bushels of corn, thus obtaining some variety in her diet. If chicken prices rise further, so that a chicken trades for a full bushel of corn, she will prefer to supply twenty chickens for twenty bushels of corn. (She has more chickens at home.) She thus has a rising supply curve: as the price of chickens rises (still gauged in bushels of corn), she trades more of them in exchange for corn.

You can add the number of chickens that each chicken farmer would freely supply, or trade, for corn—at any given price—in order to get the total number of chickens the market would supply at that price. And since each chicken farmer prefers to supply more chickens as the price rises, it doesn't matter that individual supply curves differ. Adding up how many chickens all the chicken farmers would supply at any given price, you get a rising market supply curve for chickens.

At some price, corn farmers' falling market demand curve for chickens intersects with chicken farmers' rising supply curve. At that price, chicken farmers will freely choose to supply exactly as many chickens as corn farmers freely choose to demand. The chicken market is in equilibrium.

This supply-and-demand story assumes that there are no market "imperfections." If there were production or purchasing cartels, Wicksell points out, they would set a price through bargaining. Supply-and-demand curves would not determine the price.[38] But so long as numerous chicken farmers and corn farmers individually decide how much they prefer to supply or demand at any given price, at some set of prices the market (or aggregate) supply curves and demand curves for all commodities intersect. So Jevons implicitly believed, and so Wicksell and Walras explicitly argued.[39] At those prices, the market is in equilibrium. The amount of each good that all consumers freely demand equals the amount that all producers freely supply.

Trouble in Utopia

I have told the satisfying nineteenth-century supply-and-demand parable, such as introductory textbooks still tell and economists dealing with practical problems almost always assume. However, twentieth-century neoclassical theorists concluded that it is deeply problematic. And sometimes it fails importantly in practice, as well as in theory.

One problem is that, following Jevons, I have been discussing goods in isolation. Let's switch examples to illustrate what I mean. One gallon of gasoline a day is vital to you, Jevons would say, since you need it in order to drive to work; a second gallon provides a smaller increment of utility by letting you visit friends in the country; additional gallons extend the range you can travel, but their marginal utility diminishes as you tire of driving. The problem with this story is that the marginal utility you derive from an additional gallon of gasoline depends not only on the amount of gasoline you already have but also on the other goods you own. An additional gallon of gasoline gives you far more utility if you own an Airstream camper than if you own only a motorcycle.

Once economic theory accepts this principle, Jevons's assumption of declining marginal utility no longer seems persuasive, and—trust me, again—it does *not* even guarantee that individuals maximize utility.[40] Theorists patched up this problem by inventing a more intricate assumption about preferences (I'll spare readers by not delving into it). Making this assumption, they can derive market demand, but they *cannot* derive the famous downward-sloping demand curve.[41] After investigating these problems for more than a century, the best neoclassical theorists finally concluded, as George Stigler notes, that if the market demand curve doesn't go down, it must surely go up. And if it doesn't go up, it must surely go down.[42] Rigorous theory says precious little about market demand.

This is more than just a theoretical point. Demand curves need not slope down in practice, either. A nineteenth-century British statistician, Robert Giffen, noticed that when the price of bread fell, the poor bought less of it, and when the price rose, the poor bought more of it. Why? Bread was the least expensive staple food. When bread prices fell, the poor apparently could afford a more diverse diet, including meat, so they bought less bread. When bread prices rose, they were forced to cut back on expensive foods. So, as the Victorian economist Alfred Marshall concluded, "Bread still being the cheapest food which they can get and will take, they consume more, and not less of it."[43]

Textbook economics slides over these complications. In his well-regarded intermediate-level text, Walter Nicholson properly rejects the nineteenth-century assumption of diminishing marginal utility, but later he can't resist reverting to the old downward-sloping demand curve. Listen to this slick move: "The market demand curve is negatively sloped [or downward sloping] on the assumption that most individuals will buy more when the price of a good falls."[44] Wait! If individuals buy more of a good when its price falls, then—by definition—the demand curve is downward-sloping. Nicholson's sentence would have exactly the same content if it read as follows: "The market demand curve is negatively sloped on the assumption that the market demand curve is negatively sloped." After rejecting the assumption about diminishing marginal utility, Nicholson has illicitly slipped it back in to get his downward-sloping demand curve. He fooled me until, years later, I saw what he was doing.

Macroeconomists investigating the workings of whole economies pass even more blithely over dilemmas of utility theory. In *Advanced*

Macroeconomics, David Romer presents dozens upon dozens of models incorporating equations that tally up utility on ruler-like scales and assume falling market demand curves, without so much as once suggesting that these assumptions might be problematic.[45] The fancy DSGE macroeconomic models actually used by central banks do just the same.

And then neoclassical theorists ran into the famous general-equilibrium instability problems discussed in Chapter 1. Indeed, the always thoughtful Wicksell already recognized in 1901 that there can be many different equilibria and some can be unstable, instantly coming undone and allowing prices to slip rapidly toward other equilibria. Investigations of the Arrow-Debreu model in the 1960s and 1970s revealed that no matter how perfectly competitive markets may be, a decentralized economy can have numerous "equilibria" at which supply and demand would balance. Worse, there is no good reason to believe that market trading would ever move an economy to any of those so-called equilibria. In other words, they are not equilibria in any real sense, but just sets of prices that would balance supply and demand if by some remote chance (technically a zero-probability chance) they should occur.

In *Dilemmas in Economic Theory*, Michael Mandler of the University of London explores the ongoing breach between the subtle world of proper neoclassical theory, which faces quandaries head-on, and the corrupt world of neoclassical practice, which just ignores those quandaries. After carefully articulating deep dilemmas, including several I haven't touched on, Mandler makes some real progress at dispelling at least some of them. He even reformulates the concept of utility—yet again—in a way that plausibly recaptures something of Jevons's old notion of diminishing marginal utility.

Where does this discussion leave us? In practice, we mostly do seem to purchase goods based on utilitarian motives. We do try to weigh what we desire more and what we desire less, according to our individual preferences, seeking the best buy for the dollar, given the information we can obtain about goods and our personal preferences. We mostly behave like what I will call "smart shoppers." Nor do I think this is a merely Western proclivity. I recall watching indigenous Quechua in the Ecuadorian Andes haggle over the price of potatoes and tomatoes that were spread out on carts on market day. Some of the Quechua didn't even speak Spanish; they seemed rather distant from European culture. But they seemed to care just as much about bargaining for the best buy as anybody at Wal-Mart does. Actually, they bargained harder.

Moreover, the idea of diminishing marginal utility seems generally plausible. Of course, if I buy a golf course in the desert community of Tucson, the utility I derive from an extra gallon of water would not diminish; it would suddenly skyrocket. But, in general, the assumption of diminishing marginal utility seems sensible. Just as Jevons says, the utility of the first quart of water is life itself, but, in general, the utility of more and more quarts give less and less utility. A direct logical result of this assumption gives a downward-sloping market demand curve. Adam Smith implicitly assented to the idea of the downward-sloping demand curve a century before the neoclassical project ever got underway: recall his notion that if investment is sluggish, demand for labor is low and thus wages are low. The generally plausible assumption of diminishing marginal utility leads to the coherent model of a downward-sloping demand curve. Except when it doesn't. The model depends on the assumption, and, like any model, it fails in situations where an essential assumption does not apply.

Instability concerns are far more serious. When it comes to macroeconomic models of entire economies, they should never be far out of mind. In practice, mechanisms outside of markets—perhaps social agreement on the distribution of income between capitalists and workers, perhaps convention leading us to expect continuity with the past, perhaps central bank policy—usually seem to keep economies from gyrating too erratically. Given such a stabilizing mechanism, the neoclassical theory of demand doesn't do badly for a particular market; for example, sharply higher parking-meter costs are likely to reduce the number of people who drive downtown. Even in these situations, the nineteenth-century story about supply and demand might always be amiss, but it is often a reasonable way to start out thinking about a situation.

Brave New Worldview

Nineteenth-century neoclassicals acknowledged that their theory could not declare any distribution of wealth just or unjust. But *given* individuals' initial "endowments"—the number of chickens, bushels of corn, or other commodities they start out with—if a perfect-market equilibrium could be attained, it would be an individualistic optimum. Each individual would do the best that he or she could, maximizing utility according his or her personal preferences. Jevons says: "So far as is consistent with the inequality of wealth in every community, all commodities are distributed by exchange so as to produce the maximum of benefit. Every person whose wish for a certain thing exceeds his wish for other things, acquires what he wants provided he can make a sufficient sacrifice in other respects. No one is ever required to give what he more desires for what he less desires, so that perfect freedom of exchange must be to the advantage of all."[46]

Economists believed they had uncovered some best of all possible worlds, occupying its own perfect sphere distant from the troubled social arena. Walras saw that inherent market imperfections such as monopolistic industries might argue against laissez-faire policies. But absent imperfections, he powerfully defended markets: "Freedom [of competition] procures, within certain limits, the maximum of utility; and, since the factors which interfere with freedom are obstacles to the attainment of this maximum, they should, without exception, be eliminated as completely as possible."[47]

The utopian lure of neoclassical theory recommended it to a turbulent world. That world seemed able to absorb scientific and industrial shock only by imagining utopias, whether idealized pasts or idealized futures. The construction techniques of modern industry were used to mass-produce imitations of architectural features of yore: neo- or neo-neo- or neo-neo-neo-classical, Italianate, Gothic. Catalogues of styles may have offered some sense of continuity, the art theorist and social critic John Ruskin argued, but the society that had produced those styles mattered more. He urged his readers to look again at true Gothic building: "Examine once more those ugly goblins, and formless monsters, and stern statues, anatomiless and rigid, but do not mock them, for they are the signs of the life and liberty of every workman who struck the stone."[48] Utopian socialists scribbled visions of new worlds, such as Henri de Saint-Simon's "industrial religion" (as the economist Robert Heilbroner dubbed it).[49] They founded experimental societies and led back-to-the-earth movements, such as the Scotsman Robert Owen's model factory towns and garden cities. Marx, of course, was a great utopian: "Only in community [with others has each] individual the means of cultivating his gifts in all directions; only in the community, therefore, is personal freedom possible."[50]

But neoclassical theory was perhaps the bravest utopia of all. It promised that, if only markets were perfect, there need be no struggle among capitalists, workers, and landlords, but each of us would do as well as we possibly could. And it was utopian in positing perfect markets as a Platonic ideal from which the actual economies we inhabit are mere shadowy deviations. I give Walras the last word: "A truth long ago demonstrated by the Platonic philosophy is that science does not study corporeal entities but universals of which these entities are manifestations. Corporeal entities come and go, but universals remain for ever. Universals, their relations, and their laws, are the object of all scientific study."[51]

This Imperfect World

Before proceeding to a closer examination of neoclassical production theory, I want to take up the criticism perhaps most often heard—that "economics," for short, is oblivious to real-world market imperfections. The syndicated columnist Bob Kuttner, whom I've quoted as attacking many economists for being "mathematical theorists . . . astonishingly innocent of actual economic institutions," takes this line: "Most standard economic models assume what economists call 'perfect competition' in which supply, demand and price are set by pure market forces. But in the real world, governments often intervene to promote economic development, military R&D spending spills over into commercial technology and companies conspire to set prices."[1]

Economists do not have their heads stuck in the clouds quite as firmly as critics suppose. In fact, it turns out that building models based on one imperfection or another is a good way to win a Nobel Prize. Paul Krugman won his Nobel precisely for models illustrating that, when competition is imperfect and companies exercise market power, governments may effectively intervene to promote development, and R&D spending may have positive spillovers. And just because Krugman favors more activist policies doesn't mean that his more conservative colleagues haven't noticed inherent imperfections in markets, either. Robert Lucas of the University of Chicago, famously opposed to economic activism, won his Nobel for developing models illustrating how imperfect information can drive business cycles and cause unemployment.[2] In an overview of contemporary macroeconomics, Olivier Blanchard, chief economist of the International Monetary Fund and a longtime MIT professor, defines "imperfections" as any "deviations from the standard perfect-competition model."[3] He notes that "most current research is organized in terms of what happens when one relaxes one or more assumptions in that model"—in other words, when one introduces imperfections.

Strictly for professional reasons, economists have every incentive to move beyond the standard perfect-competition model. Since it envisions an essentially unique and optimal economy, if economists really did think markets were perfect, they would long since have run out of things to do. What would they publish journals articles about? Economists are far too clever to let their discipline sink into such a grim, no-growth state. Instead, they make names for themselves by discovering clever ways to model imperfections. The math required to model them can be even more thrilling than the math required to model mere perfect markets. Economists' ingenuity in inventing imperfections should keep them employed for years to come.

Moreover, at least microeconomic models of market imperfections—models capturing the situations of particular industries—have real practical importance. For example, as electricity prices in California shot up 670 percent from June 2000 through July 2001, and the state suffered waves of rolling blackouts, Vice President Dick Cheney, apparently assuming perfect competition in the electricity generation market, blamed environmental regulations for preventing power-plant construction.[4] Not so, argued economists Paul Joskow of MIT and Edward Kahn of the Analysis Group in San Francisco, in November 2000—well before the worst blackouts appeared.[5] Based on an imperfect-competition model, they concluded that actual electricity prices had exceeded competitive levels by up to 90 percent over the previous summer. Electric utilities, often controlled by marketers such as Enron, had shut down plants that would have earned good profits. But because the market was so tight, shutting these plants down and leaving only a smaller number online allowed those marketers to collect exorbitant profits. In short, the model pointed to price manipulation. The implication was that government should cap prices at some reasonable level. After Enron collapsed, emails and other legal documents proved that Joskow and Kahn's conclusions based on their model were right.

Karl Polanyi—Hungarian soldier, journalist, and academic—developed perhaps the strongest case for the economic importance of market imperfections in his wonderful book *The Great Transformation* (1944).[6] He argued that only a sort of cabal of economists and politicians had managed to push nineteenth-century society toward the free market—"*laissez-faire* was planned"—but society itself naturally pushed back against market brutality, demanding, for example, measures to protect public health, improve working conditions, and provide social insurance. As evidence that society inherently creates what economists call "imperfections," he noted that the most disparate nations, under the most incongruent ideological banners, had adopted much the same measures:

> The supporting forces were in some cases violently reactionary and antisocialist as in Vienna, at other times "radical imperialist" as in Birmingham, or of the purest liberal hue as with the Frenchman Edouard Herriot, Mayor of Lyons. In Protestant England, Conservative and Liberal cabinets labored intermittently at the completion of factory legislation. In Germany, Roman Catholics and Social Democrats took part in its achievement; in Austria, the Church and its most militant supporters; in France enemies of the Church and ardent anticlericals were responsible for the enactment of almost identical laws.[7]

Polanyi argues powerfully and eloquently that society creates market imperfections to protect itself—above all, to protect the dignity of the individual within the community—but he says little if anything about economic theory per se. He just accepts a somewhat vague imperfectionist version of neoclassical theory.

If introducing imperfections can modify neoclassical theory to better describe the actual world we inhabit, why not just accept that approach? One problem is that the conclusions of "imperfectionist neoclassical theory," as I will call it, are notably malleable. For example, if a strategic industry such as aircraft manufacturing has two competitors—fancifully call them Airbus and Boeing—it might be tempting for governments to subsidize them, as the European Union and the United States have done to the extent of untold billions of euros and dollars. Were they wasting money, or did those subsidies increase national output? Krugman reviews models of industries dominated by two firms; about half of the models answer the question one way and the other half answer the answer the question other way.[8] In particular, if the two firms engage in "Cournot competition"—meaning that each assumes the other will set some given level of output and adjust prices accordingly—the models say the answer is probably yes. If the firms engage in "Bertrand competition"—meaning that each assumes the other will set some given price and adjust its output accordingly—the models say the answer is probably no. "The models described here are all quite special cases," Krugman concludes. "Small variations in assumptions can no doubt reverse the conclusions."[9] Assumptions about market imperfections are so easy to tweak that clever neoclassicals can invent imperfections to reach almost any conclusion they want, and other neoclassicals can invent different imperfections to reach the opposite conclusion.

To put the same idea slightly differently, market imperfections can play the role that epicycles have in Ptolemaic astronomy. Ptolemy famously held that the Sun orbits around the Earth. Astronomers had, of course, noticed anomalies in the orbits of the planets that didn't fit the model, so they added epicycles—geometric models of the variations—to explain them. Along came someone by the name of Copernicus who claimed that the Earth and the planets revolve in a circle around the Sun. But he was less than correct in thinking that the Earth's orbit is circular—the Earth actually moves in an ellipse, a kind of elongated circle. As a result of this error, the Copernican theory did a bad job of predicting future positions of heavenly bodies. For a century, astronomers did a better job using the Ptolemaic model, with its burden of epicycles, than could be achieved with Copernicus's unadorned model. Only a hundred years later, when Kepler investigated the mathematics of elliptical orbits, did a modified version of the Copernican model begin to yield more accurate predictions than the old Ptolemaic model.

Why not stick with Ptolemy rather than Copernicus? The difference is merely one of perspective: the Sun is no more the center of the universe than the Earth is. In part, the superiority of the Copernican model (as modified by Kepler) is a question of economy. If you can get the same results more simply and directly, why heap on epicycles? More important, starting from the neoclassical perfect-market model and appending imperfections is not a neutral agenda. For all the imperfections that neoclassicals can invent, when it comes to giving practical advice, they tend to revert to the unadorned perfect-market model. (Krugman is an exception here.) Thomas Palley, an economist who writes for publications such as the *Financial Times* and has held policy positions, including the directorship of the Open Society Institute's Globalization Reform Project, criticizes the imperfectionist approach. Why start from a paradigm that is "drawn from Alice in Wonderland"? he asks. "When you start in Wonderland, pieces of Wonderland stick with you and distort your vision even though you may try to shake off other pieces."[10]

Serious criticism of neoclassical theory must address the underlying perfect-market model itself, rather than imperfect deviations from it. The most penetrating critics of neoclassical theory, from Karl Marx to John Maynard Keynes, have directed their arguments pointblank against this model.[11] They argue that even if competition were as perfect as you like, economies would look profoundly different from neoclassical perfect markets. For example, Robert Heilbroner notes in *The Worldly Philosophers*, as Marx sets the stage, "we enter a world of perfect competition: no monopolies, no unions, no special advantages for anyone. It is a world in which every commodity sells at exactly its proper price."[12] Ricardo likewise assumes perfect markets, as does Keynes in his *General Theory*. The economic problems Keynes finds are not market imperfections, such as monopolistic firms or trade unions. They are the problems of the human condition: we cannot predict the future. I will therefore focus my comparison on fundamental theories of perfect markets. Imperfections can be added to any of them.

EIGHT

Entering the Realm of Production

Workers' Day, celebrated on May 1 in countries around the world, from Britain to Kenya, China to Mexico, stands as a memorial to workers' struggles to better their lives. The fact that it is not celebrated in the United States stands as a memorial to Americans' success at forgetting our role in those struggles. In 1886, a small labor group in Chicago proposed a general strike for May 1 of that year, demanding an eight-hour day for the same pay—in other words, a raise.[1] Local organizers of the Knights of Labor seized on the idea, and it spread to New York, Milwaukee, Pittsburgh, St. Louis, and other cities. On the appointed day, 200,000 workers across the country went on strike. Protesters waving red flags and sometimes carrying arms marched in support; armories had been built in U.S. cities to stockpile weapons for use against such protesters. The demonstrations were mostly nonviolent, and the campaign met with considerable success. A pro-labor weekly declared, "It is an eight-hour boom, and we are scoring victory after victory." But on May 3, after police opened fire on a crowd in Chicago, anarchists called a rally at the city's Haymarket Square. Just as the meeting was ending, someone—it has never been determined who—threw a bomb, killing a policeman. The 180 police at the rally fired on the crowd, killing one person and wounding seventy. Four "anarchists" were hanged, virtually without evidence.

In 1889 the Second International, a congress of socialist and labor parties, declared that May 1, commemorating the Haymarket Riot and Americans' strikes for the eight-hour workday, should be celebrated as Workers' Day.[2] And so it was in nations around the world, but not in the United States. To block recognition of the Second International and of the American strikes, President Grover Cleveland established a different holiday: Labor Day, the first Monday in September.

John Bates Clark, a Christian socialist who was troubled by Haymarket and who was a founder of the American Economic Association, thought that labor's challenge to capitalism deserved a better answer than a rescheduled holiday.[3] He described that challenge in 1899 in *The Distribution of Wealth:* "The indictment that hangs over society is that of 'exploiting labor.' 'Workmen,' it is said, 'are regularly robbed of what they produce.'" He conceded that "if this charge were proved, every right-minded man should become a socialist; and his zeal in transforming the industrial system would then measure and express his sense of justice."[4] To weigh the truth of the charge, Clark believed, "We must enter the realm of production. We must resolve the product of social industry into its component elements, in order to see whether the natural effect of competition is or is not to give to each producer"—capitalist and worker—"the amount of wealth that he specifically brings into existence."[5]

When Clark and his neoclassical followers advocate entering the realm of production, they introduce a strange term. When they speak about payments to workers, they use the everyday word "wages," but when they speak about payments to capital, they do not use the word "profits." Instead, they refer to the return to capital as the "interest rate." The notion is that, in free markets, the interest rate on money is driven to equality with the rate of return on capital. Neoclassicals generally reserve the term "profit" for a monopolistic return on capital, above the free-market rate. I object to this way of speaking. Interest rates are one thing, profit rates another, and they do not converge. To equate them by using the same word for both is to embed a debatable theory in a term. I therefore use the everyday word "profit"—the one that classical economists used—but when neoclassicals such as Clark refer to the return to capital as the "interest rate," I allow them their own term.

Clark's conclusion about the "natural" determination of wages and what he calls the "interest rate"—presented in the opening passage of his *Distribution of Wealth*—should come as no surprise:

> It is the purpose of this work to show that the distribution of the income of society is controlled by a natural law, and that this law, if it worked without friction, would give to every agent of production the amount of wealth which that agent creates. However wages may be adjusted by bargains freely made between individual men, the rates of pay that result from such transactions tend, it is here claimed, to equal that part of the product of industry which is traceable to the labor itself; and however interest may be adjusted by similarly free bargaining, it naturally tends to equal the fractional product that is separately traceable to capital.

Rejecting the Marxian adage, "From each according to his abilities, to each according to his needs," Clark counters: "To each agent a distinguishable share in production, and to each a corresponding reward—such is the natural law of distribution."[6] Will economists ever stop trying to promote theories by calling them "natural" laws?

Not all neoclassicals were so insistent about the moral dimension of their theory of production—some chided Clark for emphasizing it so—but they saw the indispensable need for it. In their focus on utility, the neoclassicals of the 1870s—as their friendly critic George Stigler points out—left a "fundamental defect" in their theory: "the failure to develop a theory of the prices of productive services."[7] Consumers' efforts to maximize utility might determine the price of a good, but what determined which portion of that price is paid to wages and which portion becomes interest (or profit)? The early neoclassicals had no coherent answer.[8] In fact, without a distinctive account of distribution, the neoclassical theory of utility and consumer prices could be worked in as a friendly amendment to Ricardo, who had always seen some role for supply and demand to drive short-term price fluctuations to long-term, or "natural," levels. "Jevons, so critical of the classical economists when he dealt with demand theory," chides Stigler, "was a close follower of the 'wrong-headed' Ricardo in distribution theory."[9]

A later generation of neoclassicals in the 1890s brilliantly discovered how to resolve both theoretical and moral dilemmas. The right story about production could turn it into smart shopping. Assume that firms can employ more capital and less labor, or vice versa, to produce the same output. Then firms can be modeled as shopping for factors—labor or capital—precisely the way consumers shop for potatoes or pasta at the market. Just as smart shoppers seek the best buy to maximize utility, firms could seek the best buy in the mix of labor and capital to maximize output. The smart shopping of firms in factor markets could, on the one hand, determine the wages of labor and profits of capital, and, on the other hand, ensure that each factor is paid exactly what it contributes to production.

The Best of All Possible Factories

As a mathematical assumption, the neoclassical account of production shines crystal clear. As a way to envision how goods are actually made, I find it opaque, but I will do my best to describe it. Let the technological state of the art be temporarily given. The engineers are absent, and the managers use only known techniques. The neoclassical account of production then makes two intertwined assumptions:

- First, firms know how to produce the same output by using more capital and less labor, or vice versa. Auto-plant managers know how to make the same cars by buying more robots and laying off some workers, or by selling some robots and hiring more workers.
- Second, there are diminishing returns to each factor. As you hire more labor to work with a given stock of capital, you increase output but less than proportionally. Auto-plant managers might add 20 percent more workers while keeping the same robots, and produce 12 percent more cars. Likewise, as you install more capital for a given labor force, you increase output but less than proportionally. Managers might add 20 percent more robots while keeping the same workforce and get 8 percent more cars. Diminishing marginal return to a factor is also called "diminishing marginal product" or "diminishing marginal productivity"; the terms are used interchangeably.

Economists' notions of diminishing returns can reach weird extremes. George Stigler quotes Philip Wicksteed, a pioneering British neoclassical: "The same [marginalist] law holds in intellectual, moral, or spiritual as in material matters. Caesar tells how when surprised by Nervii [a Germanic tribe] he had barely time to harangue his soldiers, obviously implying that the harangue was shorter than usual. He felt that a few moments, even at such a crisis, were well devoted to words of exhortation to his troops; but their value declined at the margin, and the price in delaying the onslaught rapidly rose: so the moment was soon reached when the time could be better spent than in prolonging a moving discourse."[10]

The assumption about diminishing marginal returns, whether in consumption or in production, is so central to neoclassical theory that the theory is sometimes called "marginalist" economics. The story of demand requires diminishing marginal utility.[11] As you buy more apples at the market, you derive increasing utility, but you derive smaller and smaller increments of utility from each apple. Likewise, the story of production requires diminishing marginal productivity. As you add more workers to a factory, you produce more output (you build more cars), but you produce smaller and smaller increments of output (fewer and fewer additional cars) for each worker.

If the following example sounds tedious, blame it on marginalist theory, and bear with me to see how all is for the best in the best of all possible factories. Suppose a firm has a large complement of capital and a minimum of labor. Since there are so few workers, managers see that their marginal product is large. Hiring one new worker for $40,000 yields a huge additional output—perhaps $1 million worth of cars. On the other hand, since the firm already has so much capital, managers see that its marginal product is low. If they spend another $100,000 on a robot, they get little additional output—perhaps only $10,000 worth of cars. They decide to hire workers and to refrain from a loss-making investment in robots. As they hire more workers, the additional output each one produces gradually declines. Perhaps the hundredth new worker produces only another $40,000 worth of cars. Here, the managers stop hiring. Another worker would produce only $39,000 worth of cars, a loss-making proposition. At the point where the last $40,000 worth of labor hired produces $40,000 worth of additional cars, the firm has maximized its output.

Moreover, in the best of all possible factories, labor is being paid exactly what it produces. But wait! Isn't it only the last worker who produces $40,000 worth of cars? Didn't workers previously hired produce larger values, so aren't they exploited? Not so. They produced larger values only when there was less then a full complement of labor. Once there is a full complement—once the optimal number of workers is hired—each and every one produces $40,000 worth of cars. Likewise, at that point, each and every $100,000 robot produces $100,000 worth of cars. Each factor is paid what it produces.

Neoclassical assumptions about production justify claims such as that of John Snow, Treasury secretary for President George W. Bush: "People will get paid on how valuable they are to the enterprise."[12] As well, impertinent political interference in the labor market only causes problems. Unions might demand $45,000 for a worker, rather than $40,000. Fine, neoclassical managers would say—but now the last worker we hired costs $45,000 and produces only $40,000 worth of cars. We will reduce our labor force until the last worker employed produces $45,000 worth of cars. In general, setting wages above the "free-market equilibrium rate," Samuelson assures readers of his textbook, "freezes workers into unemployment."[13] And he is a political liberal. Economists were so convinced of this ironclad logic that the profession reacted with astonishment when David Card and Alan B. Krueger announced the results of a statistical study in 2000 in the prestigious *American Economic Review,* concluding that a modest increase in the minimum wage in one state actually did not increase unemployment.

The "production function" formally describes the production options available to firms, analogous to the shopping options available to consumers. In a textbook version, the quantity of labor is denoted by L, the quantity of capital by K, and the quantity of output by Y. The production function specifies the unique value of output, Y, that will be produced by any given quantities of labor, L, and capital, K. Firms maximize output by shopping for an optimal combination of labor, L, and capital, K.[14]

A crucial point is that the production function is supposed to describe options available to managers, given the current state of technology; it describes the ways they *already know* to combine more capital and less labor, or vice versa, to produce output. Even if it takes time to install 20 percent more capital, managers know what to install and how much output it will yield. Just how the current state of technology was invented is a question that the neoclassical model doesn't pretend to explain. (Nor, for that matter, does the classical model pretend to explain it.) Technology is simply a given, exogenous to the market model. The market model, incorporating the production function that describes managers' known options for applying technology, then purports to determine the quantity of goods produced and their prices, as well as wages, profits, and other matters.

The production function is arguably the heart of neoclassical theory because only it can "disentangle" the distinct product of labor from that of capital, as J. B. Clark puts it.[15] Thomas Palley, a non-neoclassical economist, says there is one place that even progressive neoclassicals "dare not go": the abandonment of marginal-productivity theory.[16] The reason is clear. The classical assumption about technology sees essentially one way of producing goods, at a given state of the art, absent innovation by engineers. Specific workers use specific equipment to carry out production. The contribution of capital cannot then be separated from that of labor. As a union joke puts it, "What's the marginal product of a worker on the assembly line?" Answer: "It's the steering wheel." Thus, there can be no pure market wage or profit rate. Lack of a market wage or profit rate means that society must enter the economy. There can be no pure market realm.

Dream Factory

Economists invented neoclassical assumptions about production in the 1890s, some twenty years after the assumptions about utility. As well as J. B. Clark, some of these economists included the mathematically minded Francis Edgeworth and the theologian-economist Philip Wicksteed.[17] Why did it take twenty years longer to invent marginal productivity, and why did so many economists stumble upon it? Let me guess. The neoclassical account of utility makes a certain introspective sense; Jevons and others intuited it and tried to work out the implications. By contrast, I find assumptions about marginal productivity a peculiar way to visualize how firms actually produce goods. I doubt that economists spontaneously conceived of them as a plausible way to describe production and then proceeded to build a model. Rather, they saw a theoretical necessity for the assumptions about production to complement the theory of utility. They grasped the final shape of the neoclassical theory that they sought, and worked backward to posit the required assumptions. Indeed, Wicksteed notes that economists invented the neoclassical account of production by analogy to the account of utility.[18] This reverse engineering of assumptions, as it were, seems a dubious way to make them.

The classical account of production seems more immediately plausible. Given the state of technology, it sees essentially one efficient method to make any good. Certainly, technological innovation changes the efficient method over time. The Ford Motor Company's River Rouge plant in the 1920s required, in a real sense, far more labor and less capital to make a car than any modern auto plant does. Look at the raw muscle power and crude machinery so vividly depicted in Diego Rivera's mural of that plant in the Detroit Art Museum. In the 1920s, engineers had no idea how to use more automated equipment and fewer workers. Today, the situation is the opposite. The precise tolerances essential to modern automotive technology require computer-controlled machining centers. In 2006, when Ford opened an auto plant in Chongqing, China, where wages were a fraction of those in Germany, a spokesman for the automaker told the *New York Times* that the plant was "practically identical to one of its most advanced factories" in Germany.[19] The reason is obvious. Now Ford engineers had no idea how to build cars by using more low-wage Chinese and less capital equipment. Perhaps Ford could have reproduced the River Rouge plant in China. But who wants Model T's these days? If Ford dispensed with its computer-controlled machining centers and tried to employ workers instead, what exactly would the workers do? What simple tools would they use and somehow still make modern cars?

I pulled the example of Ford's Chongqing factory from an offhand remark in the newspaper, but the situation is essentially universal.[20] A study on the global auto industry by Harley Shaiken of the University of California, Berkeley, concludes that plants in Mexico and the United

States were using essentially the same level of automation. The computer-controlled machinery in one body shop was not only modeled on an Japanese plant, but was "designed, fabricated, and tested in Japan" and shipped to Mexico.[21]

The same principle applies in other industries. Retail might seem to be a case where relatively low-paid sales and clerical workers could substitute for laser-scanners, computerized cash registers, and inventory control systems. When I was writing a case study about a supermarket chain run by the Mexican Social Security Institute that had come under competitive pressure from Wal-Mart, the managers told me that they had rejected a labor-intensive, low-tech approach: "The latest technology is in all the stores, the same as Wal-Mart, the same as all the chains," I was told. "Isn't there some intermediate solution?" I asked. The answer: "It doesn't exist."[22] Managers had to control inventories, reorder items as they ran low, minimize spoilage and theft, and price items flexibly—sometimes as loss leaders, sometimes as profit generators. They had to tally sales daily; they had to supervise suppliers and warehouses. There were two options, the managers told me: go bankrupt or upgrade to the latest technology. They chose the second.

Looking back in history, you discover the same essential story. When the Harvard institutional economist Alexander Gerschenkron studied industrialization in underdeveloped nations of an earlier day—Germany, Eastern Europe, Russia—he concluded the state had been required to support industry because industry needed that support to adopt the latest technology: "To the extent that industrialization took place, it was largely by application of the most modern and efficient techniques that backward countries could hope to achieve success, particularly if their industrialization proceeded in the face of competition" from advanced countries.[23]

If it rarely proves possible to compete by swamping antiquated capital with a surplus of low-paid workers, the opposite approach—conjuring up futuristic automation to thin the ranks of high-paid workers—can fail, too. General Motors (GM) ran a multi-billion-dollar experiment in the 1980s, testing this sort of fantasy. Its managers blamed overpaid and recalcitrant workers for undermining GM's competitive edge against Japan. Having read too much neoclassical theory, or else too much science fiction, they supposed they could regain that edge by replacing workers with robots. Warren P. Seering, an MIT mechanical engineer (not an economist), describes the unfortunate results: "Many manufacturers believed that the United States could simply build an army of robots with humanoid features that would work in factories day and night, undercutting the advantages of cheap labor abroad. These robots, most people thought, would have manipulators that swung like human arms, grippers that grasped objects like human fingers, and sensing abilities comparable with human senses. Made in the image of humans, these robots would soon outperform humans in cost and efficiency."[24] Imagine trying to design a robotic hand to grasp a tiny light bulb without breaking it and screw it into a dashboard panel. Humanoid robots were a flop. Their unit price of more than $100,000 at the time (not including operating or repair costs), and their poor performance, rendered them useless. The MIT International Motor Vehicle Program estimated that, in the 1980s, GM wasted $40 billion on such high-tech failures.[25] Having learned its lesson, GM spent a mere $200 million on its pragmatic New United Motor Manufacturing joint venture with Toyota. Using "equipment at best described as 'medium tech,'" as one researcher put it, but Japanese "lean-production" methods, GM achieved productivity 40 percent better than its norm and the highest quality levels it had ever attained.[26]

There are situations where alternative capital- or labor-intensive techniques appear to be available at a point in time, but they are rarely legitimate examples of the neoclassical production function. Myriad low-tech street vendors choke the Mexico City subway entrances, while peasants hand-cultivating corn are found throughout much of the countryside, but they are not competing in a modern economy. To exaggerate only a little, Mexico has dual economies: a modern economy, which uses methods hardly different from those across the border, and an "informal economy," as economists hopefully call it, which uses practically medieval methods. Mexican peasants growing corn by hand methods do not compete with American Midwestern farms. Under the North American Free Trade Agreement (NAFTA), many were driven out of business and, in bad times, to near starvation. The Mexican farms that do compete with and export to the United States use the same mechanized equipment—and literally the same migrant workers to pick crops that the equipment can't handle. Looking at competitive Mexican and U.S. farms, you see no real difference.

There is a small literature on "engineering production functions," which describe trade-offs that might be made among different input factors in specific operations. Its results suggest that there are no such practical possibilities. The Harvard economist Hollis Chenery wrote the pioneering article. As his father was an executive of Pacific Gas and Electric, he could gain access to pipeline data. He studied possible trade-offs not between capital and labor, but between two different types of capital: larger-diameter pipelines with less powerful compressors, and smaller-diameter pipes with more powerful compressors. He selected this example, he notes, because it seemed to present an unusually easy case for calculating possible trade-offs.[27] He could ignore substitution between capital and labor because—be it noted—once the pipeline and compressor technology had been chosen, it determined the required amount of labor.[28] To calculate the trade-offs between pipeline size and compressor power, Chenery had to make assumptions about such imponderables as "the expected life of the gas field, demand for gas, the rate of interest, and even the property tax."[29] He used economic techniques unknown to the pipeline engineers, and had to rely on industry data already rendered obsolete by technical change.[30] Thus, he warned against using his results in practice.[31] Given that he selected what he saw as a particularly easy case, the notion of a concrete production function, actually telling managers how to make substitutions among a wide range of factors as prices vary, seems wildly improbable.

Shopping versus Innovation

I need to be clear about what I'm saying. No reasonable person would claim—and I certainly do not claim—that relative amounts of capital and labor, or of any particular productive inputs, are fixed for all time. The relative use of inputs changes as technology progresses; the very kinds of input materials and capital equipment that are available change. If you lump inputs together into some measure of aggregate capital and labor, production tends to become more capital intensive over time. For example, from 1960 to 2008, the amount of capital per member of the U.S. workforce grew something like 2 percent per year, for a total increase in capital per worker of about 200 percent.[32] This sort of secular technological change is admitted in both classical and neoclassical paradigms.

But classical and neoclassical paradigms disagree about what a given state of the art of technology looks like. The classical view holds that, at a given state of the art, firms know essentially one method to produce goods. To the extent that there are variations, this paradigm abstracts from them—that is, it ignores them. The neoclassical account of technology makes a more ambitious claim. It supposes that, *at any given technological state of the art,* firms can chose from a wide menu of alternative methods, using more capital and less labor—or more of any specific input and less of any other—to produce the same goods. In order for firms to choose an optimal combination of input factors to maximize output, just as smart shoppers choose an optimal combination of goods to maximize utility, the neoclassical paradigm must assume that the menu of alternative methods is known. Implementing alternative methods cannot depend on the uncertain possibilities for technical innovations that might work out, or, then again, might flop.

You would think that, by now, economists might have discovered arguments for why technology should somehow provide firms with a wide menu of known alternative methods for producing goods. I have never seen any such coherent argument. The notion of the production function and the possibility of substituting one factor for another seem to be a kind of academic lore passed down sotto voce from one classroom to the next.

By contrast, there are good arguments against the neoclassical account of production. To adopt a line of reasoning developed by Paul David, professor of economics and history at Stanford University, suppose that, at some hypothetical moment, managers happen to know two equivalent techniques, one labor intensive and one capital intensive, for making the same good.[33] If the price of labor falls a little, the first method is cheaper, whereas if it rises a little, the second is cheaper. One technique or the other is adopted; perhaps it is the capital-intensive one. So long as capital prices and wages do not wildly fluctuate—and in general they don't—the firm carries on production within this general technique. Furthermore, if it doesn't want to fall behind its competitors, the firm continues to make incremental improvements, "learning by doing." Managers and workers scrutinize production processes, seeking to resolve trouble spots and bottlenecks, incrementally cutting costs and improving quality. Meanwhile, no innovation takes place in the labor-intensive alternative technique, because it is not being used. If wages should now fall, firms will *not* go back to the labor-intensive technique because it has become inefficient at any plausible wage level. Indeed, the product itself has undoubtedly been improved, too, rendering the alternative technique utterly useless.

Of course, if factor prices change—say, if wages rise—firms can *try* to develop a method employing less labor and more capital. In his microeconomics text, Walter Nicholson explains the usual neoclassical account of production. Then, a few pages later, to justify it, he says that if the minimum wage increases, fast-food operations "may attempt to substitute capital equipment (automatic cooking equipment) for teenage workers." He notes that in response to a minimum-wage increase in 1977, McDonald's "adopted a new program of research on labor-saving technology and initiated several changes in its teenage hiring practices."[34] Though he was writing more than a decade after that noble experiment, Nicholson never informs us if McDonald's succeeded. As GM discovered, such experimental programs can fail. Worse from a theoretical perspective, Nicholson confuses his students by obscuring the distinction between a market choice among known options and an uncertain project of technological innovation.

The distinction between smart shopping to chose among known goods and a research project to carry out uncertain innovation is not just some methodological nicety. We may not know everything about the goods we buy—there are lemons—but a variety of choices does exist; we have some experience about the pros and cons; and we can generally obtain probabilistic information about them. For example, based on statistical estimates from the performance of actual car models, *Consumer Reports* can tell us the chance that the transmission on a given model will need repair. By contrast, a research project to develop an alternate production method involves groping. An alternative method doesn't even exist—since if it did, why undertake a research program? The firm cannot know ahead of time if the attempt will succeed or fail, or how much it may cost.

Transmuting Concrete Capital into Abstract Capital

After taking so long to invent their account of production, the neoclassicals still seemed uncomfortable about it. Consider Wicksteed's weird biblical example of substituting one factor for another: "The manufacture of bricks requires both intelligence and straw"—and presumably some clay as well—"but at the margin one may be substituted freely for the other without affecting the quality of the output."[35] Why a biblical example? You don't build bricks with straw in Britain, but I guess Wicksteed couldn't think of a British example. And just how could even our biblical forebears make bricks with more intelligence and less straw, or vice versa? If there were better ways to arrange the straw reinforcing in bricks, presumably brickmakers had earlier learned the lesson and applied it. What was additional "intelligence" to accomplish?

Alfred Marshall, the always pragmatic Victorian economist, saw marginal productivity as applying mainly to agriculture, and, even there, more as capturing historical development—technological change—than offering actual contemporary possibilities for substitution.[36] As late as the 1940s, the economist Paul H. Douglas, co-inventor of a mathematically convenient form of the production function, lamented that his colleagues "have instilled the pure doctrine of John Bates Clark during one hour, and then during the next hour have taught as economic gospel the bargain theories of Sidney and Beatrice Webb!"—the view that wages are set by bargains between employers and employees.[37]

J. B. Clark himself concedes that there may well be no practical way to substitute one concrete factor of production for another: "A given machine often requires one man to run it, and no more."[38] Subtract the worker, and the machine stops. Clark therefore struggles to imagine a marginal quantity of capital: "The cars, engines, tracks, buildings, etc. . . . embody the whole capital of [a] railroad; but when we try to find and identify the part of it that is 'final' and interest-determining"—the last increment of capital that determines the marginal product—"we cannot single out [particular pieces] of the equipment." Instead, Clark continues:

> We must try to find what is the final productive element in the whole equipment, and in each of the instruments that constitute it. What outlay would the company forgo if, in the building and equipping of a

railroad, it found that its real capital—its concrete and material outfit of instruments for carrying passengers and merchandise—must be made smaller than its original plans had called for? If it proceeded in a natural way, it would slightly reduce in quality nearly everything in its proposed outfit. It would forgo putting the final perfecting touches to cars, engines, roadbed, buildings, etc. . . . It is clear that this final increment of the capital of this industry is not one that can be physically taken out of it, as it could be if it consisted of a few locomotives or a few cars that could be sold to another company.[39]

Unable to identify actual pieces of equipment that can be added or subtracted to alter the output of a railroad—or other enterprises—Clark conceives of lumping them all together in metaphorical abstract capital. This has no particular physical manifestation, Clark hypothesizes, but "lives, as it were, by transmigration, taking itself out of one set of bodies and putting itself into another, again and again."[40] For example: "The capital that was once invested in the whale fishery of New England is now, to some extent, employed in cotton manufacturing; but the ships have not been used as cotton mills. As the vessels were worn out, the part of their earnings that might have been used to build more vessels was actually used to build mills. The nautical *form* of the capital perished; but the capital survived and, as it were, migrated from the one set of material bodies to the other."[41] Abstract capital earns a return. If you tally the value of all actual pieces of capital equipment, "the grand total will describe the permanent capital of the world. Find what part of itself this fund will earn in a year, and you have the *rate* of interest."[42]

Likewise, a mill cannot simply dispense with some of its workers. If it does just dispense with workers, Clark concedes, "There are abandoned machines, and the remaining workers cannot set them running. The capital that is in them can be utilized, however, if it will transform itself into an improvement in the machinery that the remaining workers use." Clark admits that this scenario is far-fetched, exclaiming: "How nearly unthinkable is . . . the prompt transmuting of the capital into the forms that the reduced working force would require!" Yet it happens, he insists:

"All this is done in actual industry: the world daily accomplishes this miraculous thing, automatically and without observation. By forces that run through its economic system, it gives to each industry its due portion of the whole social capital. It puts that portion, in every case, into the forms that the men of the group require." You can't deny Clark's rhetorical abilities, but you sometimes wonder where economic mechanisms end and miracles begin.

The Aggregating Quagmire

Microeconomics does not allow Clark's transmutation of concrete equipment into abstract capital, or of concrete workers into abstract labor. It sees many types of equipment and workers, treating each as a different "factor of production." It still assumes that one factor can generally be traded off against another. This story runs into an engineering problem—the one that I discussed and that Clark concedes. At a concrete level, substituting one factor for another rarely seems possible. Take the engineer away from the train's engine, and you cannot substitute more capital; the train just stops. Take the engine away from the engineer, and you cannot substitute more labor; the train just stops.

Clark proposes—and the latest macroeconomic models continue to assume—an *aggregate* production function, transmuting all concrete equipment to an abstract quantity called "capital" and labeled K, and transmuting concrete workers to an abstract quantity called "labor" and labeled L. If the microeconomic story runs into practical trouble, the macroeconomic story runs into theoretical disaster.

Actually, the aggregate production function runs into two theoretical disasters. In a long-running debate, non-neoclassical macroeconomists in Cambridge, England, attacked it, while neoclassical macroeconomists in Cambridge, Massachusetts, defended it. Paul Samuelson, to his credit, finally conceded defeat for Massachusetts.[43] Meanwhile, microeconomists, including Samuelson's MIT colleague Franklin Fisher, destroyed the aggregate production function from a neoclassical angle. Yet supposedly practical economists still use it as if nothing had happened. The latest DSGE macroeconomic models, those with the name worse than the acronym, use the aggregate production function as if it were entirely alive and well. Fisher and Jesus Felipe of the Asian Development Bank remark in an article about the problems of aggregation, "The younger generation of economists remains ignorant of these problems, with the consequence that bad habits and bad science breed bad economics and bad policy advice."[44]

The Cambridge-Cambridge debates focused on the question: What is a quantity of capital? If capital equipment includes bulldozers, software, and seed corn, how do you aggregate them into a single quantity called K? Clark said you add up their prices to get K—but a little problem arises. How do you know the price of each piece of capital equipment? Neoclassical theory requires you to already know K in order to calculate that price.[45] For example, an automaker might spend $100 million in January 2009 to build a new plant—just grant, for the sake of argument, that the prices of needed input materials and the wages of needed labor are known and add up to $100 million. But the plant can start operating only in January 2010. Neoclassical theory agrees that the automaker must make a normal profit or interest rate on its $100 million investment over that year. In other words, you need to know the profit or interest rate to determine the full value of plant, so you can aggregate it into the total value of capital, K. But you need to know the value of aggregate capital, K, to determine the profit or interest rate via the production function. There is no way around this circular logic.[46]

Neoclassicals might regard, and indeed did regard, this circularity as a sort of theoretical curiosity; but the debates reached the further conclusion that Clark's parable about diminishing returns need not hold, either. It requires that, as the firm uses more capital for a given complement of labor, the return to capital—the profit or interest rate—declines. In his concession to Cambridge, England, Samuelson presented a model of champagne making (stunningly unrealistic but logically impeccable) in which this relationship is violated. At a certain point, even as the firm continues to use more capital for its complement of labor, the profit rate continues to rise.[47] The result of this and other anomalies—or anyway what look like anomalies if you believe the aggregate production function—is that the marginal product does *not* determine the distribution of income between capital and labor.[48] Clark did not prove Marx wrong, after all.

Fisher and other neoclassical microeconomists asked a different question: Can you derive an aggregate production function specifying aggregate output, Y, produced by aggregate capital, K, and labor, L, in such a way as to correctly summarize the production of different firms using distinct capital goods and types of workers?[49] While the Cambridge, England, camp was concerned only with aggregating capital, Fisher was also concerned with aggregating labor and output. Referring to Joan Robinson, who played a prominent role in the Cambridge-Cambridge debates, Felipe and Fisher ask, "Was one woman-hour of labor by Joan Robinson really the same as one of Queen Elizabeth II or one of Britney Spears in terms of productivity?"[50] They show that you can aggregate labor only if each firm uses exactly the same complement of workers, perhaps at different scales. For example, if one firm employs one lawyer and three carpenters, another could employ two lawyers and six carpenters. All firms in the economy must employ only lawyers and carpenters, and only at a ratio of one to three. You can aggregate output only if each firm produces the same mix. One firm could produce two legal briefs and one wooden barn a month; another could produce four legal briefs and two wooden barns. Production functions must be all alike, except perhaps for efficiency—some firms can mysteriously produce more than others with precisely the same inputs.

In short, you cannot derive an aggregate production function from micro-level production functions under any remotely plausible assumptions. Moreover, as Felipe and Fisher discuss, statistical estimates about economies based on the aggregate production function—estimates that macroeconomists routinely do—can involve serious error.

Suppose the economy is very simple: it has one good that can be consumed and also serves as capital, and it has one type of labor. In short, suppose it is Ricardo's corn economy. Here, if you assume an underlying neoclassical production function, Clark could maintain his parable that each factor is paid according to its productive contribution, and he would not run into theoretical disaster. But he would not prove Marx wrong. In this same economy, Marx could also maintain the labor theory of value without running into theoretical trouble. When all industries have the same capital intensity, as must be the case when there is only one industry, all value can be measured in labor-hours. The theoretical problems with Clark's parable and with Marx's parable are equivalent. It is interesting to see how widely Clark's parable is accepted and how vehemently Marx's is rejected. The difference obviously has little to do with theoretical coherence.

Is there any justification for J. B. Clark's parable? Robert Solow once quipped, "If God had meant there to be more than two factors of production, He would have made it easier for us to draw three-dimensional diagrams."[51] It is a flip way of stating the least-bad argument for using a simple corn model. Solow agrees it is vastly oversimplified, but the toy economy can at least be understood—and in appropriate situations, it might allow economists to derive estimates about the real economy that seem at least to have the right order of magnitude. The Solow growth model is used to break economic growth down into three elements: increase in the workforce, accumulation of capital, and admittedly vague improvements in efficiency, referred to as "total-factor productivity." I will have more to say about this model, but I will say now that I find it useful, if crude. I look at total-factor productivity derived from the model when I'm trying to understand how an economy is doing—say, Mexico versus South Korea. Solow argues for using these "lowbrow" models because they "remain heuristically important for the intuition they provide, as well as the basis for empirical work that can be tractable, fruitful and policy-relevant."[52] This approach may be a fair enough way to break growth down into increase in the labor force, accumulation of capital, and efficiency. But anyone who uses it should know that it is built on theoretical quicksand. If results look doubtful, question them.

The Delusion of a Pure Market Economy

The idea of treating consumption as a market phenomenon where smart shoppers try to get the best buy for their dollar is plausible enough. It could and perhaps should be woven into a classical account of production. But production is a different kind of thing from consumption. Though there are markets for input factors—different types of labor, machinery, natural resources—the realm of production is not what neoclassical economics would try to make it: a realm where entrepreneurs can optimize their purchases of alternative combinations of factors, the way smart shoppers do. It is a far more intractable activity, hemmed in by the structure of technology, webs of human relationships and institutions, and profound uncertainty as to what real alternatives to the status quo may be discovered. At a given juncture, production is carried out according to given methods—not because they will never change, but because we cannot know how they might be changed. In this situation, the habits and customs of the people must enter into the decision as to who gets paid what; markets alone cannot make this determination.

To be clear, I am not just arguing that perfect markets would fail to be optimal. I am arguing that markets—no matter how perfect they might be—would fail to constitute *any economy at all*. There is no theoretically coherent or practically meaningful way to extricate the habits and customs of the people from the economy. These habits and customs can be useful, or they can be destructive. But they will be a factor.

NINE

What Caused Income Inequality?

The debate that heated up in the 1990s about why U.S. income inequality has sharply worsened since the 1970s features John Bates Clark in updated guise. As George Johnson of the University of Michigan wrote in the *Journal of Economic Perspectives,* the economics literature reached "virtually unanimous agreement" about the causes of this unfortunate situation: "During the 1980s relative demand increased for workers at the high end of the skill distribution and thus caused their relative wages to rise," while it decreased for workers at the low end of the skill distribution, causing their wages to fall.[1] The information revolution was supposed to have inexorably driven this result via some skill-biased twist in the production function, that neoclassical picture of aggregate technology. Since the top one hundred chief executives of U.S. corporations were paid forty times more than the average worker in 1970 and a thousand times more than the average worker in 2000, some astonishing improvement in their marginal productivity must decree that it be so.[2]

The studies that reached this nearly unanimous conclusion actually dispense with any invisible labor-supply curve, and just consider supply to equal the actual number of workers at different education levels—

such as less than high school, high school, some college, and college.[3] The supply of better-educated workers rose enormously. Johnson calculates that the ratio of "college-equivalent" labor to "high-school equivalent" labor rose from a little over a tenth in 1950 to almost half in 1993.[4] To neoclassical eyes, this improvement creates a puzzle. If the supply of a good increases and demand doesn't shift, the price of the good must fall. If the supply of better-educated workers increases relative to that of less-educated workers, their pay premium should fall. Of course, just the opposite happened. The pay of better-educated workers rose in buying power, while that of less-educated workers fell. The conclusion is evidently that demand for better-educated workers must have increased even faster than the supply, and thus drove up their pay.

To get the discussion going about income-inequality studies, grant for the moment the parable of the aggregate production function. In standard form, it tells how much output firms can produce by using more capital and less labor, or vice versa. But for purposes of using the production function to investigate income inequality, the assumption is that firms can produce the same output by employing more college-educated labor and less high-school-educated labor, or vice versa. The marginal product of each factor—the additional amount produced by one more college-educated worker or one more high-school-educated worker— determines the wages paid to that factor.

Economists derive a curve describing the demand for better-educated versus less-educated workers from such a production function. The production function has a "dual" that describes the same facts in the opposite form. Given any wage paid to a factor—in this case, college-educated or high-school-educated labor—the dual specifies the amount of that factor the firm will demand. The dual of the production function is, in principle, used to reveal the labor-demand curve in these income-inequality studies.

Actually, what this literature calls the "demand" curve I will call the "everything-else" curve. It bears practically the whole burden of capturing *everything* relevant to determining income inequality, other than labor supply—everything other than the actual numbers of workers of various types employed in different industries. For example, in a canonical paper, Lawrence Katz of Harvard and Kevin Murphy of the University of Chicago promise to incorporate in their everything-else curve "the effects of technology, product demand, and other nonlabor inputs."[5] Such an everything-else curve can capture institutional changes, such as the weakening of organized labor; shifting trade patterns, such as rising trade deficits in manufacturing industries that pay higher wages to less-educated workers; evolving industrial shares, such as growth of financial industries that tend to employ many better-educated workers; and, of course, technological change.

Economists face the perennial challenge that they cannot measure technological change in any remotely direct way—or at least have not managed to do so. Their strategy for isolating the effects of technological change is like that of the fictional detective who eliminates a list of shady suspects to discover the real culprit. Eliminate everything else, and the effects of technological change are what's left—the "residual." Alas, real-life income-inequality studies encounter certain difficulties that fictional detectives avoid. Detective writers give all their suspects names and faces and roles in the plot. Authors of income-inequality studies may have a tough time working even identifiable suspects such as manufacturing trade deficits into their models, and they may fail so much as to imagine other important suspects. To the extent that studies do not adequately tally up the nefarious actions of other suspects, they overstate the effects of technology.

Economists are game for almost anything. Take a look at Katz and Murphy's effort. After tallying up shifts in the everything-else curve— or, in their terms, the overall demand curve for labor—they identify one principal component of those shifts that is not attributable to technology. This component is the change in demand for workers between different industries, such as increasing demand for retail-sales workers, who tend to earn lower wages, and declining demand for manufacturing-production workers, who tend to earn higher wages. The authors net these shifts in demand out of their everything-else curve. They are left with what they see as changes in demand for different types of labor within given industries—say, increased demand for better-educated women or decreased demand for less-educated men within retail. These changes are the unobserved residual, left after one nets out more visible factors. These "difficult to measure changes," as Katz and Murphy infelicitously put it, turn out to account for "the majority of the required demand shifts in favor of more-educated workers and females."[6] They proceed to label these changes "technological" shifts in demand for different types of workers that drive income inequality. But "technology" is essentially a label attached to the unexplained. There is no obvious reason it couldn't just as well be labeled "politics."

John Bound of the University of Michigan and his colleague George Johnson do an unusually comprehensive detective job.[7] They build a model to identify different factors that affect the wages of thirty-two groups of workers, distinguished by educational level, years in the labor market, and sex. Along the way to uncovering the invisible effects of technology, they conduct an impressive hunt for more-visible factors. The shifting employment shares of U.S. industries matter importantly. For example, manufacturing of durable goods (automobiles, refrigerators, and so on) and mining employed 19 percent of workers in 1973 and 14 percent of workers in 1988. Since these industries are more unionized and pay less-educated workers higher wages, their declining share of employment erodes the wages of this group. Next the authors want to gauge how much more each of the thirty-two groups of workers is paid in manufacturing and mining than in services—and, generally, to gauge wage disparities for each group across different industries. Unable to determine the disparities across industries for each of the 32 distinct groups, they are forced to lump all workers together and gauge average wage disparities across industries. For example, in 1973, wages were some 36 percent higher in construction than in education, but this is just an average for all workers in these industries.[8] High-school dropouts might have been paid 50 percent more in construction and college graduates 10 percent less.

Finally, Bound and Johnson investigate a dimly lit but not quite invisible culprit: shifts the demand for different industries' products. For example, demand for business services grew the fastest among the seventeen industries identified. Since a large percentage of business-service employees are well-educated, increasing demand for those services should raise the wages of this group of workers. While Katz and Murphy find that shifts in demand between different industries tended to worsen income inequality, Bound and Johnson find the opposite. I have no idea who has the better case.

In any event, the end results are similar. The visible culprits Bound and Johnson identify leave most of the deterioration in income inequality unexplained. "Obviously, something else is going on," they conclude.[9] What could that something else be? In this framework, it can only be the invisible residual, labeled "technological change." The problem is that many unidentified culprits could be lurking there.

The labor movement's overall decline in strength since about 1980 could, for example, be one of the lurking culprits. The wage premium that workers enjoy in one industry versus another does capture some of the effects of unionization as between one industry and another. But Bound and Johnson cannot identify economy-wide erosion of labor-union strength.[10] For example, when the air-traffic controllers went on strike in August 1981, in a powerful political act, President Ronald Reagan fired the more than 90 percent of controllers who went on strike; he broke the union and decertified it. It was the first step in a sustained attack on organized labor almost across the economy. Bound and Johnson's model accounts for the direct effect on air-traffic controllers' wages— trivial because there were only 13,000 of them—or other specific unions, but not for the general force of the bully pulpit on labor relations. Com-

pare President John F. Kennedy's use of the bully pulpit in 1962. Just after the United Steel Workers had agreed to moderate raises, U.S. Steel
increased prices by what Kennedy considered an exorbitant $6 a ton. He
lambasted the company's "wholly unjustifiable and irresponsible defiance
of the public interest."[11] U.S. Steel backed down. In effect, he warned
business that it had better not raise profits far out of line with wages.
While higher profits do not immediately feed into top executives' wages,
they undoubtedly do over the longer term.

Another economy-wide political fact that Bound and Johnson's model
cannot capture is the women's movement. Since the 1970s, only one
broad group saw its pay keep up with economy-wide productivity growth:
female college graduates.[12] The median wages of other groups (high-
school-educated men and women, as well as college-educated men) fell
steadily behind.[13] Why might college-educated women have done better? One factor that Bound and Johnson can capture is that women
increasingly stayed in the labor force after 1970, gaining experience and
becoming more productive. But didn't they also launch a campaign
against being paid only 59 cents on the dollar? Didn't the government
pass an Equal Pay Act? While the labor movement's ability to push for
raises faltered, the women's ability to push for them strengthened.

Too Many Unexplained Facts

There are good reasons to believe that political decisions, rather than just
technology working its way through the production function, have powerfully worsened income inequality. One problem with the story blaming
technology as the prime culprit is that income inequality has not worsened across the developed nations. In a broad-based comparison, David
Howell of the New School notes that, while earnings have become more
unequal in the United States and the United Kingdom, they have become more equal in Germany and Belgium, while in the fourteen other
advanced nations for which data are available, there have been no changes

or minor changes, tending as much one way as the other.[14] These countries went through the same technological revolution that swept the United States, so why didn't they experience broadly worsening income inequality?

Neoclassicals have a response when confronted with Europe's relative income equality. Europe was able to sustain it, the University of Chicago economist Gary Becker ominously warns, only by making a devil's choice to "drown in joblessness."[15] The neoclassical production function tells him that if wages are pushed to supposed above-market levels, workers should be unemployed. The only problem, aside from the theory, is a matter of facts. The 1980s and 1990s saw worsening unemployment in most developed nations, but Germany and Belgium, where incomes became more equal, had some of the smallest increases in unemployment.[16] And by the way, while the United States ran large trade deficits along with its worsening income distribution, Germany ran significant trade surpluses along with its improving income distribution.

Compare the Nordic countries with the United States. Income distributions are often measured by the "Gini index," which would give a country with perfect equality a value of 0 and a country with perfect inequality a value of 100. The Nordic countries, with a Gini index of around 25, have much more equitable distributions than the United States, with a Gini index of about 40.[17] According to the Economist Intelligence Unit, since 1980 (the earliest year for which it provides data), Finland's unemployment was sometimes better and sometimes considerably worse than that of the United States; Sweden's was better about half the time and worse about half; Denmark's was almost always better; and Norway's was better in every single year.[18] Unemployment rates in all of the Nordic countries were lower than the rate in the United States following the global financial crisis.

Moreover, if Becker were right, unemployment should work precisely the way the production function says it should work. The "flexible" low wages for less-educated workers in the United States that he so admires should have rescued those workers from high unemployment, while the floor under European wages should have worsened unemployment specifically for less-educated workers. In fact, that is just the opposite of the picture that emerges from a study by the Organisation for Economic Co-operation and Development (OECD). The relative unemployment rate for less-educated workers in the United States posted the absolute worst record among rates in all nations for which there are data.[19]

Not only is the story about technology worsening income inequality hard to square with European experience; it is also hard to square with U.S. experience, once you look beyond the most superficial accounts of the information revolution. How exactly is that revolution supposed to explain why the median wages of all workers with a high-school education, as well as the median wages of men with a college education—that is, the median wages of three-quarters of the U.S. workforce—have fallen increasingly behind average productivity? Such a continuing change looks much more like loss of bargaining power than a result of changes in marginal productivity.

Also, the timing is wrong for the story identifying information technology as the culprit raising the marginal productivity of better-educated U.S. workers and lowering it for less-educated workers. Information technology would not seem to have been adopted widely enough in the 1980s to have broad effects; and during that decade, economists ritually lamented the dismal performance of U.S. productivity. But that was the decade when U.S. income inequality took its sharpest turn for the worse.[20] The information revolution was widely seen as taking hold in the "new economy" of the late 1990s, as productivity growth finally picked up, yet those years actually saw some amelioration of income inequality. Why should income inequality have worsened when productivity was doing badly, and why should it have been ameliorated when productivity improved?

For that matter, why were huge technological advances from the 1920s through the 1970s compatible with dramatic improvement in income equality?[21] You have to use quite a contorted production function to generate all these possibilities.[22] And this marvelous production function has yet another twist to incorporate, as Ian Dew-Becker and Robert J. Gordon of Northwestern University point out. If technological advance was behind the premium that college-educated workers earned over the non–college educated, why did high-tech occupational groups, including "engineers" and "math/computer," account for only 17 percent of the premium, while "managers" accounted for half of it?[23]

Particularly since the 1990s, rising incomes of the top 1 percent of U.S. earners accounted for the lion's share of worsening income inequality, and they fit the technology story even worse.[24] Since the welfare state never limited the earnings of top executives, why didn't their pay surge in Europe?[25] The more plausible story about U.S. executives is that they form a sort of cabal. Each committee that recommends high pay includes friendly executives who will receive a like favor in return; it also includes contractors to the firm who depend on it for hundreds of millions of dollars worth of business.[26]

A More Hopeful View

In 2008, Harvard economists Claudia Goldin and Lawrence Katz shifted the debate with *The Race between Education and Technology* (Katz's views had evolved considerably since he'd co-authored the 1992 article mentioned above). They echo other researchers in seeing a race between technology's demand for increasing skill levels and the U.S. educational system's ability to supply workers with those skills. They argue, however, that technological demand for skills did not substantially surge after 1980 so as to worsen income inequality. On the contrary, there was a more or less steady rise in the demand for skills throughout the twentieth century. Demand for higher skills was driven just as fast by early industrial developments—such as synthesizing chemicals, refining petroleum, and manufacturing office machinery—as by the information revolution. But the enormous progress of American education earlier in the century reduced income inequality, and the deterioration of education after about 1980 worsened the problem. While the demand for skills continued more or less on course, a narrowing supply of better-skilled workers drove up their wages, and a broadening pool of less-skilled workers drove down theirs.

One of the most powerful aspects of this study is its historical sweep. A century-long perspective reveals insights that the view of a few decades can miss. In the early twentieth century, except for a tiny elite, the critical degree was the high-school diploma. Among the examples Goldin and Katz discuss, they show that more than 40 percent of workers had high-school degrees in the industries that constituted high technology in 1940—including chemicals and the others just mentioned, as well as aircraft, photographic equipment, and electrical machinery, to name a few more—while only 10 to 15 percent had high-school degrees in traditional sectors such as textiles and logging.[27] Evidently, technological advance did demand a better-skilled workforce. A standard neoclassical approach to gauging technological demand for better-skilled workers suggests that its upward trend was relatively steady throughout the century and did not suddenly accelerate after 1980.[28] This historical account tells at once an unusual story and a plausible story.

The spread of education across the broad American workforce, supported by universal public education, unquestionably far outpaced that of other nations in the early twentieth century—and played a critical role in propelling the United States to economic leadership. How significantly the reach of American education narrowed after 1980, raising the skills of university graduates while leaving a broad swath of other workers behind, might be questioned. By Goldin and Katz's gauge, the ratio of college-educated to high-school-educated workers grew 3.8 percent a year from 1960 to 1980, and only 2.0 percent a year from 1980 to 2005—still growth, but at only about half the rate.[29] In a simple calculation I did using Census Bureau data, that ratio grew 1.0 percent a year before 1980 and actually picked up to 1.9 percent a year after 1980.[30] However, by my calculation, the percentage of the workforce with high school or some college—in effect, the new high school—grew much faster before 1980, at 2.1 percent a year, than afterward, at only 0.3 percent a year. My calculations are crude; theirs take into account hours actually worked, experience on the job, and other factors.[31] Moreover, Goldin and Katz argue persuasively that the quality of U.S. education deteriorated. In one of the most important international tests, the Third International Math and Science Study, U.S. high-school seniors placed a dismal fifteenth out of twenty nations.[32] Although the best U.S. students did extremely well, the average had failing scores.

In any event, Goldin and Katz's account of the vicissitudes of American education and the workforce is fascinating, and in principle the numbers can be counted. The deeper problem—the perpetual problem in neoclassical efforts to pinpoint causes of income inequality—is identifying technological demand for better-skilled versus less-skilled workers. As always, the demand curve is an intellectual construct. It cannot be observed but depends on your model. As always, Goldin and Katz's neoclassical production function allows firms to trade one factor for another, hiring more skilled workers and fewer unskilled, or vice versa. The production function that, they estimate, best describes the U.S. economy yields a particular falling demand curve for labor. For example, if wages of unskilled labor fall, say, 10 percent compared with those of skilled labor, firms hire 16 percent more unskilled labor.[33] Firms would thus absorb a growing pool of unskilled workers, at the cost of worsening income inequality.

I have spent enough time lamenting the implausible neoclassical production function at the level of the firm, and its theoretical impasse at the aggregate level. Suppose the classical account of production is true and, at a given state of the art, there is no real trade-off, or at least a limited trade-off, between one factor and another. If the Mexican government retail chain wants to compete with Wal-Mart, or just avoid massive losses in the face of Wal-Mart competition, it has to adopt a broadly similar approach to managing its entire operation, based on intensive use of information technology.

Goldin and Katz's claim that demand for better-skilled versus less-skilled workers steadily rose during the twentieth century might still be valid within this classical account. The classical account does *not* say that the same use of factors persists forever, but only that change requires uncertain and time-consuming technological innovation. For decades, the Mexican government retail chain made a profit—and forced small-town monopolists to lower their prices—using practically no information technology at all, but by the turn of the twenty-first century, those labor-intensive methods no longer worked. Now the chain required fewer workers, and many of them needed computer skills. More generally, though production methods become fairly standard at any given state of the art, progressive change in the state of the art over the twentieth century can well require more high-skilled workers as compared with low-skilled workers. (Interestingly, Goldin and Katz argue that advances in the early nineteenth-century industrial revolution did not require more skilled workers, but rather replaced skilled with unskilled workers.)

Yet a classical interpretation of Goldin and Katz's results would differ in one crucial respect: how much workers are paid still depends substantially on some social determination, whether wage bargaining, minimum-wage legislation, or convention. It is not realistically possible for firms to shop for 16 percent more high-skilled workers and comparably fewer low-skilled workers, or vice versa, based on their respective marginal products, because they do not have marginal products in any real sense. The retail methods developed by Wal-Mart and adopted by the Mexican government retail chain in the early 2000s have fairly fixed requirements for given types of workers. All of them contribute, and it cannot be determined just how much each contributes. A particular way of organizing production does not automatically translate into relative wages. Construction workers earned 36 percent more than teachers in 1973, according to Bound and Johnson, but this premium could not have been because they had some imaginary higher level of marginal productivity. In fact, surely many fewer construction workers held college degrees, so they should have been lower-skilled and had lower marginal productivities in a neoclassical account. They earned higher wages because they had stronger unions. There remains considerable room for social and political determination of relative wages.

A classical interpretation of Goldin and Katz does agree that a nation needs to improve its educational system so as to provide the skilled workers required by the latest technologies. A nation that lacks a sufficient number of skilled workers will simply fall behind in many industries. Given the evidence that Goldin and Katz marshal about the U.S. education system, the United States has plenty of educational work to do.

The Treaty of Detroit

Just what political and institutional changes might have driven increasing income equality from the 1920s through the 1970s and increasing inequality since? In 2007, the MIT economists Frank Levy and Peter Temin wrote a widely cited article discussing these possible changes.[34] The short version is that the New Deal in the 1930s set the nation on a course of improving income equality and the Reagan revolution in the 1980s set the nation on the opposite course. These were political responses to circumstances—the Great Depression of the 1930s and the stagflation of the 1970s—but not inevitable responses. Responses to similar circumstances differed across nations.

In a slightly more detailed version, the 1935 National Labor Relations Act, with broad public support, established a framework for unions to organize the workforce; and after the unusual labor conditions of World War II, President Harry Truman made it clear that the government would mediate between business and labor to sustain a balanced relationship. "Labor unions are woven into our economic pattern of American life, and collective bargaining is a part of the democratic process," declared none other than the president of the U.S. Chamber of Commerce in a statement after one round of meetings with Truman: "I say recognize this fact not only with our lips but with our hearts."[35]

The "Treaty of Detroit," as *Fortune* magazine dubbed a 1949 settlement between General Motors and the United Auto Workers, established that wages should rise in line with productivity gains plus inflation.[36] Increases of this sort, typically set by the largest firms in major industries such as autos and steel, would spread by means of "pattern bargaining" to other unionized firms. Nonunionized firms such as IBM also accepted them, so as not to provoke their workers to organize. And they spread even through smaller firms via custom and minimum wage.[37] Meanwhile, the highest income earners were taxed at marginal rates that would be regarded as exorbitant today: 90 percent in the 1950s.[38]

As growth slowed and inflation rose in the 1970s, partly as a result of two oil crises, a neoclassical resurgence blamed New Deal "rigidities" such as unionization, excessive regulation, and high marginal tax rates.[39] The crudest forms of neoclassical theory tend to sally forth when economists don't understand what's happening. This was not exclusively a Republican affair. Paul Samuelson, a Democrat, declared, "The evidence from heavily unionized European countries suggests that, when unions succeed in raising money wage rates, the main impact is to trigger an inflationary wage-price spiral."[40] When the House passed a bill seeking to preserve the Treaty of Detroit, President Jimmy Carter failed to support labor the way Truman and Kennedy had, and the measure was killed.[41] Reagan recruited a management consultant who had specialized in breaking unions, and appointed him to the chair of the National Labor

Relations Board.[42] As government threw its weight behind business, the minimum wage fell from a range of 25 to 30 percent of average labor productivity in the 1950s and 1960s to less than half that level: 10 to 15 percent of average labor productivity.[43] Such a drastic change seems far out of line with any conceivable labor-demand curve.

Technology Is Malleable, Too

The classical account and the neoclassical account concur implicitly on one point. They both see technology—or, more broadly, the organization of production—as a sort of autonomous force that proceeds according to some predetermined logic. In real life, technology does seem to proceed partly according to some such logic; but to an important extent, it seems to be influenced by its social context, including how wages are set.

Robert Solow makes this point. He participated in a research project comparing low-wage jobs in the United States with those in several European countries. The American team would ask European colleagues how they organized a particular type of work—which individuals performed it, how much they were paid, what training they were given. One case was hospital work. The French had few low-wage workers in their hospitals, and the Dutch had none. In general, European governments run hospitals and set higher wages for categories of workers such as nurses aides than U.S. hospitals pay. As a result, hospitals are managed and organized differently, so that nursing aides do work that justifies their wage, Solow says. He argues that any U.S. hospital could do the same:

> If we passed an ordinance tomorrow that nobody who worked at Beth Israel Medical Center could be paid less than $22 an hour, the first thing that would happen is a lot of people would be fired. The next thing that would happen is that managers would realize they can't run the hospital without those people. So they would sit down and say,

"How can we reorganize this hospital so we can pay $22 an hour and get the rooms cleaned and still be viable?" You can't describe the production function of a hospital; the situation is a lot more complicated than that, as in most things. The whole organization of the production process would respond to the higher wage. And that's just a way of saying production would have to be organized so the enterprise hired the amount of unskilled labor that corresponded to $22 an hour on the demand curve.[44]

Solow describes the situation in quasi-neoclassical terms; I would interpreted it as organizational and technological innovation within a classical account. But the broader point is that production technology does respond, in some real measure, to its social context and, in particular, to the relative wages that a society establishes.

Suppose the United States did set higher wages for less-skilled workers. Depending on possibilities for managerial and technological innovation, something like the changes Solow suggests might well begin to spread, no doubt more in some industries than in others. Once the U.S. Chamber of Commerce realized that businesses would have to pay higher wages at the bottom of the scale, it might stop funneling millions of dollars into campaigning for candidates who clamor for tax cuts for the rich, and instead it might even lobby to improve public education, so that better-trained workers would be available to justify the higher wages. As several successful European countries—such as the Nordic nations and Germany—have shown, setting a reasonable floor under the wage scale can work. Wages certainly can be raised too fast, but the Treaty of Detroit did not do so. It raised them in line with economy-wide productivity growth. The Reagan revolution pushed the wages of nearly all workers further and further behind economy-wide productivity growth. That trend persisted, and has not ensured anything like full employment. Reversing it—and also improving education—is in order.

TEN

Understanding an Uncertain World

Born near the end of the Victorian age and reaching adulthood in the Indian summer of the Edwardian age, neither John Maynard Keynes nor his contemporaries imagined the cataclysms awaiting them. World War I destroyed a generation of men and what had seemed a pan-European order. England fell into deep recession in the 1920s, as unemployment hardly dipped below 10 percent, and then, along with the rest of the world, sank into the Great Depression. Economic doldrums ended—as a result of World War II. The uncertainty of the human condition, deflating the confident predictions of neoclassical theory, shaped Keynes's vision. His great contribution was to comprehend the implications of uncertainty, yet still show that reason—and not only reason, but considered models—can somehow help us to understand and cope with our economic world.

It wasn't easy becoming the greatest economist of the twentieth century. Called Maynard by friends, Keynes entered adulthood as a brilliant, arrogant, and insecure Eton boy, in my reading of Robert Skidelsky's fine biography.[1] He began reading mathematics at Cambridge University but soon turned his attention to practically everything else, notably moral philosophy. As exams neared, he weighed his options. One was the Moral Sciences Tripos. Another was the Economics Tripos; a few weeks of study with Alfred Marshall convinced the great economist that Keynes must be recruited to the profession. In the end, although Keynes was not a true mathematician—reading his *General Theory of Employment, Interest, and Money*, you sense a mild distaste for the subject of math—he settled on the Mathematical Tripos and passed in twelfth place. A year later, he took the civil service exam to enter government.

After university, Keynes led a double life. One life was his official and academic persona. He clerked at the India Office, a top civil-service post, and pondered a dissertation about probability in the face of uncertainty, a work he would not publish until fifteen years later. If such a thing as first-hand knowledge of finance exists, he hardly had it for India—he never traveled farther east than Egypt—but he learned economics as an administrator, not just as a theorist. After two years, he accepted a lectureship sponsored by Arthur C. Pigou, professor of economics at Cambridge. Epitome of the early twentieth-century neoclassical, Pigou became Keynes's life-long friend—and his opponent in *The General Theory*. Then on to Treasury, where Keynes served as principal assistant to the powerful chancellor of the exchequer Reginald McKenna.

In his private life, via friendships established at Cambridge, Keynes entered the Bloomsbury group, a clique of writers, critics, and artists who took their name from the then low-rent district of London where they congregated. Including the novelist Virginia Woolf, the biographer Lytton Strachey (whose *Eminent Victorians* would take aim at Victorian pretensions), and the art critic Clive Bell, among others, they led the English modernist movement. Their revolt had parallels to that of the generation of the 1960s, but unlike the later generation, they were dogmatically apolitical, centering their interests on culture. Their upscale existence required a retinue of servants. Skidelsky writes that they joined in a "sexual merry-go-round"—with members of the same or the opposite sex—"as friends became lovers and then went back to being friends."[2] Homosexual during this era, Keynes fell in love with a handsome, free-spirited painter named Duncan Grant.

Something of an outsider to the "Bloomsberries" as an economist and—worse—a public official, Keynes saw his life torn apart even as World War I tore Europe apart. The Bloomsberries' attitude toward the war was a murky mixture, again not unlike that of the 1960s movement toward Vietnam: it is immoral, and we don't want to risk our skins. At Treasury, he labored day and night to sustain the war effort, while using his pull to help his Bloomsbury friends get conscientious-objector status. In an economy stretched beyond capacity, with not a resource to spare, mobilizing a new military division could mean failing to supply another unit of the armed forces. Keynes very well knew what economists have sometimes charged him with ignoring: supply constraints can bind an economy. On the monetary front, as Britain kept borrowing from the United States, Keynes kept warning politicians about the dangers of inflation and financial crisis. Torn by moral objections to the war and by guilt about his exemption from military service as a Treasury official, he wrote Duncan Grant, "I work for a Government I despise for ends I think criminal. . . . I pray for the most absolute financial crash (and yet strive to prevent it—so that all I do is a contradiction with all I feel)."[3]

These gathering frustrations came to a head in 1919, at the Treaty of Versailles. Keynes concluded that the devious French prime minister, Georges Clemenceau, wanted to force Germany to pay exorbitant reparations, partly in revenge for France's defeat in the Prussian War, partly to force Germany, in effect, to repay French war debts to the United States. The British prime minister, David Lloyd George, knew Germany could never pay the proposed reparations to France and England, but ceded to electoral pressures at home and pressed for them anyway. And the U.S. president, Woodrow Wilson, stuffed with his ten abstract principles, was bamboozled by wily Europeans, in Keynes's view. Wilson refused to forgive American loans to France and England in exchange for their releasing Germany from impossible reparations. The resulting multinational disaster—Germany was required to repay more than it ever could to France and England, while they were to use their nonexistent receipts to repay the United States—would ultimately contribute to the Great Depression and the failure of German democracy. Frustrated by what he saw as politicians' conniving, as well as his own sense of complicity, Keynes fired off an instant book, *The Economic Consequences of the Peace.* It was an international bestseller.

Keynes saw that economics was serious stuff. As Britain sank into postwar recession—the worst since the recession after the Napoleonic Wars had motivated Ricardo—Keynes vehemently opposed the plan to restore sterling to the prewar exchange rate, or "parity," of $4.86 dollars to the pound. At that price, to prevent speculators from selling pounds and buying dollars, the Bank of England would have to maintain high interest rates, Keynes argued, cutting off economic recovery. He pressed his view in newspaper articles and on commissions, as well as with economist colleagues. Bank of England officials argued that it was naïve of him to see the interest rate as a sort of switch that could turn the economy up or down: lowering it might just undermine business confidence and do harm. Keynes conceded the point about the importance of business psychology, but his advice was ultimately proved right. After the pound was restored to prewar parity in 1925, high interest rates wrought havoc on the British economy. Even Winston Churchill, the chancellor of the exchequer who restored the pound to parity, later conceded he had made a terrible mistake.

Keynes felt he had lost the debate when it counted—throughout the 1920s—because he had not gotten his model right. As the world sank into the Great Depression, he sat down with a circle of friendly critics to get it right. "The new theory emerged through a process of intellectual argument, marked by a sense of high responsibility from all concerned," according to Skidelsky.[4] This was no mere academic exercise. On the argument depended policy; and on policy depended millions of livelihoods.

Keynes's life now turned more conventional. His marriage to a famous Russian ballerina, Lydia Lopokova, distanced him from the Bloomsberries. It was hard to say which sin they considered worse: settling down with any woman at all or settling down with a ballerina—hardly educated, let alone intellectual, though sharp as a whip by all accounts. Keynes moved into the world of officialdom and business. A product of the English university tradition, he had looked down on business, but dealings with executives and bankers on government commissions had slowly changed his mind. The entrepreneur, hazarding investment in the face of uncertainty, defeating "the dark forces of time and ignorance which envelop our future" to move the economy forward, would become, in some sense, the hero of *The General Theory*.[5]

The General Theory

Keynes's book *The General Theory of Employment, Interest, and Money* is not light reading. Paul Samuelson famously opined:

> Any layman who, beguiled by the author's previous reputation, bought the book was cheated of his 5 shillings. . . . It abounds in mares' nests and confusions: involuntary unemployment, wage units, the equality of savings and investment, the timing of the multiplier, interactions of marginal efficiency upon the rate of interest, forced savings, own rates of interest, and many others. . . . Flashes of insight and intuition intersperse tedious algebra. . . . When it finally is mastered, we find its analysis to be obvious and at the same time new. In short, it is a work of genius.[6]

The book isn't all that bad. What's so confusing about involuntary unemployment? Well after Keynes's *General Theory* appeared, Samuelson found room for involuntary unemployment in his textbook.[7] The equality of savings and investment that seemed to puzzle Samuelson is today presented as an indisputable accounting identity in every macro text, including Samuelson's. Nor are the other concepts so terribly difficult. Samuelson's review unwittingly reveals how deeply *The General Theory* revolutionized economics.

Perhaps Samuelson's essential complaint about *The General Theory* is that he thought mathematically, and Keynes did not. On that matter, Samuelson has a point. After Keynes's careful discussion of his assumptions, when you finally get to Chapter 18, "The General Theory of Employment Re-Stated" (Keynes had sketched it earlier), he refuses to spell out a mathematical model. Even I feel like grabbing him by the lapels and demanding one. If Keynes had provided one, he certainly would have saved countless economists decades of still-unresolved debate about what he really meant.

Keynes had his reasons for not spelling out his argument in algebra. He had been explaining for two hundred pages that his model assumes that conventional expectations provide a measure of stability, temporarily holding at bay the fundamentally uncertain future. These conventions can be counted on to hold—until they suddenly shift. To inscribe a model in algebra could suggest that it rests on a far more solid foundation than mere fragile conventions covering up uncertainty. It might suggest that you can just pull a few levers to "fine-tune" the economy, precisely the hubris that Samuelson's generation fell for, and that the current generation of economists fell for even worse.

The uncertain world of *The General Theory* affects economic decisions that will turn out to have been good or bad, depending on what the unknown future brings. When conventions crumble and uncertainty looms, entrepreneurs cannot make investment decisions based on any confident calculation about expected profits. Investment depends on mere "animal spirits"—fragile gambles in the face of the elemental unknown—and may well falter. As it falters, the economy weakens. A dismal condition can settle in. No automatic forces operate to restore growth or employment.

But Keynes did believe he presented a model that would help people to better understand an economic world surrounded by uncertainty. A model can never prove that you are right, since it is only a simplified picture of an actual economy, but it provides a "useful check" on thoughts, at least ensuring consistency, as Skidelsky describes Keynes's view.[8] *The General Theory* is difficult partly because it is pioneering work—at once profoundly new yet somehow obvious, just as Samuelson says. Sometimes, the intellectual pioneer burdens readers with unnecessary and circuitous detail; at other times, he fails to bring critical points into sharp focus. Unfortunately, Keynes himself had little time to remedy any initial lack of clarity. Shortly after publication of *The General Theory*, he had a heart attack. On recovering, he was called on to help Britain finance World War II. As the war ended, he was enlisted as the central intellect to shape the postwar international financial system adopted at the conference in Bretton Woods, New Hampshire. And not long afterward, he died. Ambiguity remains.

The way I understand *The General Theory* is based on my own repeated readings of it, informed by the interpretations of his former students and colleagues at Cambridge University. Several of them, such as Joan Robinson, belonged to the "Cambridge Circus" of younger colleagues who periodically met with Keynes to hash out the concepts. Luigi Pasinetti, an Italian economist who received his doctorate at Cambridge, and who has been associated with that university though teaching primarily in Milan, laid out the structure of the model particularly clearly.[9] These interpretations filtered down to me when I studied with Lance Taylor at MIT and Murray Milgate at Harvard in the 1990s. (Taylor later moved to the New School and Milgate to Cambridge University.) Majority opinion in Cambridge, Massachusetts, led by Paul Samuelson and Robert Solow, arrived at a quite different interpretation of Keynes that I will discuss later.

Effective Demand

A rough and ready summary of *The General Theory*—but only a first take, requiring modification—is the theory of "effective demand." It's a very simple theory. President George W. Bush described it well enough: "When people have more money, they can spend it on goods and services. And in our society, when they demand an additional good or a service, somebody will produce the good or a service. And when somebody produces that good or a service, it means somebody is more likely to be able to find a job."[10] The Obama administration's roughly $800 billion stimulus plan—which entailed government spending and tax breaks, and which was passed in 2009 to shorten the recession—rested on the theory of effective demand.

More precisely, effective demand comprises all spending on goods and services produced by domestic industries, located within the nation, whoever the owner may be. For the United States, the purchase of a Honda built in Ohio is part of effective demand; the purchase of a Ford built in Brazil is not. Thus, effective demand includes household spending on domestically produced consumer goods or residential construction; business spending on domestically produced capital equipment and other productive inputs; and all government spending—on roads, salaries, pencils—except for the purchase of imported items. Effective demand also includes goods manufactured by domestic industry and sold abroad.

The theory of effective demand hypothesizes a cause-and-effect relationship: effective demand *determines* national economic output.[11] If consumption, investment, or government expenditures on domestically produced goods increase, economic output increases. If exports of domestically produced goods increase, economic output increases.

This theory can stir controversy. Why doesn't it count saving among the factors that increase economic output? An interchange between Robert Henry Brand, a banker who chaired a committee in 1930 to advise the British prime minister on the Depression, and Keynes himself, a committee member, poses the question. Keynes argued that if households spend income rather than saving it, they may benefit the economy. Brand had doubts: "I have always assumed that if I save money, those savings go in some form, either by my own investment or by the bankers' investment, back into industry."[12] Not necessarily, replied Keynes. "What happens to my savings?" asked the puzzled banker. Keynes replied, "The fact that you do not spend money means that some businessman fails to sell you something he hoped to sell you . . . and is, therefore, poorer by the exact amount that you are richer." Keynes might have gone on to argue that, as businesses across the economy see inventories piling up, they reduce their production, and output declines. Brand replied, "That is a strange doctrine to a Scotsman."

A Prelude to Theory

In long discussions with members of the "Cambridge Circus" and other colleagues in the 1930s, Keynes sought to get his model right. But before getting to the model itself, he wanted to clarify his definitions and accounting. Economists had been using the terms "investment," "saving," and "consumption" loosely; they had spoken of saving as exceeding investment, or investment as exceeding saving, without being clear what they meant. Keynes argued—and all economists now agree—that if you define the terms precisely, saving must always equal investment. This equality does not prove cause and effect. It could be, as neoclassicals usually hold, that increased saving is channeled into investment, *causing* investment to rise. It could be, as Keynes held, that increased investment raises national output, *causing* saving to rise. Or other factors could also play key roles in the cause-and-effect relationship. But it's important first to get the definitions and accounting clear.

Suppose there is an economy with no government or trade. This simplification is unimportant; it merely avoids some algebra and makes the point easier to see. With no government, exports, or imports, the total value of output, or the domestic product, must equal consumption expenditures, often denoted C, plus investment expenditures, often denoted I. Simply, these are the only things produced and sold. Thus, the value of output, or domestic product, equals $C + I$. (What I have called the domestic product is the same thing as the gross domestic product, or GDP. Net domestic product is the gross domestic product minus depreciation of capital equipment. It is less often used, since depreciation, or the wear and tear on equipment, can be only roughly estimated.)

Now view the economy from another perspective. Instead of considering the domestic product, or what is produced, consider domestic income, or what is earned. Domestic income (still assuming no government and no trade, for simplicity) is wages plus profits. And domestic income must equal domestic product. Why? All expenditures on consumption and investment goods must be paid either to workers as wages or to firms as profits. Simply, there is no one else to collect earnings from sales.

Domestic income is used for saving or consumption. All retained business profits are saved. If firms deposit profits in a bank, they are saved but not immediately invested; if firms use profits to buy capital equipment or productive inputs, they are saved and immediately invested. (Even office-party expenses are treated as investment. This rather far-fetched device saves statistical agencies from splitting hairs.) Households spend some income on consumption goods, either nondurable goods such as food or durable goods such as cars. All these goods are counted as consumption. Whatever income households do *not* spend on consumption, they save. They can do two things with savings. They can invest them in the only thing statistical agencies allow households to invest in: residential construction. Or, instead of investing their savings, households can hoard them as cash, put them in a bank account, or use them to buy a financial instrument such as a stock. Buying a stock is not investment, properly speaking, since it does not constitute the purchase of capital equipment or other productive inputs.

On the income side of the economy, consumption spending by households is still denoted C, the same symbol used to denote consumption on the production side. Whatever products are sold as consumption goods, households must buy as consumption goods. Saving is denoted S. It includes saving by households (whether deposited in a bank or invested in residential construction) plus saving by firms (whether deposited in a bank or invested in production). Thus, domestic income equals $C + S$.

If the value of domestic income is $C + S$, and the value of domestic product is $C + I$, and domestic product equals domestic income, then saving must equal investment.

Wait a second! If investment equals saving, it means that if one fine day I decide to save $1,000 rather than buy a couch, my act in and of itself necessarily increases domestic investment by $1,000. Keynes acknowledged that this way of phrasing things sounds paradoxical. He responded, "The reconciliation of the identity between saving and investment with the apparent 'free-will' of the individual to save what he chooses, irrespective of what he or others may be investing, essentially depends on saving being, like spending, a two-sided affair."[13] Whether I spend $1,000 and buy a couch or save $1,000 and forgo the couch affects not only my own bank account but also the bank account of the firm that hopes to sell the couch.

An example illustrates why saving equals investment just as a matter of accounting. Keep in mind that investment is *defined* to include business spending not only on fixed capital equipment, but also on inventory—the value added to goods as they move through production in preparation for sale. Keep your eye on inventory.

Suppose a furniture maker has already spent $800 on labor and materials to build a couch ready for sale. The inventory value of the couch is $800. I come along and spend $1,000 to buy the couch. What happens to domestic saving and investment? First, why do I pay $1,000 for the couch rather than the $800 the firm has spent on labor and materials? The extra $200 is the firm's profit, its incentive for making the couch. It receives its profit only when it sells the couch. What happens to domestic saving? My saving is clearly down by $1,000. The furniture maker had previously saved and invested $800 in the couch—those transactions were already carried out—but its profits are up $200. Its savings are therefore up $200. With the firm's saving up $200 and mine down $1,000, domestic saving is down $800. What about domestic investment? It is also down $800, because the firm's inventory investment falls by $800 as I walk out the door with my couch.[14] Both domestic saving and domestic investment are down $800.

If all economic activity were a matter of selling inventory, the economy would soon grind to a halt; but fortunately the furniture maker, flushed with success at the sale, now decides to replenish the inventory. Suppose that the necessary input materials, such as wood, springs, and cloth, have already been purchased for $400. The furniture maker takes $400 from the bank to pay employees to make the couch. The firm's saving does not change—the firm has merely taken money from the bank to invest in inventory—but the value of its inventory does go up by $400. Thus, domestic investment is up $400. Where does the extra $400 in saving come from? The instant the employees are paid—our imaginary real-time national accounts catch them before they rush out to buy anything—their saving is also up $400. Thus, saving and investment, always equal, are both up $400.

Keynes's Model

The key relationships in Keynes's model are among consumption, investment, and saving, so let's continue to imagine an economy with no trade or government. Again, this assumption has no substantive importance and just avoids complications. I will make several other assumptions that are important: change them and the whole picture of the economy changes. For the moment, I will slip these in with little or no discussion, to paint the overall picture. I will then return to weigh the assumptions.

The economy is slouching along with high but steady unemployment—the year could be 2011. Saving equals investment, and both are fairly stable. Some promising development leads firms to expect the economy will improve to the extent that they can sell an additional $30 billion of output next month, over and above what they have been selling. They gear up and expand production, expecting that additional sales will yield $30 billion of income, including $20 billion of wages and $10 billion of profits. They collectively expect that the $10 billion of profits will be reinvested by businesses that receive them to produce more goods. The entire $30 billion of additional output would be sold if households spent all $20 billion of their salaries on consumer goods. But households are only spending 90 percent of their income and saving 10 percent, partly as a contingency against layoffs. Households therefore spend $18 billion on consumption goods and put the other $2 billion in bank accounts. Sales could fall $2 billion short of what firms had expected. Who could borrow the $2 billion in bank accounts to purchase goods? It can only be businesses, borrowing the savings through the financial system and investing them in additional production. Recall Robert Henry Brand, chair of the committee to advise the prime minister on the Depression, who thought that the banking system would channel all his savings into investment.

Will firms make that additional investment? Their decision depends on two factors: the interest rate they know they can receive by buying a bond, and the real return they *expect* to get on investment. The return they expect on investment had better be higher than the interest rate, or why invest? The interest rate was low in the United States in 2010, thanks to the $2 trillion or $3 trillion worth of loans the Federal Reserve had injected into the financial system. What about the return on investment? Firms might expect they could make a 5 percent return, no return at all, or a 5 percent loss. Because the world is fundamentally uncertain, Keynes assumes, they cannot calculate their probable return, let alone be sure what confidence to place in any educated guess: "Our knowledge of the factors which will govern the yield of an investment some years hence is usually very slight and often negligible. If we speak frankly, we have to admit that our basis of knowledge for estimating the yield ten years hence of a railway, a copper mine, a textile factory, the goodwill of a patent medicine, an Atlantic liner, a building in the City of London amounts to little and sometimes nothing; or even five years hence."[15] In a world where we face fundamental uncertainty, Keynes argues, "most, probably, of our decisions to do something positive . . . can only be taken as a result of animal spirits—of a spontaneous urge to action rather than inaction, and not as the outcome of a weighted average of quantitative benefits multiplied by quantitative probabilities."[16]

If animal spirits dim, as well they may, investment falters. To return to our example, the final $2 billion worth of income—$2 billion that households save rather than spend—goes into the banking system. Since in 2010 the banking system was already holding a trillion dollars of cash at the Federal Reserve, there the $2 billion may stay.[17] As a result, $2 billion worth of inventory goes unsold. Failing to sell this portion of their output, businesses cut back production. As employees lose jobs, the extra $2 billion in savings dissipate. Eventually, the $2 billion inventory sells, but the economy is right back where it started. Now, once again, saving balances investment at a more or less steady level. The only problem is that the same high level of unemployment has returned.

To sum up: households spend a portion of their income on consumer goods, but they also save a portion. To keep the economy going—and even more so to advance it—entrepreneurs must borrow and invest those savings. They are the engineers, and their investment is the engine of growth. Their decisions to invest are based on two factors: the interest rate and the return they expect on investment. If the return they expect on investment is below the interest rate, they fail to invest and the economy falters. If the expected return is above the interest rate, they invest and the economy improves. Their expectations are fickle. In an uncertain world, they depend not on any confident calculation of future profits, but on animal spirits. This is Keynes's essential model.

Keynes had two principal policy recommendations for ameliorating a depression. The central bank should lower interest rates, if they were not already low, and the government should invest in infrastructure—railroads, bridges, education. Keynes was cautious about increasing government consumption, such as by raising unemployment insurance payments or cutting taxes to encourage household spending. His World War I experience helping to manage an economy running at maximum capacity lurked as a warning about the dangers of inflation. Government investment would lay groundwork for sustaining growth in the long run, while it would raise animal spirits in the short run by providing workers money to buy goods that investors might venture to produce.

Say's Miraculous Law

I turn to assumptions underlying *The General Theory*. First, it helps to spell out the principal neoclassical assumption Keynes argued against: Say's so-called law, which I touched on earlier. One way to express it is that supply creates its own demand. All goods that the economy produces are sold because wages and profits earned in producing them provide just enough income to buy them. Say's law accounted for "the celebrated *optimism* of traditional economic theory," writes Keynes.[18] It "has led to economists being looked upon as Candides, who, having left this world for the cultivation of their gardens, teach that all is for the best in the best of all possible worlds provided we will let well alone."

Ricardo assumed Say's law. Workers consume all they earn. Extravagant landlords consume all their rental income, and then some, sometimes falling into penury. Capitalists invest all their profits. Every pound of income is spent on consumption or investment; everything that firms produce is sold. Unfortunately, the theory did not work in practice. The industrial revolution initiated the cycle of booms and busts. A deep depression followed the Napoleonic Wars, just when Ricardo was writing his *Principles*.

In the twenty-first century, Say's law hardly seems obvious. Savings are deposited in banks. What happens next? As Maurice Dobb of Cambridge University quips, "To the ears of common sense [Say's law] was a strange, if not monstrous, assertion. Was income never 'hoarded'? Did individual thrift never take the form of holding money or adding to bank deposits? Everyday observation suggested that this was certainly a common case. Whose magic wand decreed that every increase of bank or savings deposits would be forthwith matched by increased investment by businesses?"[19]

Some supply-and-demand story about investment and saving was needed to rescue Say's law. Keynes himself had been teaching it for years before writing *The General Theory*, without (as he says) quite thinking it through. He explains it succinctly: "Investment represents the demand for investible resources and saving represents the supply, whilst the rate of interest is the 'price' of investible resources at which the two are equated."[20] If households' saving starts piling up in bank accounts, the interest rate falls. A lower interest rate promotes investment and discourages saving, until the forces of supply and demand restore investment and saving to their equilibrium levels.[21] The mechanism works just as well in the opposite direction. All is for the best in the best of all possible worlds.

Uncertainty

Frank Knight, a University of Chicago economist of the generation before Milton Friedman, drew a distinction between "risk" and "uncertainty." Risk describes the world of *Consumer Reports*. In particular, the used-car section, which I like to consult, not only tells you about gas mileage and safety features, but also gives the probability that a given component—the brakes or transmission—of a given year and model will fail. These probabilities, based on actual experience, are reasonably reliable. Occasionally, when the sample is insufficient, an asterisk indicates that repair records cannot be calculated. Risk also describes the world of insurance. Actuaries estimate the number of years an individual will likely live, basing their estimates on the person's sex, place of residence, medical history, and other factors.

Calculations of risk assume that underlying features of the world, omitted from the model used to make the calculations, remain more or less constant. If those underlying features of the world suddenly shift— say, the automaker introduces an entirely new car under the same model name, or the individual with a given sex, domicile, and medical history goes to war—all risk calculations are off. Insurance companies call such changes in underlying features of the world "acts of God," and do not insure against them. God does not supply ex ante probability distributions for His acts.

Financial models, first developed in the 1960s and applied in the early 2000s more widely than ever before, assumed that finance is a world of risk, not uncertainty. Prices of financial instruments can be probabilistically estimated on the basis of past performance. It turns out that all models (or nearly all) assumed the same crucial underlying features of the world. When those features suddenly changed, the models fell apart. In 2009, on the basis of its model, one financial institution that owned a particular bond said it was worth 97 percent of its face value; Standard & Poor's said it was worth somewhere between 87 percent and 53 percent of face value; and it actually traded for 38 percent of face value.[22]

Keynes insists that we live in a world of uncertainty. Quite simply, there is no Oracle at Delphi. Or if there is, it's useless. We may well want to be smart shoppers, trying to get the best buy for the dollar, given our tastes in style and features, reliable information, and the limits of our patience. The problem is that, in contrast to our situation when buying a car, we may not be able to ascertain with any known confidence the outcomes of important economic decisions, notably investment, that will be affected by an uncertain future. There is no *Investor Reports* comparable to *Consumer Reports*. The probability that a given component of a car will break down can be reliably estimated based on past performance—but as the realistic lawyers who write the small print on mutual-fund reports say, when it comes to investment, past performance is no guarantee of future results.

People like me, who believe in the existence of economic uncertainty, can easily find examples to buttress our view. In two years, from 2003 to 2005, the median sales price of a house in Fort Myers, Florida, soared from $130,000 to $320,000. It hesitated for a couple of years, fell to $260,000 in 2007, and plunged to $100,000 in 2008.[23] If in 2003 home buyers could have calculated home values with any meaningful confidence, how could prices possibly have risen and then plummeted so? Or take Mexico's 1994 crisis. "The time to be invested in Mexico is now," declared Maria-Elena Carrion, managing a portfolio of Latin American investments for Bankers Trust, in August 1994.[24] Three months later the peso crashed, losing half its value.

There's a deeper point: not only do we often fail to predict the future; it may be inherently unpredictable. For example, I share the view of many observers that the 1994 Mexican peso crash could perfectly well *not* have turned out to be nearly so bad.[25] The economy was held together with pins, as finance secretary Pedro Aspe reportedly conceded. A rebellion in southern Mexico and the assassination of a presidential candidate certainly didn't help. Aspe volunteered to stay on for a year to stabilize the economy, but after the presidential candidate was assassinated, he was replaced by Ernesto Zedillo, a political enemy of Aspe. On becoming president, Zedillo fired Aspe. For good measure, he also fired all the undersecretaries below Aspe, 90 percent of the director-generals below them, 79 area directors, and 176 subdirectors, obliterating institutional memory. No president had ever before so completely wiped out the Ministry of Finance, not even when power had changed hands during the Mexican Revolution. Inexperienced finance officials bungled an attempt to devalue the peso 15 percent. Key businessmen learned about it ahead of time and pulled billions of dollars out of Mexico. The government devalued in the middle of the week, not on Friday afternoon, when it would have had time to explain its plan and calm investors. In fact, there was nothing to explain, since the government had no plan. The finance minister refused phone calls from U.S. mutual-fund managers. Markets went berserk and the peso plunged far worse than necessary. The probability of a disaster that did not have to happen could never have been determined.

Despite some serious mistakes as chairman of the Federal Reserve, Greenspan was a pragmatic observer. Here is what he says about uncertainty:

> The Federal Reserve's experiences over the past two decades make it clear that uncertainty is not just a pervasive feature of the monetary policy landscape; it is the defining characteristic of that landscape. The term "uncertainty" is meant here to encompass both "Knightian uncertainty," in which the probability distribution of outcomes is unknown, and "risk," in which uncertainty of outcomes is delimited by a known probability distribution. In practice, one is never quite sure what type of uncertainty one is dealing with in real time, and it may be best to think of a continuum ranging from well-defined risks to the truly unknown.[26]

Keynes did not say that we face stark uncertainty in every decision. Instead, we develop social conventions as a bulwark against uncertainty: "In practice we have tacitly agreed, as a rule, to fall back on what is, in truth a convention. . . . [The] conventional method of calculation will be compatible with a considerable measure of continuity and stability in our affairs, so long as we can rely on the maintenance of the convention."[27] The convention holds—until it collapses: "A conventional valuation which is established as the outcome of the mass psychology of a large number of ignorant individuals is liable to change violently as the result of a sudden fluctuation of opinion due to factors which do not really make much of a difference to the prospective yield."[28]

Consumption, Investment, and the Interest Rate

Keynes assumes that if our income increases, we consume a fairly predictable proportion of the increase and save a fairly predictable portion. Milton Friedman responded with his "permanent-income hypothesis." He assumes that consumers maximize utility subject to the caveat that lifetime consumption must equal lifetime earnings. You can't take it with you, or leave any of it behind. "Like much of good macroeconomics," say Rudiger Dornbusch and Stanley Fischer in their textbook, this hypothesis pays "careful attention to microeconomic foundations."[29] It is supposed to reflect what optimizing individuals do.

Utility maximizers' optimal choice, it turns out, is to consume exactly the same amount each year of their lives. Why? Recall diminishing marginal utility. You gain less utility by consuming an extra amount one year than you lose by giving up that amount another year.[30] The implication is to upend Keynes's assumption about consumption. For example, suppose output begins to fall in a recession. We are assumed to know that the decline will be temporary, since the economy must return to equilibrium. As our income begins to decline, we obey the permanent-income hypothesis and continue consuming the same amount. Nationwide, we consume a larger portion of our income and save a smaller portion. Effective demand remains just what it had been, and—presto!—the recession ends, if it could ever have gotten going in the first place. The permanent-income hypothesis also says that a temporary tax cut, such as the $800 per taxpayer that was part of the Obama stimulus package, has practically no effect on the economy, since we know it's temporary and we spread the windfall out evenly over the rest of our lives.

The only problem is that the permanent-income hypothesis is based on wild assumptions, and its predictions fail. A key assumption is that a decentralized market economy is supposed to be stable, in direct contradiction of general-equilibrium theory based on the Arrow-Debreu model, so we are supposed to know that it will snap back to equilibrium. We are supposed to know what our future earnings will be. Somehow, none of us is supposed to fall into that 9 percent or 16 percent of the workforce, depending on how you count it, that is still unemployed three years after the 2008 financial crisis.[31] We are supposed to know how to calculate the amount we should spend each year so as to maximize our lifetime utility. And if maintaining a constant level of consumption should exhaust our bank accounts for a few quarters or years, we are supposed to be able to borrow freely until the economy picks up, our earnings increase, and we pay the money back. Actually, such access to borrowed funds seems far-fetched even to economists, so when the permanent-income hypothesis isn't borne out in practice, they blame the problem in part on "liquidity constraints."[32]

To be fair, Dornbusch and Fischer, neoclassicals with a Keynesian bent, concede that Friedman's hypothesis is hard to square with the data. For example, in the 1990 edition of their text, they note that Italian households were saving 24.0 percent of their income; Japanese, 16.4 percent; and Americans, 4.3 percent.[33] How could such differences be plausibly consistent with the savings calculations over approximately the same life spans?

Keynes's hypothesis isn't quite right, either. For one thing, he doesn't make clear what time span he was thinking of: the short run over the course of a business cycle, or the long run across a series of business cycles. Over the long run, Americans tend to save 5 to 10 percent of their income. This gross pattern is observed in the data.[34]

The short-run picture during a business cycle is different. As the economy improves, the data show that we Americans may consume a smaller share of our income, as the Friedman hypothesis supposes, but only because we pay a larger share in taxes.[35] The saving share tends to stay about the same. But household investment matters, too. As the economy improves, we Americans invest more of our savings in new houses, strengthening demand. In this stage of the cycle, what I will call the "household saving gap" (our savings over and above our housing investment—in other words, savings that we do not directly use to buy output) is small. Business investment need only fill this small gap to support demand, and it has no trouble doing so. But as the economy worsens, we invest less of our savings in housing—in 2008, housing investment fell 20 percent. Now the household savings gap increases: our savings rise significantly above housing investment, weakening demand. Business investment has to fill this larger gap to sustain demand. But as the economy sours, its investment falls off, too. The economy would head straight downhill if something didn't stop it. That something can be government spending, not only a specific stimulus plan but automatic "stabilizers" such as unemployment insurance.

Thus, Keynes's picture of the propensity to consume was not literally correct, but his essential story works. Indeed, since households' residential investment falls as the economy enters recession, the saving gap that Keynes saw business as needing to fill grows even larger than he thought; the shortfall in aggregate demand is even worse than he thought. Keynes wins the argument about consumer spending and saving.

Turn now to Keynes's assumption versus the neoclassical assumption about investment. In the neoclassical view, entrepreneurs' expectations about the return to investment are based on known facts or confident predictions. The simplest story says the return to investment simply equals that fanciful quantity, J. B. Clark's marginal product of capital. For example, Casey Mulligan of the University of Chicago saw no reason for concern even after financial crisis struck in 2008, because the marginal product of capital was 10 percent, well above the norm.[36] Of course, business would keep investing, he advised readers: "So, if you are not employed by the financial industry (94 percent of you are not), don't worry." Though few neoclassicals would have made such a rash prediction at that moment, they do hold that, as the economy moves to equilibrium, capital earns its marginal product. In every long-run model in David Romer's popular graduate-level text *Advanced Macroeconomics*, capital earns its marginal product.[37] Romer doesn't even hint that there might have been, once upon a time, any doubt about the Clark parable. A more elaborate neoclassical story about the return on investment treats it as analogous to consumers' calculations of lifetime utility. Investors perform probabilistic calculations of the projected marginal product of capital over an infinite sequence of economic periods receding into the future. We don't need to get into details.

Even if you grant the J. B. Clark production function parable, neither investment story works if the future is uncertain in Knight's sense, because neither certainties nor confident probabilities about future returns can be calculated. Keynes does not deny that firms might *like* to invest like smart shoppers, but he says they simply cannot tell with any confidence what return they would get on their investment.

"Only a little more than an expedition to the South Pole, is [an enterprise] based on an exact calculation of benefits to come," Keynes wrote in 1936, when expeditions to the South Pole were rather hit-or-miss. "Thus if the animal spirits are dimmed and the spontaneous optimism falters, leaving us to depend on nothing but a mathematical expectation, enterprise will fade and die;—though fears of loss may have a basis no more reasonable than hopes of profit had before."[38] Indeed, "if human nature felt no temptation to take a chance, no satisfaction (profit apart) in constructing a factory, a railway, a mine or a farm, there might not be much investment merely as a result of cold calculation."[39]

Finally, I'll turn to Keynes's account of the interest rate. He argues that it does *not* adjust to equate the supply of saving to the demand for investment. To begin with, recall what saving is. A decision to save is a decision not to consume: if you don't buy a couch for $1,000, you save $1,000. Then comes a crucial second decision. You can keep your savings in cash in a bank account and receive little or no interest, or you can receive more interest buying a bond or other financial instrument, lending your money out for a fixed term so a business can more readily use it to invest in production. The decision to hold cash or lend it out for a fixed term might have been made by a wealthy individual in Keynes's day. Today it is more often a bank or other financial institution that decides whether to hold cash or to purchase a longer-term bond or other instrument that will, presumably, channel the cash into real business investment. The principle is the same.

Why would individuals or financial institutions hold cash and receive no interest on it? One reason is the simple "transactions" motive: to hold ready cash to pay foreseen bills as they regularly come due. You can calculate reasonably well how much money you need for this purpose, and the greater the total economic output, the greater will be the economy-wide transactions demand for money. In this respect, money is a "convenience which is devoid of significance or real influence," Keynes says.[40]

Keynes discusses two other reasons for holding cash: the "precautionary motive" and the "speculative motive." The speculative motive operates, for example, if you think the prices of stock, bonds, or other financial instruments will fall. Suppose you think stock prices will fall as the economy appears to be heading into recession. You sell your stock portfolio for cash. More than that, you might short stock. That is, you borrow shares of a stock via your broker, sell them for cash, and plan to repurchase them later at a cheaper price and return them at a profit. After shorting stock you are thus holding even more cash. And since essentially the same mechanism operates with respect to bonds or other financial instruments, speculators tend to desire to hold more cash at precisely the wrong time for the economy: when it appears to be souring.

The precautionary motive, as Keynes sees it, operates at a deeper psychological level than the speculative motive, and arises even more essentially from uncertainty about the future. Individuals may keep their savings in cash at a federally insured bank or mutual fund (the government insured them in 2008) because if they unexpectedly need savings in an emergency, they have immediate access to them. If they had put their savings in a bond, they could sell it but might lose money, particularly if the economy is going bad. Financial institutions hold cash in case instruments they hold go sour—perhaps derivatives bundling mortgages together or guarantees insuring those derivatives—and they have to pay off their creditors or put up collateral. Banks were holding a trillion dollars worth of cash in reserves at the Fed in 2010 and earning virtually no interest on it, apparently for just this reason. Inability to put up required collateral drove American International Group (AIG) and other institutions under.

The interest rate is therefore *not* a return to saving, as the usual supply-and-demand story would have it. If individuals and financial institutions hold savings as cash out of precautionary fears or speculative gambles about an uncertain future, they are saving but do not receive interest. Rather, interest is a reward for "not-hoarding," as Keynes put it.[41] Interest is the reward for relinquishing access to savings for a specified period and lending them out in a form that can be channeled into real business investment.[42] Only an increase in the amount of money lent out for fixed periods can lower the interest rate. People are most likely to hoard rather than lend money, and thus are more likely to keep the interest rate high, just when the economy is going badly and a low interest rate is most needed to promote investment. There is no market interest rate that balances the supply of saving and the demand for investment.

Keynes eloquently explained the hoarding instinct in a reply to some of his critics:

> Partly on reasonable and partly on instinctive grounds, our desire to hold Money as a store of wealth is a barometer of the degree of our distrust of our own calculations and conventions concerning the future. Even tho this feeling about Money is itself conventional or instinctive, it operates, so to speak, at a deeper level of our motivation. It takes charge at the moments when the higher, more precarious con-

ventions have weakened. The possession of actual money lulls our disquietude; and the premium which we require to make us part with money is the measure of the degree of our disquietude.[43]

After leaving the Fed, Alan Greenspan discussed the moments of disquietude he had observed on his watch. He noted that crises such as the October 1987 market crash, the panic caused by Russia's debt default in the fall of 1998, and the terrorist attacks of September 11, 2001, precipitate "efforts of market participants to convert illiquid assets into cash."[44] People try to convert stocks, bonds, futures, or any other financial instruments that mature over a period of time, into hard dollars. "When confronted with uncertainty, especially Knightian uncertainty, human beings invariably attempt to disengage from medium to long-term commitments in favor of safety and liquidity." Having learned Keynes's lesson about the precautionary motive, Greenspan had the Fed buy bonds at those moments, flooding the economy with cash precisely so the gut-level instincts to hoard it would *not* drive interest rates up.

Those were minor episodes compared with the financial crisis that erupted after Lehman Brothers folded in October 2008, and money markets froze around the world. They froze because money market funds and other institutions were so seized with disquietude that they refused to lend, even to the most credit-worthy firms with triple-A ratings, at any interest rate. The Fed bailed out banks, guaranteed loans between banks, guaranteed the savings households deposited in mutual funds, and itself lent money by buying bonds—a few trillion dollars' worth over the course of the crisis. Despite the Fed's efforts, the mercury in banks' thermometer of disquietude—the reserves of cash they held at the Federal Reserve over and above the legally required minimum—surged from $2 billion dollars in August 2008 to $1 trillion in June 2010.[45]

All three faces of uncertainty can thus bring a disquieted economy down: the propensity of anxious households to save rather than to buy goods; the financial system's flight to safety as it hoards cash; and firms' reluctance to invest for fear of the future. The Great Recession began in the last quarter of 2007, and GDP stopped falling after the second quarter of 2009. During this time—contrary to Friedman's permanent-income hypothesis and quite in accord with Keynes—on an annual basis, in real 2005 dollars, consumption fell by $175 billion, as personal saving soared and eroded demand.[46] Housing investment had the same effect, falling $180 billion (and far more than twice that from its peak in 2005). Could business channel all this saving into investment? On the contrary, investment in fixed plant and equipment fell $300 billion, and inventory investment fell another $170 billion. The only improvement was a $230 billion amelioration of the trade deficit, as exports increased. The combined private-sector hit to aggregate demand was about $600 billion dollars per year. Spending by state and local governments barely budged—they are prohibited from running deficits. The federal government was the only domestic actor working to ameliorate the downward trajectory.

Money

Keynes's model revolves around money. Why should we hoard money or, in an earlier day, gold—and not another commodity? At some level, Keynes saw our instinct to hoard gold or money as mythologically printed on our psyches. But we could be taught subconsciously to hoard a commodity such as gold or money only if it has two characteristics. First, it must be durable and nearly costless to store: corn wouldn't serve, because it is expensive to store and it rots. Second, the commodity must not be easily produced. Compared with the size of the economy, gold reserves yield the barest trickle, and money cannot be legally created at all except by central banks.

These characteristics define what can serve as money. For example, suppose we bought and sold goods by exchanging a commodity that could be readily manufactured—say, wampum beads. Wampum beads would have a great advantage. There would never be a long depression, because idle firms and workers could turn to manufacturing them; and since wampum beads served as currency, people could buy whatever they needed. The depression would soon end. But wampum beads would also have a great disadvantage. As firms set about producing them, they would create inflation. The reason producible wampum beads would *not* fill the role of money or gold is that they *could* be manufactured. Money is essential to a modern economy. But the very characteristics that make it money also cause depressions, close down factories, and throw workers out of jobs.

ELEVEN

In the Long Run

Never imagining that a single Mexican citizen had quite forgiven the United States for grabbing half that nation's land in 1848, I was taken aback by a conversation with a Mexico City taxi driver in 2009. On a radio talk show blaring in the background, a woman was explaining how she had suffered from cosmetic surgery gone bad. The doctor had not been legally licensed to do the operation. She had gone to another doctor to have the problems fixed, but he had only made them worse. The second doctor wasn't properly licensed either. On and on the gruesome story of medical consequences went, until I asked the driver if we couldn't change the station: "Such horrible things upset me."

"You *norteamericanos*—you North Americans!" he exploded. "You just don't get what a disaster it is here. Up there things work, doctors don't ruin patients' lives, people can get somewhere. Here nothing works, everybody's lazy, we get nowhere. When the United States invaded Mexico, I wish it had just taken over the whole country!"

I burst into laughter. I said it's not true that Mexicans are lazy. Mexico City traffic starts barreling down thoroughfares at six in the morning. University classes begin at seven; if you held a class that early in the

United States, not a single student would show up. And some things do work in Mexico. The Mexico City Metro is faster, quieter, and more efficient than the Boston subway. In Boston, some garbled voice habitually chimes in over the speakers to explain (if you could hear it, but you know what it says from experience) that the train is delayed because of a disabled car. Obviously, the car wasn't properly maintained. Cars don't get disabled regularly in the Mexico City Metro. In two years riding that metro, I recall one unscheduled delay: a voice over the speakers explained that we had to pause because of a *temblor*, a minor earthquake.

And yet there was something to what the taxi driver said. In the 1950s and 1960s, Mexico had been the South Korea of the day, growing more than 6 percent a year. You tossed a seed, and a tree sprouted, one economist told me. Millions of Mexicans whose fathers had been laboring on estates as peons (a Spanish word) came to till their own fields. Workers in cities found jobs in burgeoning industries. In the first decade of the 2000s, the economy did badly. Growth averaged a dismal 2 percent a year. Seas of vendors hawking T-shirts, boom boxes, and such items proliferated ever further on the sidewalks. They belonged to the so-called informal economy, comprising something like half the labor force, workers who did not pay taxes or receive social security.

What had gone wrong? Harvard Business School students struggled with that question in some essays I read. They recited woes culled from a case study they were assigned.[1] Monopolistic sectors—telecommunications, electricity, oil, cement, even beer—were strangling growth. Well, maybe monopolistic breweries, which after all exported to 100 countries around the world, did not threaten the economy. Mexican cement makers had factories in the United States and Europe, and oil was sold at world prices. State-owned utilities charged 10 to 12 U.S. cents per kilowatt-hour, compared with 8 cents in the United States, but that disadvantage did not seem inordinate.[2] The telecommunications tycoon Carlos Slim, who in 2008 was declared the world's richest man by *Forbes*, controlled 96 percent of the fixed-line market, 76 percent of the mobile market, and 68 percent of broadband.[3] A typical basket of business calls cost twice as much as in the United States, but only 10 percent more than in Britain.[4] Cell-phone calls cost slightly less in Mexico.[5] Broadband coverage was available to only 9 out of 100 Mexicans, compared with 26 out of 100 Americans, and the service was slower, but costs were comparable.[6] In the end, it was not clear how much damage Slim really was doing.

The students noted that Mexican labor laws were "rigid." When a formal-sector business dismissed workers, it had to pay at least three months' severance.[7] The state-owned oil-company and electric-utility unions were militant and corrupt. However, outside of those unions and the irresponsible teachers' union, Mexican organized labor was not strong, and the huge informal-sector workforce wasn't unionized at all. The president of the Mexican Business Council said, "Mexican workers have world-class flexibility and are very productive if you create the right environment."[8]

Mexico was famously waging a war against drug cartels. But the homicide rate was the same as the U.S. average in Mexico City—about 6 per 100,000 inhabitants—lower than the U.S. average in most Mexican states, and higher in only six states, mainly along the northern border. And despite the crime, some of those border states continued to receive among the highest levels of foreign investment in the nation.[9]

The specific problems you could count off did not seem overwhelming, yet Mexico had not done well. Chile, considered a Latin American success story, grew 4 percent on average in the first decade of the 2000s— twice as fast as Mexico.[10] That was the difference between progress and stagnation. Chilean investment had increased 10 percent per year; Mexican investment, only 4 percent. Labor productivity (output per worker-hour) had not done spectacularly in either country, but at least Chile had improved at a decent 1.6 percent growth rate, Mexico at a mere 0.4 percent.

After reciting all the depressing data, many students concluded in their essays that Mexico had lost its "competitiveness," a buzzword popularized by the World Economic Forum's annual *Global Competitiveness Report.* But even here, Chile's score of 4.70 versus Mexico's of 4.19, on a scale of 1 to 7, involving dozens of subjective judgments, hardly seemed the stuff of success versus failure.[11] If Mexico had somehow lost "competitiveness" in the 2000s, what precisely did competitiveness consist of?

Two approaches to modeling long-run growth at least provide a framework for thinking about it. These models attempt to describe long-run growth, over perhaps a decade or more, but at least over a full business cycle. They do not purport to say anything about short-run fluctuations during the course of a business cycle.

The canonical neoclassical growth model, published in 1956 by Robert Solow of MIT and independently developed by the Australian economist Trevor Swan, assumes that three factors, and only three factors, can drive growth: labor, thrift, and ingenuity. Labor—the size of the workforce—doesn't really get an economy anywhere. It just means that more output is divided among more people.

The old-fashioned virtue of thrift—national saving—can raise per-capita growth in the model. Saving is assumed to depend on individual preferences: how much individuals desire to store up for the future rather than consume today. All saving is then assumed to be transformed directly into real investment. In other words, Say's law operates in the long run. The resulting investment causes output per worker to grow.

That other old-fashioned virtue of ingenuity, or rather the resulting technological innovation, is assumed to be the other possible cause of per-capita growth. It is usually called "total-factor productivity" or "multi-factor productivity." "New-growth theories," developed since the 1980s, try to break down this somewhat nebulous concept by modeling, alongside technological innovation, other factors that might be more directly gauged: educational attainment of the workforce; "social capital," such as consistent enforcement of property rights; and even the avoidance of "rent seeking"—that is, corruption, lobbying, and other unproductive activity.

Colleagues of Keynes developed alternative growth models. Actually, the frequent claim that Keynes cared only about the short run, citing his infamous quote that "in the long run we are all dead," is a gross misinterpretation. He wrote that line years before *The General Theory*, while he was still a neoclassical economist and saw the economy as gravitating toward an optimal equilibrium but too often getting stuck along the way. In his *General Theory* he dropped this notion of equilibrium, concluding that the economy can indefinitely settle into a bad situation. In an uncertain world, only animal spirits supporting investment can rescue long-run economic prospects.

A growth model developed by Nicholas Kaldor, of Cambridge University and the London School of Economics, emphasizes investment as the driving force.[12] Economic institutions or social custom, outside of markets, might support a predictable environment and entrepreneurial optimism to sustain animal spirits—or they might not. The strength or weakness of animal spirits governs the amount of investment. Investment is the economic engine, determining how fast the economy grows. And as output rises, saving rises, hauled along like the caboose. Thus, investment determines saving. Keynesian growth models, unlike neoclassical models, deny Say's law.

How might something as intangible as social custom sustain animal spirits and investment? Consider why Japan invested vastly more and grew much faster than Britain for several decades after World War II. When Japanese firms lost sales, the sociologist Ronald Dore argues, moral norms held them responsible for still employing workers and retaining suppliers.[13] Smaller suppliers and more marginal workers might be squeezed, but not dispensed with except for uncorrected productive failures. Japanese firms therefore urgently sought new avenues of investment. By comparison, when British firms lost sales, their responsibility was to maintain short-term profits for stockholders. To that end, they laid off workers, dropped suppliers, and cut investment. Deeply held beliefs seem to have contributed importantly to the sharp divergences in investment and growth.

Kaldor cared just as much about productivity growth as Solow, but, again, saw cause and effect the opposite way around. His model assumes that healthy investment causes rapid productivity growth. Investment is supposed to support the incorporation of technological advances already available and the development of new technologies. Investment thus promotes productivity growth as well as saving. It is a brave claim.

Is Macroeconomics Possible?

Before comparing long-run growth models, I don't see any way around an initial question: Is macroeconomics possible? There are serious doubts.

In recent decades, neoclassical macroeconomists have been proclaiming success at basing their "general-equilibrium" models on "microfoundations." That is, they claim to base their models on assumptions about the rational individuals and profit-maximizing firms that populate the Arrow-Debreu world. But before you blink, they homogenize all that diversity into one "representative agent," thus assuming away the whole point of markets. Why trade if we are all alike? They give this agent cardinal utility, measured on a ruler-like scale. Never mind that neoclassical theorists rejected any such notion a century ago or that every decent micro text declares it illicit. Blithely ignoring "insurmountable aggregation problems," as Felipe and Fisher summarize the literature actually investigating the matter, macroeconomists willy-nilly homogenize all distinct consumer and capital goods into one uniform type of stuff.[14] They amalgamate diverse firms into one megafirm converting homogenized labor and capital into homogenized output, via J. B. Clark's parable of the aggregate production function—"a tool whose lack of legitimacy was demonstrated decades ago," Felipe and Fisher note.[15]

Some of these moves may be more defensible in practice than in theory (even if it's a strange defense for an economist) and some of the worst moves apply to models of "short-run" business cycles rather than models of "long-run" growth. What boggles the mind is how blithely macroeconomists make these moves. Felipe and Fisher believe that most macroeconomists don't even realize that theorists have declared the J. B. Clark production function illegitimate.[16] Indeed, in his graduate-level macro text, Romer doesn't so much as mention these aggregation questions, let alone try to address them.

Is there a sounder foundation for macroeconomics? Recall that Piero Sraffa developed a formal classical model. If wages of different workers can be aggregated as multiples of one standard wage—if it can be determined how many standard wages the economist Joan Robinson, Queen Elizabeth II, and Britney Spears is each paid—then Sraffa provides a consistent theory of the prices of diverse consumer and capital goods. Gauged in terms of a basket of goods that he calls a "standard commodity," these relative prices even remain invariant when the profit rate and wage change. Once you have such invariant prices, you *can* theoretically aggregate consumer or capital goods.

There remains the little matter of determining the relative wages of Joan Robinson, Queen Elizabeth II, and Britney Spears. (Do they actually pay Elizabeth for being queen?) You might make progress on this front by supplementing Sraffa's model with consumer preferences—they could be incorporated—hence market demands for commodities.[17] Perhaps commodity demands could then translate back into demands for specific workers who produce them, hence wages. Perhaps. But let's stop playing games. Sraffa's model really depends on the idea that relative wages are socially determined, not set in auctions like commodity prices on the Chicago Board of Trade. This may be a plausible idea. In the textbook I so regularly criticize, Samuelson says that "100 percent of all labor" is priced in administered markets: "Most firms administer their wages and salaries, setting fixed pay scales and hiring people at an entry-level wage or salary. These wage scales are generally fixed for a year or so, and when they are adjusted, the pay for almost all categories goes up by the same percentage."[18] Samuelson sees such procedures as a source of "sticky" wages that refuse to fall, causing unemployment. But if nonmarket administrative procedures do determine wages, Sraffa's model may provide a theoretical basis for aggregating. It will work with Ricardo's classical model and Keynes's *General Theory* model, but it will not work with J. B. Clark's neoclassical parable.[19]

Doubts remain. An interviewer suggested to Kenneth Arrow that it's impossible to base a macroeconomic model on microfoundations. "True and unfortunate," Arrow agreed.[20] Even if you can aggregate wages and commodities, how do you aggregate people's diverse ideas about how economies work and their expectations about the future? As Keynes emphasized, our economic actions depend on these ideas and expectations. Neoclassical macroeconomics decrees such problems out of existence. The Oracle at Delphi proclaims that the economy is moving toward an ordained equilibrium, and the representative agent recognizes the oracle's truth.[21]

Classical economics is more sophisticated. At least it acknowledges some diversity but assumes that economic thoughts and actions depend on class: capitalists, landlords, or workers. If, as classical theory also assumes, society somehow determines the real wage—setting a living standard that, custom decrees, it is indecent for creditable workers to fall below—then equilibrium prices are thereby fixed. Neoclassical instability problems, arising from trying to make markets do everything, are overcome.

Keynes also divides society into classes, though of a conceptually different kind. He envisions entrepreneurs whose collective optimism or pessimism drives investment; speculators whose fickle opinions about the future can wreak havoc; and workers who mostly spend their salaries but save some portion. He therefore sees class actions partly in terms of people's mentalities. For the most part, Keynes holds, people don't actually think much, in part because the future is so uncertain anyway, but rather follow convention. The famous quants (quantitative analysts) who advise hedge funds how to invest are not thinking about the future, but trying to identify conventional views about the future. If you bet on the side of convention, you profit, at least for a time. Nor is convention a bad thing, Keynes adds, because it provides some stability—until it changes.

In effect, Keynes and Ricardo deny that macroeconomic models can be built on micro-level assumptions about individuals. They make macro-level assumptions about people's beliefs and habits. Ricardo assumes that the three classes, capitalists, landlords, and workers, behave in typical ways. Keynes assumes that conventions—entrepreneurs' animal spirits; speculators' instinct to hoard; workers' proclivity to save a bit out of wages—dictate how these groups act, at least until conventions change.

Positing macro-level assumptions seems legitimate, so long as you admit what you're doing. Sciences with a better claim to the name than economics make macro-level assumptions. Ecology posits macro-level models seeking to capture patterns without accounting for every individual plant and animal. Weather cannot be forecast based on observations at the micro level, because it is chaotic. In principle, the famous flap of a butterfly's wings in Brazil can cause a hurricane in the North Atlantic; the most minute failure to measure some initial condition leads to drastic forecasting errors. Yet for centuries, crude models have been used with some success to predict weather patterns in the short term. When the barometric pressure is low near the surface of the Earth, the air is less dense—it weighs less per cubic inch—and tends to rise. As it cools in the upper atmosphere, water vapor condenses out, forming clouds. If the mercury falls sufficiently low—and if this mechanism operates forcefully enough—as mariners have known for centuries, a storm is likely to develop. This macro model ignores micro-level complexity, yet retains some validity. Forecasters continue to draw weather maps incorporating macro-level models not so unlike this one, if more sophisticated.

How might economists use macro-level assumptions to construct models? Government data breaking the domestic product down into consumption, investment, government spending, exports, and imports are not meaningless, as Felipe and Fisher agree.[22] Nor are the data meaningless that break domestic income down into employees' wages and benefits, corporate profits, interest paid to lenders, and other streams. And the dollar value of the domestic product equals the dollar value of domestic income (give or take a statistical discrepancy). What on one side is the sale price of a product becomes, on the other side, income collected by some party.

These numbers convey important information about an economy, but you cannot find cause-and-effect relationships in the data. The national accounts require that investment must equal saving, but they do *not* prove whether saving determines investment, investment determines saving, or the connection between them is more involved.

Causal relationships can be posited by imposing assumptions on the skeleton of the national accounts and other data such as the financial "flow of funds." Imposing such assumptions on data constitutes a model.[23] We make assumptions anyway in voicing practical opinions—a higher profit rate increases or reduces growth; a fiscal stimulus does or doesn't ameliorate a recession—so we might as well make them explicitly. It is possible to weigh such assumptions based on arguments about whether they are realistic enough, and whether the resulting model is at least not egregiously contradicted by experience. Model-building seems less unattractive than shouting back and forth opposing notions about what we insist "common sense" dictates.

A Pragmatic Solow Model

Michael Mandel of *BusinessWeek* sees the Solow model as providing one of the most important insights in economics. Think about Malthus, who argued that people would never stop breeding, so we would run out of land and mass starvation would ensue. More broadly, the Malthusian argument applies to all limited resources, says Mandel:

> And he's right if there isn't multi-factor productivity growth. If you don't have new technologies, you don't have any spare resources. Whatever problem you run into first knocks you down. When the flow of technology slows down, as it did in the 1970s, people say, we're doomed. And you know what? They're right. We have two problems now: healthcare and energy. If we don't have new technologies—that magic factor—then we have global immiseration ten or twenty years down the road. That magic factor, multi-factor productivity growth, is just an extra 1 percent. It doesn't sound like a lot, but it's an enormous amount. With this extra 1 percent, all of your economic models get you to the same place, which is things are good. Without it, they all get you to the same place, which is things are bad.[24]

Solow's model can be stripped down to a pragmatic version that does not assume Say's law and just provides a "growth accounting" framework—a way to break growth down into three components: growth of the workforce, investment, and the magic factor. (Actually, in his seminal 1956 article setting out the model, though Solow assumes Say's law, he acknowledges that it might not be valid.)[25] Let's start by imposing a minimum of assumptions on national data to get this pragmatic Solow model; neoclassical twists can be added later. The pragmatic version is not novel. Herbert Simon, one of the rare skeptics about neoclassical theory to win the Nobel Prize in economics, pointed to it in his Nobel lecture in 1978.[26]

This pragmatic model starts with simple accounting: economic output equals labor costs plus capital costs. Now break these costs down further: labor costs equal the average wage times the total number of workers. Capital costs equal the profit rate—earnings on a dollar's worth of capital—times the total value of capital. With apologies to William Strunk, Jr., who enjoined writers to omit needless words, I repeat: total output equals the wage times the total number of workers plus the profit rate times the total value of capital. These numbers are readily derived from standard government data.

The model translates this breakdown of *output* into a breakdown of *growth*.[27] To do so, first, it must assume that the profit share of total output and the wage share remain roughly constant. Concretely, in the United States, profits have typically accounted for about one-quarter of total output, and wages for about three-quarters of total output.[28] Second, the model must assume that capital and labor each grow at a roughly steady rate. Concretely, over long time spans, the U.S. capital stock has grown about 3 percent a year, and the labor force about 1 percent a year. The model assumes it is possible to assign some such numbers to an economy.

Using these particular estimates for the United States for the sake of concreteness, how much do growth of the capital stock and growth of the workforce contribute to overall economic growth? Since the capital stock grows 3 percent a year and profits on capital are a quarter of total output, capital accumulation contributes 3 percent times one-quarter, or 0.75 percent, to annual growth. Since the workforce grows 1 percent a year, and wages are three-quarters of total output, increase in the amount of labor contributes 1 percent times three-quarters, or another 0.75 percent, to annual growth. Together, these two factors therefore contribute 1.5 percent to growth. But growth has averaged around 3 percent per year. So something else—the magic factor, total-factor productivity, call it what you will—has to contribute around 1.5 percent per year to growth, or half of the total. Whether it's 1 percent or 1.5 percent, as Mandel says, it's huge. Absent the magic factor, an economy is in trouble.

Neoclassical Growth Theory

The neoclassical version of the Solow model adds several assumptions. As mentioned, two factors are assumed to determine long-run per-capita growth: national saving, which on the assumption of Say's law translates directly into investment, and total-factor productivity. For poor nations, the model emphasizes the importance of saving. Since they have a small capital stock per capita, a high saving rate substantially increases investment and growth. For rich nations, the model emphasizes the importance of total-factor productivity. These nations already have a large capital stock per capita. The model assumes the neoclassical production function, so adding to a large capital stock yields less and less incremental output. Total-factor productivity becomes the principal economic engine. If this magic factor enters the model as an "exogenous variable"— an independent actor stepping into the drama from outside—growth increases. If the magic fails and it doesn't enter, growth founders.

This story raises doubts. Total-factor productivity is simply any portion of national growth that cannot be measured. Literally, it is calculated by netting out the effects of labor and capital and calling what's left total-factor productivity. It is also commonly called the "Solow residual": the portion of growth that cannot be explained by quantifiable factors. Or, as the Stanford economist Moses Abramovitz famously said, total-factor productivity is a "measure of our ignorance."[29]

Productivity growth does tend to parallel economic growth, but economic growth often seems to be the horse, and productivity growth the cart. For a rough look at why it might be so, turn to the more usual measure of productivity—namely, labor productivity, or output produced per worker-hour—since it's simpler to measure, and the data are more widely available. Moreover, in the Solow model for an advanced economy, where the effects of capital accumulation are supposed to be small, the two measures of productivity growth closely parallel each other.

When the United States entered the Great Depression and economic output shrank in the years 1929 to 1933, productivity declined disastrously, at 2.2 percent a year. As World War II approached and the economy boomed in the years 1939 to 1945, productivity grew stupendously, at 3.7 percent a year.[30] It seems unlikely that technology spontaneously failed after 1929 or suddenly surged after 1939. In fact, the economic historian Alexander J. Field argues that the 1930s saw more rapid technological advance than any other decade of the twentieth century—for example, with the invention of television and the development of the DC-3, the first viable commercial airliner.[31] But because the economy was doing so badly, few of those products were produced or sold, so the advances were not evident in productivity data. Rapid growth put that technology to work; for example, some ten thousand DC-3's were built for military transport during World War II, and after the war, purchases of televisions soared. It took growth to incorporate technological advance on a wide enough scale to be counted in productivity data.

The notion that faster economic growth causes faster productivity growth—in other words, the direct opposite of the neoclassical Solow model's assumption—is called Verdoorn's "law," after the Dutch economist Petrus Johannes Verdoorn. It isn't a law (I wish economists would stop calling things laws), but despite neoclassical economists' protestations to the contrary, there is good evidence that Verdoorn often does a good job of describing events.

Consider the "New Economy" of the late 1990s, when, after decades of medium-lousy performance, the United States suddenly seemed to do spectacularly. In accordance with the Solow model, economists' diagnoses centered on productivity growth. Even the notoriously opaque Alan Greenspan got the point across. "Huge investments in technology are yielding substantial gains in productivity," as one reporter summarized his congressional testimony in June 1999. The result was "a fundamental and far-reaching improvement in the way the economy functions."[32]

President Bill Clinton's Council of Economic Advisors argued: "The unexpected surge in productivity growth has led to several positive developments: it has restrained inflation, allowing the unemployment rate to fall lower than it otherwise might; it has increased economic growth, with positive effects on the Federal budget balance; and it has boosted stock market valuations."[33] The council even thought productivity growth might support the good times almost indefinitely. "An expansion is only as old as it feels, and this one still feels young," the council opined in January 2000.[34] It hadn't noticed the dot-com bubble, which brought the expansion down a year later.[35]

The economist Ray Fair of Yale disagrees, concluding that virtually the only unusual aspect of the late 1990s was the dot-com bubble.[36] Using a macroeconomic model he has developed and tested over decades, and that I find very plausible, he simulates an alternative scenario. What if the stock market had followed its historical pattern instead of soaring in a bubble? He concludes that the economy would have continued much as it had since the 1980s. The stock boom alone explains a significant increase in consumption (as households' portfolios rose in value), a boost to investment (driven by healthy consumer demand and lower costs of raising equity capital), higher growth, lower unemployment, and, incidentally, the surge of imported goods that occurred.

What about the productivity surge? There wasn't much to it, Fair notes. Productivity seemed to surge if you leave out the recession of the early 1990s and count only the New Economy from 1995 to 2000. But productivity growth fluctuates a lot over the course of business cycles, so accepted practice is to gauge it from cyclical peak to peak. (Thus, the famous 1970s slowdown is usually dated from 1973 because that year marked the peak of the final business cycle that had begun in the 1960s.) Fair points out that the difference between productivity growth in the 1980s and productivity growth in the 1990s—counting full peak-to-peak business cycles—was modest, merely rising from 1.5 percent annually to 1.8 percent annually.[37] Although Fair doesn't make this argument, as the stock market bubble raised growth and investment, it could well have driven that modest improvement in productivity growth. Why did informed economists, who well know that productivity should be gauged from peak to peak, get so excited about the upswing after 1995? In their relief to see something going well, they must have just reached for their favorite long-run growth theory: the Solow model.

Adding Epicycles

Neoclassical economists noticed that the Solow model can predict crazy things. Some of the trouble comes from assuming a production function with diminishing returns, so that the more capital a nation has per capita, the less any additional increment of capital yields. Suppose the United States has something like ten times greater GDP per capita than a middle-income country such as Mexico. (This rough order of magnitude serves to illustrate the point.) If profits are about a third of total output (also a rough number), and both countries have access to the same technology—after all, multinationals operate globally—then the Solow model says the United States must have something like a *thousand* times more capital per person.[38] This conclusion is clearly preposterous. Also, if saving is automatically transformed into investment, as the model assumes, then saving or investment—they come to the same thing—have an unbelievably small effect. An enormous 10 percent increase in the U.S. saving rate boosts growth by only 0.15 percentage points over the first seventeen years—and then dwindles off even further.[39]

To try to do better, the new growth theories add epicycles. One approach is to reconstrue the Solow residual. It is treated as disembodied knowledge, which can be assumed to grow faster the more knowledge a nation has (knowledge breeds knowledge), or slower the more knowledge a nation has (knowledge has diminishing returns), or at the same rate no matter what. Disembodied knowledge can be assumed to grow faster if the population is larger (more people make more inventions), or not, as you wish. It can be assumed to grow faster if the capital stock is larger (something like Kaldor's assumption that investment embodies technology), or not, as you wish. These models still keep running into trouble. If a middle-income country has a tenth the per-capita income of the United States because it lacks access to the same knowledge, the model says it has to be a hundred years behind.[40] Another nonstarter.

Next, the new growth theories search for characteristics that block poor countries from absorbing technology. One could be inadequate education. Economists plug education into a neoclassical production function with diminishing returns. Why would education have anything to do with such a production function? Anyway, if you do plug education into such a model, of course, it turns out to have diminishing returns and produces little effect, just like saving.[41] Even in the new growth theories, educational differences might explain only a quarter of the income gap between the very richest and very poorest countries—that would be the United States versus Haiti, not versus Mexico—while differences in the amounts of capital might explain a sixth.[42]

To fill in the biggest gap, the new growth theories turn to "rent seeking"—lobbying, corruption, or other ways to capture what others produce. Rent seeking can be a problem, but it can also be the last resort of desperate economists. Wading deeper into metaphor, they discover lack of "social capital." Under this rubric, they propose problems such as weak enforcement of property rights, distaste for entrepreneurship, unfortunate colonial legacies, excessive litigation (but don't lawyers protect property rights?), and even (I hope not too seriously) too much philosophical speculation.[43] They have too many models and too many stories, and don't explain enough.

Keynesian Growth Theory

Kaldor's model provides a useful framework for understanding the growth experiences of at least some nations. It sees investment as driving growth and saving—Keynes's conclusion about the most plausible direction of causation—and, at the same time, as embodying technological advance. In other words, total-factor productivity is not a distinct essence that mysteriously enters to infuse efficiency into capital and labor, but rather a way of gauging improvements embodied in more advanced capital equipment, greater skills on the part of workers, and who knows what else.

Certainly, the Kaldor view has its limitations. Investment does not always produce technological advance. One such situation occurred when, as mentioned earlier, General Motors wasted $40 billion on robots that cost more and did a poorer job than autoworkers. Nevertheless, in a capitalist economy where competition tends to drive innovation—and particularly in any economy not at the cutting edge, where technologies known to be more efficient can be harnessed essentially by investing in them—investment itself often does seem to drive efficiency improvements.

To see the same point from a different perspective, think back to the conceptual scheme of the neoclassical Solow model. It is set up to account for the contribution of capital by assuming that the kind of capital being used never changes. Thus, if the world had started circa 1950, the model assumes that, in 2010, airlines still flew 21-seater DC-3s, room-sized computers ran on vacuum tubes, and doctors put polio victims in iron lungs. The model depicts combining total-factor productivity with that same old capital to yield greater output. Since, obviously, by 2010 laptops had vastly outstripped the fastest 1950 computer, jets had replaced DC-3 prop planes, and polio vaccines had obviated the need for iron lungs, the capital had changed radically. That capital itself—that investment itself—embodied much of the Solow residual. Improved managerial methods, workers' skills, and other elusive factors embodied the rest. The Solow residual simply *tabulates* separately the huge amount these advances contributed. As a rough tabulation of their importance, the pragmatic Solow model sheds important light. As a dramatic account of how productivity plays the *deus ex machina,* either descending to make an economy grow or getting lost backstage and leaving the economy in peril, the model makes little sense.

Growth Stories

The governments of virtually all currently wealthy nations had something like Kaldor's model in mind as they developed. Concretely, they all harnessed industrial policies—policies intended to simultaneously promote investment and technological advance—as Ha-Joon Chang of Cambridge University documents in a broad-based study.[44]

The development stories of the Asian tigers such as South Korea are now well known. As they rose from impoverished to developed nations, they wielded policies including protectionism, subsidies, state ownership of firms, and state allocation of credit. In the 2000s, China's statist model captured attention. As the prime minister, Wen Jiabao, said, "The socialist system's advantages enable us to make decisions efficiently, organize effectively, and concentrate resources to accomplish large undertakings."[45] While private firms compete in export assembly plants and consumer goods, the state dominates strategic sectors such as finance, transportation, telecommunications, and energy. And China is said to have long manipulated its currency to promote exports. It may run into problems as other nations have, but it has made extraordinary progress.

As Chang argues, Britain and the United States, the great advocates of neoclassically inspired market policies today, themselves ardently deployed industrial policies. The Washington Consensus might be Washington's prescription for developing nations, but it was not Washington's prescription for the United States. As mentioned, what Adam Smith attacked as mercantilism included, along with large doses of injustice and waste, industrial policies that made Britain the global economic leader. Its former American colonies took notice. The first industrial policy theorist was not, as often said, the German historical economist Friedrich List, but U.S. Treasury secretary Alexander Hamilton. In fact, List picked up his ideas largely from Hamilton's *Report on Manufactures.*[46] The famous Asian model is actually the U.S. or British model.

The American use of industrial policies, remarkably like the so-called Asian model, is so often forgotten that a whistle-stop historical tour seems useful. Given authority to regulate foreign commerce, the U.S. Congress raised tariffs in 1792 to a modest 12.5 percent. Southern plantation owners were opposed, as tariffs forced them to pay more for manufactured goods. Congress doubled tariffs to raise revenue during the War of 1812 and, noticing the salutary effect on manufacturing, raised them to 35 percent in 1816.[47] Disputes over tariffs, and in some broad sense over economic destiny, may have played a role in causing the Civil War. Chang argues that abolition of slavery was only a theoretical possibly when Abraham Lincoln was elected; he had never explicitly supported it. But he had long favored industrial protection and wooed several Northern states during his campaign by promising to strengthen it.[48] The certainty that he would raise tariffs after taking office may have encouraged Southern states to secede. Between the Civil War and World War II, the United States maintained industrial tariffs in the range of 40 to 50 percent.[49] Already the global economic power by 1930, America set a terrible example with the infamous Smoot-Hawley tariff, triggering a cascade of protectionism, but this tariff merely adjusted the level from the lower end to the higher end of the post–Civil War range.[50] Only after World War II did the United States seriously liberalize trade.

As elsewhere, protectionism was far from the only U.S. industrial policy. In a long-running effort, the armories at Watertown, Massachusetts, and Harper's Ferry, West Virginia, forced recalcitrant machinists to adopt the "American system" of interchangeable parts.[51] Its benefits spread far beyond the military. In the late nineteenth century, the U.S. government gave railroads a land area larger than the state of Texas, or thirty-five times larger than Massachusetts.[52] The government thereby bought not only an efficient transport infrastructure but also an industrial engine that provided a market for steel, steam engines, glass, and other manufactured goods.

The United States hardly relinquished industrial policy after World War II. AT&T's Bell Labs, effectively a public research institute financed by profits from the highly regulated telephone monopoly, invented the transistor. The U.S. Army funded the transistor's decade-long transition into commercial reality. The U.S. Air Force provided the initial market for integrated circuits in its Minuteman missile, followed by the National Aeronautics and Space Administration (NASA) for the Apollo Moon shot. And the Defense Advanced Research Projects Agency (DARPA) paid for development of the Internet, in good part at MIT. Private-sector ingenuity was critical to innovation behind all these technologies, but so was government support.[53]

Aircraft manufacturing provides another example of the crucial role U.S. industrial policy has played.[54] The U.S. Postal Service subsidized air transport, but demanded planes large enough to carry passengers commercially; it was uninterested in the *Night Flight* adventures celebrated by Antoine de Saint-Exupéry. Under the authority of the 1930 McNary-Watres Act, postmaster general Harold Brown forced a consolidation of private air carriers, forging an oligopoly that could support development of a transcontinental transport. The result was the DC-3. A pressurized cabin, retractable landing gear, and other innovations made it the first effective commercial aircraft.

As the same aircraft manufacturers supplied military and civilian markets, advances paid for by the armed forces were commercialized, but the Civil Aeronautics Board (CAB) also played a key role. Each time Boeing developed a new jet transport, it was betting the company. It could expect negative cash flow for six years and the break-even point, if it occurred, only a dozen years later. Boeing could not make such all-or-nothing bets without a commitment from airlines to front 20 to 30 percent of launch costs. The airlines, in turn, sought assurance that they could recoup their expenses. Before deregulation, the CAB provided that assurance, setting fares high enough to cover those expenses. The CAB thereby not only rewarded airlines that ordered new planes, but punished those that did not. The laggards, forced to charge the same fares for poorer service, lost market share. Pan American and some other airlines maintained large engineering staffs, who worked with aircraft and engine manufacturers to develop new technology. Barely more than two decades after the 28-passenger DC-3 was launched, Pan Am inaugurated the first workhorse of the jet age, the Boeing 707, flying from New York to Paris. In another decade, the 550-passenger Boeing 747 entered service.

The Washington Consensus proscription against industrial policy—since neoclassical theory sees no serious possibility for state promotion of investment and technological advance—has often not worked well. Jaime Serra, Mexico's secretary of commerce under Carlos Salinas and holder of a Ph.D. in economics from Yale, famously declared, "The best industrial policy is no industrial policy."[55] Certainly, many former Mexican industrial policies, distorted by warring factions of the state, should have been ended; but as an overall strategy, renouncing industrial policy did not succeed well. Actually, even though he didn't call it industrial policy, Salinas had one: using NAFTA to lure U.S. investment to Mexico. It worked for a few years after the 1994–1995 crisis, but in the end it failed because the factories that located in Mexico were weakly linked to the economy—they mainly imported parts and exports assembled products—so it fell apart in the 2000s, when Chinese labor undercut Mexican labor in many industries.

Which Model Is More Persuasive?

My industrial-policy stories tend to support the Kaldor model, but have I proved anything? The new growth theories don't even mention industrial policies—at least not as even possibly promoting development, investment, and growth.[56] Quite aside from some of the questionable results of those theories already mentioned, I find it hard to see how an approach to understanding growth could be credible if it omits such a prominent feature of the most successful stories. A legitimate response might note that neoclassical "strategic-trade" theory does leave room for effective industrial policies. Assuming that industries are monopolistic or affected by other market imperfections, strategic-trade theory develops neoclassical models depicting how protection and subsidy may move investment from sunset industries to sunrise industries, boosting national growth. Paul Krugman won his Nobel Prize for developing models along these lines.

However, on closer examination, these models do not work very well to explain the success of any consistent use of industrial policies. In contrast to the situation in Keynesian models, in these models, industrial policies *cannot* increase total investment, since national saving, a result of individuals' preferences, determines total investment. Policies can push investment only from one industry to another, and if they push investment the wrong way—namely, from sunrise to sunset industries—they undermine growth. To make such policies work, in these models, politicians would have to be unbelievably astute and publicly motivated. First, they might well fail to identify sunrise industries: Just which new energy technologies will be winners? Second, even if the right sunrise industries are identified, armies of lobbyists for existing sunset industries will descend on Washington to highjack subsidies. Thus, neoclassical models make it very hard to imagine how actual politicians could succeed in deploying trade and industrial policies. However, if Keynesian models are right when they claim that such policies can increase total investment, there is more room for error-prone real-world politics. This room is not unlimited: pushing enough investment in stupid enough directions will do harm. But somewhat sensible efforts falling far short of perfection might work. Since industrial policies so often have worked, despite politicians' frequent ineptitude, the Keynesian view seems more plausible.

Another way to compare theories is to look at the way people, including economists, talk. Neoclassical theory says that trade always benefits a nation; protectionism is like filling harbors with rocks. Imports can hurt certain sectors, but they cannot erode investment because trade doesn't determine investment; saving does. Trade only moves investment from inefficient to efficient industries, neoclassical theory says, while protectionism only does the opposite. But you would never guess the theory from the way trade negotiators, many of them economists, talk. When they allow one of their nation's markets to be opened, in the language of trade negotiation, they call it a "concession," which they grant only in exchange for a hard-fought concession from the trading partner. This view might be attributed to pressures from interest groups facing increased imports, but if the national benefits of trade were so certain, placating narrow interests would not seem to require such enormous bargaining efforts.

In fact, neither proponents nor opponents of free trade make their case in neoclassical terms. U.S. officials' unending laments that China has manipulated its currency to boost exports—hence investment—at the expense of other nations is Keynesian. And when trade officials advocate trade, they often do so in Keynesian terms. Listen to former commerce secretary Donald Evans: "I have businesses from all over America come and talk to me about their future and their growth and the importance of opening up markets. . . . Those leaders come to me and say, 'Our future growth is outside the borders of the United States.' Certainly there's some here, but they look to foreign markets to continue the growth they've experienced over the last five to ten years."[57]

Economists call trade cutoffs such as those triggered by the 1930 Smoot-Hawley tariffs (as one nation adopted protectionist measures, another responded, and on the cycle went) "beggar-thy-neighbor" policies. The Cambridge Keynesian Joan Robinson invented the term.[58] She was right, and neoclassical economists who use the phrase are right to use it. Trade contraction *is* a beggar-thy-neighbor policy because it destroys demand and investment, in a vicious circle. The problem is neoclassical theory. If it were right—if saving determined investment and if rounds of protectionism only moved investment from more efficient to less efficient industries—then trade contraction would not be nearly so serious. When economists themselves dismiss the practical conclusions of a theory that they claim to espouse, the theory looks doubtful.

TWELVE

In the Short Run

All economists who espoused Keynesian theory in the 1930s saw in it a hope to combat the Depression, but they disagreed about what it meant. When it left Cambridge, England (I use that town to designate Cambridge University and its allies), it was a theory about a profoundly uncertain future, an indispensable but perilous thing called "money," and an economy that might settle at almost any level of unemployment, good, bad, or indifferent. When it arrived in Cambridge, Massachusetts (I use that town to designate Harvard, MIT, and their allies), it was an addendum to neoclassical theory. It assumed that economies gravitate toward a unique equilibrium but may be impeded along the way by imperfections, such as a temporarily excessive interest rate that discourages investment, or temporarily high wages that cause unemployment. Cambridge, England, saw capitalism as inherently troubled; Cambridge, Massachusetts, came to see capitalism as merely in need of "fine-tuning."

What happened on the way to Cambridge, Massachusetts? It did not help that Keynes's ideas straggled into town half-formed before *The General Theory* was published. The Canadian economist Robert Bryce had attended the "Keynes Club," a series of Monday-evening talks given by Keynes at Cambridge, and summed them up in what he called a "clandestine" essay.[1] Arriving to do graduate study at Harvard in 1935, Bryce saw himself as the only "expert on Keynes's work" at the university, and organized informal seminars based on his essay.[2] In those discussions, he probably made a point that he surely stressed later: "*The General Theory* wasn't written to be easy to understand; it was written to try to carry a detailed argument through to conclusion. Anyone who studies that book is going to get very confused."[3]

Bryce's warning seems have resonated at Harvard. Paul Samuelson, studying there at the same time, would later famously declare *The General Theory* "obscure" and "arrogant." His initial feelings toward the book were hostile, he recalled years afterward: "My rebellion against its pretensions would have been complete except for an uneasy realization that I did not at all understand what it was about."[4] The sense that Keynes was confusing and confused lived on. Gregory Mankiw, a prominent "New Keynesian" who was further removed from Keynes than the Samuelson generation, remarks, "One might suppose that reading Keynes is an important part of Keynesian theorizing. In fact, quite the opposite is the case. . . . I am not sure that even Keynes himself knew completely what he really meant."[5] A rising young Harvard economist whom I had dinner with several years ago volunteered the same view.

Samuelson's sense of confusion probably resulted from the simple fact that he could not accept Keynes's central theoretical claim. As he says, "What I resisted in Keynes the most was the notion that there could be equilibrium unemployment."[6] That notion could not be reconciled with the neoclassical theory that Samuelson had learned at the University of Chicago before coming to Harvard and that he would espouse throughout his career. Yet he believed that Keynes's policy recommendations, such as spending on public works, were vital for creating employment amid a depression. As it happened, on essentially pragmatic grounds Frank Knight and other University of Chicago economists were already bucking majority U.S. economic opinion to call for deficit spending.[7]

Samuelson saw how to resolve his theoretical concern about Keynes— "just stop worrying about it," as he later put it—while justifying key Keynesian policy proposals.[8] He could shoehorn Keynes into neoclassical theory. He notes that he "was content to assume that there was enough rigidity in relative prices and wages to make the Keynesian alternative to Walras operative."[9] "Walras" is a moniker for the assumption that the economy gravitates to a unique and optimal equilibrium. In an aggregate neoclassical model, "rigidity" in prices or wages can sufficiently impede the economy's movement toward equilibrium to justify some Keynesian policies.

Samuelson did not invent the neoclassical interpretation of Keynes's *General Theory*. In embryonic form, the idea that imperfections, particularly an excessive interest rate, could cause business cycles went back at least to Knut Wicksell and, indeed, to Keynes's earlier work. British economists contributed importantly to the neoclassical version of Keynesian thinking; they included Sir John Hicks, who published a seminal model in 1937 seeking to capture it. But Samuelson would help to cement this version in the canon.

American resistance against foreign entanglements seems to have nearly finished off alternative interpretations of Keynes in the United States in the 1930s. If Americans had even heard of Keynes, many confused him with Marx, never mind that he was adamantly anti-Marxist.[10] "In the eyes of many economically illiterate but deeply patriotic (and well-to-do) citizens," Harvard University president James Conant reflected years later, "to accuse a professor of being Keynesian was almost equivalent to branding him a subversive agent."[11]

Lorie Tarshis, a Canadian economist who saw Keynes more along British lines, ran into Keynes phobia almost the moment he began teaching at Tufts University in 1936. Along with several Harvard economists, but not Samuelson, he co-authored *An Economic Program for American Democracy*, which wound up on Franklin D. Roosevelt's nightstand.[12] Soon the president of Tufts began warning Tarshis that alumni were

canceling donations because his name appeared on the book. "I was regarded as an absolute Red," says Tarshis. "When you read the book now,
there's no Red in it! We were trying to save capitalism."[13]

That episode was only the prelude to the textbook Tarshis next wrote.
When it appeared in 1947, he initially received delighted notes from the
publisher, Houghton Mifflin, as one university after another adopted it.
But soon Merwin Hart, who supported the fascist regime in Spain and
opposed outlawing child labor, organized a "National Economic Committee" to attack the text.[14] The committee sent letters to the trustees of
every university that had adopted it, and many universities began canceling orders. After Yale refused to cancel its order, William F. Buckley devoted a chapter in his book *God and Man at Yale* to lambasting Tarshis.
Tarshis recalls, "The amount of distortion is enormous. He would pick a
phrase and tack it onto a phrase two pages later, another [a] page later,
another . . . four pages earlier, and make a sentence that I couldn't recognize as anything I'd written."[15]

Samuelson himself deplored the attacks on Tarshis.[16] When his own
textbook came out, it was attacked, too.[17] Speaking of himself in the
third person, he notes: "There were a lot of complaints that Samuelson
was playing peek-a-boo with the Commies. The whole thing was a sad
scene that did not reflect well on conservative business pressuring of col-
leges."[18] He adds: "For some reason that I have no understanding of, the
virulence of the attack on Tarshis was of a higher order of magnitude
than on my book."[19]

Samuelson's *Economics* survived partly because, as he says, he wrote it
"carefully and lawyer-like."[20] His neoclassical version of Keynesian theory would strike neoclassical economists as clear. His text highlighted
the so-called "Keynesian-cross" diagram, with one curve going up and
another going down. These curves had practically nothing to do with
microeconomic supply-and-demand curves for goods—but how would
committees intent on attacking Marxist-Keynesians ever know the dif-

ference? Samuelson's approach looked more scientific and proved easier to defend against right-wing attack. If he hadn't spread Keynesianism to America, someone else who thought much the same way would have.

The assumption that economies gravitate toward a unique equilibrium lies at the core of the "grand neoclassical synthesis" that Samuelson announced in the third edition of his text.[21] Henceforth, this synthesis promised, neoclassicals and Keynesians need no longer debate philosophical imponderables such as our knowledge of the future or the relationship between market and society, because, in the long run, the economy gravitates toward its center of repose. Granted, in the short run, sticky prices, wages, or interest rates might impede this natural progress, causing unemployment for a considerable time. The right policies—the proper "fine-tuning"—could ease the economy on its way to its long-run equilibrium and thus alleviate short-run suffering. Economists could debate how steep this curve or how shallow that curve might be, and whether fiscal or monetary polices might be more appropriate. These debates would be technical, not ideological.

Joan Robinson of Cambridge University famously branded the American neoclassical synthesis "bastard Keynesianism." It crucially supposes that individuals' efforts to maximize utility and firms' efforts to maximize profits in markets lead the economy, as if by an invisible hand, toward a unique equilibrium. "Structural" market imperfections such as labor unions or monopolistic firms can keep this equilibrium from being quite optimal, but it is the best that can be achieved under the circumstances.

The "unique-equilibrium assumption," as I will call it, turned out to be just that—pure assumption. No model ever demonstrated that an economy of diverse individuals and firms, producing and trading various goods, would be led as if by an invisible hand to equilibrium, let alone a unique one. About a quarter of a century after Samuelson first published his textbook, theorists gave up the effort that Arrow and Debreu had launched to model the invisible hand. But by that time, the macroeconomic project assuming a unique and stable equilibrium had gone too far to be easily abandoned.

Short-Run Keynesianism

I will call the American view "short-run Keynesianism." Despite my criticism of the way it has been synthesized into the long-run neoclassical model, I think it's not a bad model *if* you restrict it to picturing the short run—anywhere from a few quarters to a few years. In effect, over this short-run period, it is just the theory of effective demand.[22] Suppose the economy is in a slump, so industry has the capacity to boost production. If effective demand increases—that is, if consumer, investment, or government spending to purchase goods and services produced by domestic industries increases—these industries will generate the goods and services. Output rises, and more workers find jobs. Moreover, as firms and workers spend their income, their additional demand will further boost output and employment. This "multiplier" effect has a limit, since some income is saved and some demand is directed to imports. The size of the multiplier effect depends on circumstances.

Short-run Keynesianism leads to a policy prescription for ameliorating a recession. Since individuals reduce consumption during a recession as they lose jobs, and firms reduce production as sales fall, the principal economic actor that can put some floor under the downturn is the government. It can cut taxes or increase spending, for example, by providing unemployment insurance, sharing revenue with states to pay for services such as education and policing, or investing in infrastructure. Short-run Keynesians relied on this essential argument to support the 2009 Obama stimulus package—and many continued to support additional stimulus at least through mid-2011.

This model raises a theoretical question for neoclassicals. Notice that it has nothing whatsoever to do with optimizing by individuals or with economic equilibrium, but just posits an assumption about the macro-economy—namely, the theory of effective demand. How can a model that has nothing to do with neoclassical theory be transformed into a long-run neoclassical model based on notions about optimization and equilibrium?

I would not argue that the model of effective demand could remain valid for an indefinite period of time. A large enough stimulus, maintained for long enough, will raise government debt, cause inflation, and create other trouble. However, I will argue that the way the American neoclassical-Keynesian synthesis merges the short-run model of effective demand into a long-run neoclassical model is muddled. It confuses our understanding of economies.

Readers will be astonished to hear that the route from the short-run model to the long-run model involves two curves, one going up and the other down. The first is called an aggregate supply curve; the second, an aggregate demand curve. One little problem is that no remotely plausible aggregate demand curve actually goes down. The other little problem is that, although the aggregate supply curve does plausibly go up, you have to torture neoclassical theory to get it to tell that story. In effect, the upward-sloping supply curve provides good evidence that neoclassical theory is wrong.

These aggregate curves look like the usual supply-and-demand curves for goods, but are different sorts of things. The aggregate curves depict supply and demand not for any particular good, but for total output—the dollar value of all goods produced. And they concern not a particular price, but the average price level of all goods. A price level is an index—such as the consumer price index (CPI)—that gauges the average price of a basket of goods. The index is arbitrarily set at a value of 100 in some base year; for example, the Economist Intelligence Unit (EIU, of *The Economist* magazine) currently sets the CPI at 100 in the year 2005. By itself, this number is meaningless, but the percentage change in the index gauges the average inflation (or deflation) of that basket of goods.

For example, in 2006 the EIU estimated the CPI at 103.2, for a consumer-price inflation of 3.2 percent. If the CPI had dropped to, say, 97.0, there would have been about 3.0 percent deflation. The index used to gauge the average price level of all goods that constitute the GDP, not just consumer goods, is somewhat awkwardly called the "GDP deflator."

Start with the supposedly falling aggregate demand curve. As the price level falls—in other words, as deflation sets in—consumers and firms are supposed to offer to buy more goods. Theory aside, it makes some sense that when the price of a particular good falls (say, the price of gasoline falls from $4.00 a gallon to $2.00), people likely spend more money on it (say, to drive longer distances on summer vacation), so demand increases. But why should aggregate demand for total economic output increase when the average price level falls, and deflation sets in? I recall staring at aggregate demand curves and puzzling for hours. Since I have never personally experienced deflation—though there was a scare about it in the early 2000s—how was I to visualize it? Worse, before World War II, the term "deflation" was used as a synonym for "depression." For example, during the Great Depression from 1929 to 1933, according to the U.S. Census Bureau, the GDP price level index fell 25 percent—there was 25 percent deflation—and GDP declined 27 percent.[23] How could aggregate demand possibly have increased under those circumstances?

An answer was provided by the economist Franco Modigliani. In his Ph.D. thesis, written at the New School for Social Research and published in 1944, he presented a theory about how falling prices might increase aggregate demand.[24] The mechanism is supposed to work this way: If the price level falls and deflation sets in, people's real savings—the "real balances" in their bank accounts—are worth more. Consumers are supposed to respond by spending more, thus increasing aggregate demand.[25] This effect is not theoretically impossible. It has been observed when anti-inflation plans have been implemented in countries such as Brazil. Wages, contracts, and other prices that had been indexed to rise with inflation, so as to maintain their real value, are suddenly de-indexed by legal fiat. Real balances in savings accounts do seem to rise (or anyway stop eroding), and people spend more. However, the United States had better not count on the real-balance effect. If a family has a $200,000 mortgage and $30,000 of savings in a money market account, deflation works the wrong way.[26] The higher real cost of mortgage payments will discourage far more spending than the higher real value of savings will encourage. Nonfinancial businesses are usually net debtors, so their real debt burden rises, and they are not likely to invest more. Moreover, they are loath to invest because they will have to sell goods at falling prices. Under typical circumstances, as prices fall, aggregate demand does not increase. A falling aggregate demand curve is implausible.

An upward-sloping supply curve is often observed in practice. The business pages regularly report that rising real output in a business-cycle upswing causes inflation, or, in other words, an increase in the price level. Similarly, policymakers often worry that if the economy "overheats," it will ignite excessive inflation. Thus, you get the upward-sloping supply curve: as real output increases, the price level rises.

However, the neoclassical production function is difficult to square with this typical behavior. A nation's capital stock is accumulated over decades, even centuries. During a business upswing, firms put dormant capital stock to work, but the volume of capital remains relatively stable. By contrast, firms use substantially more labor, hiring workers who may have lost jobs during a prior recession. Thus, as a business upswing proceeds, firms employ relatively more labor to operate a relatively fixed stock of capital.

From here things get a little intricate, not because the actual economy is so intricate but because the story of the production function is intricate. The production function says that to induce firms to employ more labor with a relatively fixed capital stock, as happens during a business upswing, the real wage must fall. But if the real wage falls, how can the price level rise and trigger inflation? In theory it's not utterly impossible, but in practice it doesn't happen. Money wages rise, along with prices, during a business upswing. Real wages—real buying power after discounting money wages for inflation—may remain roughly stable or may rise. But the one thing real wages do *not* do is fall—just the thing the neoclassical production function insists they must do.[27]

Leaving neoclassicals to try to untangle dilemmas of their own creation, let's just for a moment hypothetically grant their assumptions that aggregate supply-and-demand curves operate as supposed. Then, how do they see a short-run Keynesian economy as moving toward a long-run neoclassical economy? Picture the economy as starting out in long-run optimal equilibrium. We could suppose that the government spends an extra trillion dollars on goods and services—but the logic will be more direct if we borrow Milton Friedman's metaphor and suppose that helicopters drop a trillion dollars from the sky.

Americans collect the trillion dollars and spend most of them to buy goods. (We hope the top 1 percent of the income distribution doesn't grab 90 percent of the dollars and stash them in their hedge funds.) With more money in circulation, firms discover that they do not lose sales even if they raise prices, so they go ahead and raise prices. Wages are sticky, fixed by union contracts or longer-term agreements, so workers' *real* wage falls. (As mentioned, this phenomenon is rarely if ever actually observed, but, remember, this is just model.) Now, noticing that they are paying lower real wages, firms hire more labor to increase output, in accordance with the neoclassical production function. So far, prices have risen somewhat, and output has also risen.

Before long, two unfortunate effects come into play. Workers notice that their real wages have fallen and push for raises. As the real wage rises, firms lay off workers and reduce production. Meanwhile, increasing inflation erodes the "real balances"—that is, the real value of savings. Since we are supposed to want to maintain the same level of real balances (ask not why; in the model we do), we begin saving more and spending less. As a result, aggregate demand declines. Before long—within a few months to a few years—the economy is back at the optimal long-run equilibrium where it started, except that the price level is higher. Monetary expansion stimulated aggregate demand in the short run but dwindled off over the long run, leaving only a higher price level.

I posited an economy that started at long-run equilibrium. If instead it started in recession, it would be heading toward its optimal equilibrium, in the neoclassical view, but perhaps too slowly for the unemployed. Either a monetary expansion, generally favored by monetarist such as Friedman, or a fiscal expansion, often favored by Keynesians such as Samuelson, will temporarily bump up aggregate demand. The bump in aggregate demand gives the economy an extra push toward equilibrium. This push dwindles off in the long run, causing some inflation, but reducing unemployment in the short run might well be worth the cost.

The Rational-Expectations Revolution

In the 1960s, presidents John F. Kennedy and Lyndon B. Johnson, advised by the Keynesian Council of Economic Advisors, seemed to do a remarkably good job of economic management. Beginning in the late 1960s, Johnson's policies of spending on "guns and butter"—Great Society social welfare programs and the Vietnam War—were seen as causing inflation to increase (as, in fact, Keynesian economists warned). And the 1970s saw rising inflation and inflationary fears. Monetarists, led by Milton Friedman, argued that government efforts to manage the economy often did more harm than good, and in particular they blamed the Federal Reserve for printing too much money. Their claim is debatable. Large shocks to oil prices in 1973 and 1979, as well as shocks to prices of other commodities, such as a failure of the Russian wheat harvest that drove up food prices, certainly contributed. Moreover, in the context of the late 1990s, when there were no such large shocks, loose monetary policies did not cause high inflation.

In any event, a speech Friedman gave in 1968 as president of the American Economic Association was later seen as predicting the inflation of the 1970s. He argued that no matter what monetary or fiscal policies the government pursued, unemployment would settle at its "natural rate" in the long run. He defined this as the level that would occur in a general-equilibrium model of decentralized trading, provided that "the actual structural characteristics of the labor and commodity markets"— the level of the minimum wage, workers' resistance to moving in order to fill job vacancies, unions' capacity to push for raises—were embedded in its equations.[28] The more intrusive such structural imperfections, the higher the natural unemployment rate. Government monetary and fiscal policies might temporarily lower unemployment below its natural level at the expense of causing higher inflation, but they could have no effect on the natural rate in the long run.

Robert Lucas, a former student of Friedman's, agreed with Friedman but wondered precisely why expanding the money supply should boost output and lower unemployment in the short run, while just causing inflation in the long run. His puzzle could be rephrased is as follows: In the long run, money is supposed to be "neutral," merely a unit of account. Doubling or halving the money supply is supposed to double or halve prices, but have no real effect on employment or output. In fact, developing nations that have experienced high inflation will occasionally lop three zeros off their currency with no obvious real effect. However, in the short run, money is not neutral. Increasing the money supply is supposed to raise employment and output; and sharply decreasing it, as none other than Friedman argued, can cause a depression. Granted, "sticky" wages and prices are supposed to explain why money has real effects in the short run. But—as Lucas protested—"if everyone understands that prices will ultimately increase in proportion to the increase in money, what force stops this from happening right away?"[29]

Lucas made two theoretical points. First, he objected to the approach that virtually all economists were taking, from Milton Friedman at Chicago to Joan Robinson at Cambridge. They were doing just as I have suggested: building macroeconomic models by imposing assumptions that they considered realistic on national accounts or other data, in order to tell a cause-and-effect story. Lucas found this approach vague. Why impose one set of assumptions rather than another? What is the justification? He believed that macroeconomic models must be based on assumptions about utility-maximizing individuals—people who want to earn money but also seek leisure, who want to spend earnings but also desire to invest for the future. In short, Lucas wanted a model based on "microfoundations."

Second, Lucas wanted a model that allows individuals to think rationally about the future. If they know the Federal Reserve is printing money—and perhaps read the newspaper headline, "Inflation Worries Mount"—the model should allow them to take that information into account. If prices are expected to rise, the model shouldn't assume that they stupidly believe prices will stay put. More broadly, if individuals can benefit by basing pocketbook decisions on their understanding of the economy—on their model of the economy—they should be allowed to do so *within* the model itself.

"Rational-expectations" models assume that the rational individuals depicted in the model understand the model and make decisions to optimize utility in accordance with it. Lucas imported this approach into macroeconomics from a paper published in 1961 by Richard Muth, his colleague at Carnegie-Mellon (then the Carnegie Institute of Technology). Muth had argued that hog farmers know a thing or two about how the price of hogs and the price of corn feed interact. They have an implicit model of the corn-hog market and take it into account in projecting next year's hog prices, rather than just extrapolating from last year's prices.[30] Such rational expectations do not require perfect foresight. They require that individuals understand the structure of the modeled economy and be able to plug in past data to project future developments. But they must be able use historical data to make confident probabilistic projections of the future.

In answer to his question about the short-run versus long-run effects of an increase in the money supply, Lucas came up with a famous rational-expectations model.[31] Individuals produce goods and buy goods from others. There are no sticky prices; prices adjust flexibly and immediately, so that the supply of each good produced just equals the demand for it. In other words, the economy not only moves toward its unique equilibrium, but remains instantaneously in equilibrium.

The catch is that individuals have imperfect information. Producers experience two kinds of changes in money prices for their goods. One arises from a shift in preferences that alters demand for their goods relative to demand for other goods. This year, one producer's smart phone is more popular, so its price rises; next year, it's less popular, so its price falls. When a shift in preferences increases demand for a good, its real price rises compared with that of other goods. The producer's optimal strategy is to take advantage of the situation, work harder, and sell more; the producer thus receives greater real income in exchange for giving up some leisure. The other kind of shift in market prices for goods is caused by an increase in the general money supply, affecting all goods equally. In this case, each producer's optimal strategy is to do nothing, since the real price of the good doesn't change. Increasing output would mean that the producer would have to give up leisure time without compensating greater real income.

But producers can't tell one kind of price change from another. When the market price of their good increases, they know how big the increase is, but they cannot tell what part of it is due to a change in preference for their good and what part is due to a change in the money supply. As Lucas puts it, producers have one "bit" of information (the market price of the good), but need two "bits" of information (the change in the money supply and changes in preferences) in order to decide their optimal strategy.[32] Faced with this dilemma, producers use knowledge of the model, the laws of probability, and past data to estimate how much of the price increase is most likely due to each factor. They hedge their bets, raising output somewhat, but less than they would if they knew that the entire price increase was due to a change in preferences. Thus, economy-wide output does rise in the short run. But it returns to its long-run level as producers learn to separate the effects of changes in the money supply from changes in preferences. Even though individuals understand the model and use it to rationally project future developments, and despite perfectly flexible prices, the money supply does have real short-run effects but does not have real long-run effects. Lucas solved the puzzle he set out to understand.

"My friends say people don't have rational expectations," concedes Thomas Sargent, a pioneer of the rational-expectations revolution. A few months after Lehman Brothers collapsed and the world was plunged into crisis, he agreed that assuming rational expectations would be doubtful: "Today, in this situation, we're completely off the map. People don't have the vaguest idea what's going on. But, that said, when would rational expectations be a good approximation? If you are living in pretty normal times, and things are going up and down, but in ways that you've experienced before, so you've spotted patterns and can trust them—that's what rational expectations are good for."[33]

Lucas, Sargent, and other pioneers of the rational-expectations revolution in the 1970s believed that the macroeconomic market model was reasonably stable and known. In their view, the principal economic threats consisted of external shocks that strike from outside markets themselves, including the erratic printing of money and large government budget deficits that cause inflation. For that matter, oil-price spikes driven by Middle East politics could be added to the list of shocks in the model. Rational-expectations models were intended to guide policy to limit inflation under those circumstances.

The rational-expectations hypothesis, by itself, has much to recommend it. We do try to understand how the economy works—we do envision some model of the economy—and try to make pocketbook decisions in accord with it. As Sargent himself has often pointed out, the rational-expectations theory simply assumes we are already enlightened about the real model of the economy. It has no explanation of how we got enlightenment. But if the economy always gravitated toward a unique equilibrium—or were always in instantaneous equilibrium—we should notice that fact and come to apply it in practice.

The rational-expectations theory runs into trouble if the economy does not have, or at least head toward, a unique and stable equilibrium. If it has many possible equilibria, or if it does not necessarily reach any equilibrium at all—as the research following up on Arrow and Debreu's model of diverse agents producing and trading in a decentralized economy concludes—then what is there to rationally expect?

The rational-expectations model of monetary policy has not stood up well to experience, even at times when the economy was moving along fairly steadily. The model makes an important prediction that Lucas has emphasized. Fully expected changes in the money supply have no real effect. If everybody knows the money supply will increase 10 percent, firms just raise prices 10 percent, workers demand 10 percent raises, and the only thing that changes is the price level. The real economy just goes on as before. Only unexpected increases in the money supply have short-run effects because, as firms notice increased spending, they believe that at least some part of it results from a shifting of preferences toward their particular goods, so they raise output.

In practice, fully expected changes in the money supply do have an effect. Indeed, one might have harbored such suspicions based on Friedman and Schwartz's own *Monetary History of the United States*. In Lucas's words, they found that every U.S. depression from 1867 to 1960 "was associated with a large contraction in the money supply and that every large contraction in the money supply was associated with a depression."[34] Can the monetary authorities really fool all the people all the time, as the model implies they must in order to achieve such an unblemished record? After 1979, when Fed chairman Paul Volcker clamorously warned he would contract the money supply to wring out inflation, so anybody who read a newspaper should have expected the contraction, he still managed to cause the deepest recession since World War II. Christina Romer and David Romer identified six such deliberate contractions in the money supply—contractions that were announced and should have been expected. All six of them caused recessions.[35]

Regardless of whether the particular model by Lucas that I just described is realistic, his approach to modeling swept macroeconomics. Most macroeconomists accept that their models should be based on microfoundations—that is, on an account of how individual consumers maximize utility and firms maximize profits. And models should incorporate rational expectations: agents in the model should use the model to maximize utility and profits.

John Bates Clark Redux

In the 1980s and 1990s, economists Finn Kydland and Edward Prescott took another giant step toward the latest and greatest mainstream macroeconomic models. Those who believe the neoclassical production function faced the dilemma of how business cycles can occur. I find this dilemma difficult to keep in mind, since it arises not from the nature of things but from a belief in what I find an intricate and implausible theory of production. So let me recap the dilemma. The production function says that the real wage must fall during an upswing in the cycle, in order for firms to hire additional labor and increase employment. But empirical studies agree that the real wage does not fall in an upswing. If you believe the neoclassical production function, how can business upswings possibly occur?

Kydland and Prescott won the Nobel prize in 2004 for developing "real business-cycle" (RBC) models that resolve the dilemma. They accept Lucas's insistence that macro models be built on microfoundations of optimizing agents, and that models incorporate rational expectations: agents in the model understand and use it to calculate their optimal strategies. Lucas's model is monetary—it assumes an unchanging technology—but Kydland and Prescott incorporate technology. In particular, they assume that the same "real" force that neoclassicals see as driving long-run growth also drives business cycles: technology-induced changes in productivity. Positive technological shocks increase productivity, causing upturns and increasing wages, thus encouraging everyone to work more and sacrifice some leisure. Negative shocks reduce productivity, causing downturns and reducing wages, thus encouraging everyone to work less and enjoy more leisure. On this theory, even though Kydland and Prescott preserve the neoclassical production function, the real wage can actually rise during upswings, as it is often observed to do.

There are just a few problems. Well, quite a few. RBC models suppose that productivity shocks generate business cycles, but they measure productivity by the Solow residual. Nothing says the Solow residual—that measure of our ignorance—actually captures technology. It just rises and falls when growth rises or falls.[36] As mentioned, it ran backward during the Great Depression, presumably because the economy shrank, and then it surged during World War II, presumably because the economy surged. RBC models are a tautology: business cycles occur because growth surges and declines.

Worse, not only are these models a tautology—they are a tautology that turns out to be wrong. They say that employment rises or falls because actors choose to work more when productivity is high and less when it's low. This idea is nuts. The Yale economist Truman Bewley interviewed hundreds of corporate officials, union leaders, temp-agency managers, and job-search advisors about layoffs. They told him firms lay off workers "because of financial setbacks, technical improvements, and declines in product demand, never because of declines in productivity."[37] Advisors to the unemployed told Bewley that their clients, far from choosing leisure, "were desperate for work and miserable being jobless."[38] This is the kind of anecdotal evidence that many economists scoff at, but in this case it is too overwhelming—and Bewley was too systematic—to be ignored.

The real-business-cycle theory of downturns, as Paul Krugman remarked, says that workers caused the Great Depression by taking an extended holiday.[39] Robert Lucas adds—and when Lucas and Krugman agree, there has to be something to the idea—that it's impossible to see how a massive productivity failure could have caused the Great Depression.[40] Kydland and Prescott revised their view, claiming to explain only 70 percent of the business cycle and attributing the rest to other causes.[41] They merely show, it seems to me, that the Solow residual is highly correlated—maybe 70 percent correlated—with the business cycle. A useful insight into the Solow residual.

Keynesians Go High-Tech

Although few macroeconomists think productivity shocks drive business cycles to the extent that Kydland and Prescott's model supposes, most adopt their approach to modeling. A new generation of Keynesians (whose resemblance to Keynes, if any, had become practically coincidental) saw that they could inject market imperfections and monetary policies into the structure of Kydland and Prescott's model to forge what they advertised as a "new neoclassical synthesis." Thus were born the famous dynamic stochastic general-equilibrium (DGSE) models that central banks such as the Federal Reserve use to set monetary policy. They are tricky to capture in words. Actually, they're rocket science, albeit hauled in from the 1960s.[42] I struggled through several of the models to satisfy my curiosity.[43] You won't hear about them in undergraduate texts, but it's worth trying to get the gist of them. They aren't even quite as bad as they sound.

DSGE models are dynamic, picturing an economy as moving frame-by-frame over time, as if in a jerky moving picture. Each frame might depict one economic quarter. As the economy proceeds from frame to frame, it is hit by stochastic, or random, shocks. Following Kydland and Prescott, these models allow positive technological shocks, which tend to increase growth, and negative technological shocks, which tend to decrease it. As always, the neoclassical production function describes technology. The models also allow fiscal shocks, as the government might spend more in one particular period, tending to increase growth, and less the next, tending to decrease it. Contemporary Keynesians also incorporate monetary shocks that produce real short-run effects. There can be other shocks, as well, such as a "cost-push" jump in oil prices.

The key thing about these shocks is that they are all described by well-behaved bell curves, like the automobile defects described in *Consumer Reports*. You can't tell exactly how big next year's shock will be, any more than you can tell exactly what defects a particular car will have. But you do know the average size of shocks that will hit, as well as the deviation of individual shocks from this average.

Shocks may jar the economy somewhat from the outside—better or worse technology, more or less government spending, a larger or smaller money supply—but DSGE models assume that the core economy is stable. Never torn by destructive internal mechanisms such as speculative bubbles, runs on banks, or sovereign-debt traps, the economy always moves smoothly toward its unique equilibrium. In fact, in every time frame depicted by the model, the economy has already reached a stable equilibrium. Keynesian variants of DSGE models allow market imperfections such as monopolistic firms, so this may not be an optimal perfect-market equilibrium. But the economy is always in instantaneous equilibrium. Supply always exactly balances demand.

In DSGE models, actors do not merely optimize utility for the current time period—they use the model to optimize over their endless life spans. Why on earth assume that agents live forever? And how can agents optimize utility until the end of time? Actually, it turns out to be mathematically easier to optimize until the end of time than over a human lifetime. This assumption keeps the math do-able. And an endless lifespan is perhaps not as crazy an assumption as it sounds, since agents discount the future—that is, they consider a dollar next year to be worth less than a dollar today, and so on forever. People discount in the real world, too. If you lend me a dollar today, I must pay it back with interest, since both of us consider having a real dollar next year worth less than having that dollar now. The interest rate I'm willing to pay in some sense gauges how much more I want the dollar now rather than later, or how much I discount the future. In these models, because of discounting, the future ceases to weigh heavily after what would be a normal human lifespan.

In choosing how much labor to supply, as in RBC models, individuals weigh the relative utility of income versus leisure. If productivity leaps up during one period, the real wage rises, so they chose to work harder and take advantage of earning opportunities. If productivity lags, the real wage falls, so they chose to work less and take advantage of leisure opportunities. They also weigh how much to invest in a particular year, versus how much to spend. The return on investment depends on the marginal return on capital, in the famous neoclassical production function. When the return is higher, agents save and invest more, in order to take the opportunity to amass wealth for the future. When the return is lower, agents take advantage of the chance to spend more, since there is less opportunity to amass wealth for the future. Given market imperfections, all is for the best in the best of all possible worlds.

Back to an Uncertain Future

Robert Solow, a first-generation short-run Keynesian, notes that he cannot understand why macroeconomists have bought a DSGE model "that seems to lack all credibility." He speculates, "Maybe there is in human nature a deep-seated perverse pleasure in adopting and defending a wholly counterintuitive doctrine that leaves the uninitiated peasant wondering what planet he or she is on."[44] He scoffs at contemporary macroeconomists' claim to base DSGE models on microfoundations, calling it a "swindle."[45] He complains particularly about the "representative agent"—the model has only a sole actor, or maybe two or three—that is somehow supposed to summarize or average all diverse individuals in an economy. Indeed, in an essay making the most eloquent possible case for microfoundations, Lucas himself runs headlong into this problem.[46] He starts out envisioning multitudinous individuals and firms inhabiting a panoramic world; but in order to get anywhere, he must begin aggregating them, and soon the world narrows to a representative agent inhabiting a tunnel. Diverse expectations have been obliterated.

You can make a one-agent model economy stable, but what is a one-agent economy?[47] If diverse agents disagree about the economy, the assumption built into rational-expectations models—that everybody believes the same model—obviously falls apart. Even in a relatively stable world, like the economy of the 1970s, which rational-expectations was invented to understand, policymakers, firms, and individuals may well disagree about the model. Was inflation in the 1970s caused by oil shocks? Loose monetary policy? Budget deficits? Cost-of-living increases built into union contracts? The exhaustion of Fordist mass-production technology? Such competing views were then and still are maintained. Especially when the economic world precipitously changes, as it did in the 2008 financial crisis, it is inconceivable that any representative agent could summarize diverse views of the economy.

The original sin of contemporary macroeconomics is perhaps to believe such models literally. In "The Science of Monetary Policy: A New Keynesian Perspective," Richard Clarida of Columbia and Jordi Galí and Mark Gertler of New York University set out a DSGE model of the type used by the Fed. They concede that "the key stumbling block for policy formation is limited knowledge of the way the macroeconomy works."[48] But they immediately equate limited knowledge of the economy with mere disagreement among different DSGE models: "Results that are highly model-specific are of limited use." They claim that a "science of monetary policy" can be distilled from "results that are robust across a wide variety of macroeconomic frameworks." If they meant a wide variety of macroeconomic frameworks, I might not object; but they actually mean frameworks that all make the same basic assumptions: the economy instantly reaches unique equilibrium, a representative agent stands in for diverse individuals, the J. B. Clark production function rules, and so on. That confidence is breathtaking.

When the 2008 crisis struck, DSGE models were obviously useless. As Paul Ormerod, director of Volterra Consulting in London, says: "The American authorities paid no attention to academic macro-economic theory of the past thirty years. Real business cycle theory, dynamic stochastic general equilibrium models, rational expectations—all the myriad of erudite papers on these topics might just as well have never been written. Instead, the authorities acted. They acted imperfectly, in conditions of huge uncertainty, drawing on the lessons of the 1930s and hoping that the mistakes of that period could be avoided."[49] In October 2008, the New Keynesian Gregory Mankiw conceded that the Great Depression caught economists at the time "completely by surprise." What's worse, he continued, is that "modern economists, armed with the data from the time, would not have forecast much better. In other words, even if another Depression were around the corner, you shouldn't expect much advance warning from the economics profession."[50] Mankiw deserves credit for the admission. But how could DSGE models ever predict—or even comprehend—a crisis if they start out positing a stable economy?

Bastard Keynesianism: Not a Bad Model?

Although I don't see how you get a long-run neoclassical equilibrium from the short-run Keynesian model of the generation of Samuelson and Solow, and although that model is no sure-fire recipe, it seems like a practical starting point for understanding the short run. Some objections to it are silly. One is so-called Ricardian equivalence, an idea that Ricardo articulated only to reject, but that was named after him anyway. Consider it in the context of the debate over President Barak Obama's stimulus plan. In 2009, Christina Romer, chair of the Council of Economic Advisors, estimated that the plan would increase GDP by 3.7 percent and employment by 3,675,000 jobs by the end of 2010, as compared with the situation the country would otherwise face.[51] Based on Ricardian equivalence, Robert J. Barro, a Harvard macroeconomist, estimated in 2009 that the stimulus would have no effect at all.[52] The reason, he said, is that we know the $840 billion stimulus plan will increase government debt by $840 billion, so the government will have to pay that debt off or pay interest on it. And who will pay the debt or interest? We will. Knowing our tax liabilities must increase, we cut our spending and save an extra $840 billion now to cover future liabilities. "Real GDP is given," says Barro. "And a rise in government purchases requires an equal fall in the total of other parts of GDP."[53] The stimulus program simply moves some activity out of the private sector into the public sector.

If I now sound like a broken record, it's because some economists' models repeat like broken records. Barro's model works if we are identical agents who know the economy is instantaneously and forever in equilibrium; if we foresee future deviations from that equilibrium and can calculate the probability that those deviations will occur; if we always can get a job that pays our true marginal productivity; and if we maximize utility (measured on a scale of utils, of course) over our theoretically infinite life spans. I have already belabored these assumptions. But, as well, would the same Americans who used their houses as ATM machines really worry so about distant tax obligations? And let me protest, again, the notion of the representative agent. If some of us cannot save even a penny during the recession, if we expect our tax rates will remain low enough that we will pay less than our per-capita portion of the debt, or if we imagine various other possibilities, we just might spend some of that $840 billion after all.

A less silly concern about the Obama stimulus is that U.S. government debt, largely owed to foreigners, might reach a dangerous tipping point. As I write these pages, the Greek government has clearly reached such a point; the question is not whether it will default, but what evasion will be used to describe default and how large the default will be. The United States isn't Greece. For one thing, U.S. debt is in dollars, which the Federal Reserve prints, while Greek debt is in euros, which Greece cannot print. Printing dollars to pay debt can cause inflation, but just 1 percent higher inflation pays off lots of national debt. For another thing, at the end of 2010, U.S. government debt owed to the public stood at 62 percent of GDP, the famously frugal German government already owed 82 percent of GDP, and the average debt in the euro zone was 86 percent of GDP, according to the Economist Intelligence Unit.[54] Granted, estimates vary considerably and are not comparable across nations, because large items such as future social-security liabilities are counted differently. But Greek debt was far higher, about 150 percent of GDP. Interest rates on U.S. debt were low at record lows, indicating that financial markets saw the government as creditworthy.

Counterbalancing concerns that U.S. debt might reach a tipping point is the concern that austere government spending will increase unemployment and decrease output, not only in the short run but over the long run. Problems described by the short-run Keynesian model can affect the long run. Workers out of jobs for several years may never be able to return to the workforce or may never earn anything like what they once did. Investments postponed for several years may forever make GDP that much lower than it otherwise would have been. Since what matters is not the money value of debt but the value of debt as a percentage of GDP, lower GDP increases its real weight. In fact, U.S. government debt at the end of World War II, which stood at 109 percent of GDP, was never actually paid off but simply dwindled as GDP grew and as inflation eroded its value.[55] Too small a stimulus is just as much a danger as too large a stimulus.

Note that this disagreement turns not on some inexorable march of the economy toward equilibrium, but on uncertain assessments about how deep the recession is, how large a stimulus might ameliorate it, how much the stimulus might contribute to overall government debt, and at what level global financial markets might get spooked by that debt. There are no certain answers.

Short-run Keynesians of the Samuelson-Solow generation also believed their model too literally. When Keynesians of the 1960s advised Kennedy that they could manage business cycles by "fine-tuning" the economy, theirs was much the same hubris that led DSGE economists to proclaim the arrival of the Great Moderation in the early 2000s. The earlier Keynesians, who had lived through the Depression, were actually more pragmatic than their rhetoric. If only they had stuck with the pragmatic claim of having a somewhat helpful model, useful in thinking about important aspects of the economy while missing others! Unfortunately, their rhetoric made politicians and the public think economists knew more than anyone could. It ultimately resulted in worse disillusionment with their approach than was deserved.

THIRTEEN

The Puzzle of the Golden
Age of Capitalism

In the 1950s and 1960s, sometimes called the Golden Age of capitalism, the world economy grew faster and more steadily than ever before or since. As Western Europe emerged from depression and war, growth per person surged from almost nothing to 4.1 percent a year; Asia did nearly as well.[1] U.S. and Canadian growth per person rose from 1.6 percent a year over the previous two decades to 2.5 percent a year, and Latin America did better. The implications were profound. In those years factory workers bought homes and cars and sent their children to college, and the ranks of the American middle class kept increasing. South of the border, those years came to be known as the Mexican Miracle. The lives of peasants and urban workers alike improved, and, not coincidentally, migration across the border was a relative trickle. By 1970, fewer than a million Mexican migrants resided in the United States; by 2007, nearly 12 million did.[2]

After 1973, per-capita growth slowed around the world—in North America, Western Europe, and especially Latin America. Despite the successes of the Asian tigers, even in Asia per-capita growth, on average, fell from 3.9 percent in the 1950s and 1960s to 2.9 percent a year from the 1970s through the 1990s. The slowdown, like the earlier Golden Age, meant far more to people than just data. The U.S. middle class began falling steady behind, and economic insecurity seemed to rise inexorably. More and more Mexicans found no better recourse than to pour across the border in search of jobs.

Why? The conventional view, based on the Solow model, saw the answer in faltering productivity growth. Averaging 3 percent a year in the 1950s and 1960s in the United States, it sank to barely 1 percent in the 1970s and 1980s.[3] "Why is U.S. prosperity eroding?" asked the *New York Times* editorial page. Why were foreigners investing $700 billion more in America than Americans invested abroad? Why were so many children growing up poor? The problems had one "common root," the *Times* concluded: "Productivity growth has collapsed."[4] Peter Passell, an economist writing for the *Times*, titled one column, "What Counts Is Productivity and Productivity." "The only way to raise living standards and pay for dreams like universal health care and welfare reform," he wrote, "is to increase productivity—how many cars, hamburgers and everything else Americans make per hour."[5] The prescription sounded arithmetically irrefutable. If only we could make more cars, hamburgers, and everything else per hour, we would be richer.

I have pointed out that "total factor productivity"—usually interpreted as technology-driven productivity growth—is in good part the "measure of our ignorance": it is any portion of growth that cannot be ascribed to increases in the capital stock or labor force. To what extent does it capture physical improvements in productivity—the number of cars, hamburgers, and everything else we produce per hour? Not very well, Martin Baily and several co-authors suggested in a paper published by the National Bureau of Economic Research. Standard data say that productivity in transportation—airlines, railroads, trucking—grew 3.6 percent a year from 1948 through 1972, but merely inched ahead at 0.4 percent a year from 1972 through 1986. However, physical measures of productivity (for example, in the case of airlines, passenger-miles flown per employee-hour) held up fine. In physical terms, productivity grew

3.3 percent a year from 1948 through 1972 and—not missing a beat — continued at 3.3 percent a year from 1972 through 1986.[6] More broadly, the authors found it difficult to identify a slowdown in physical measures of productivity growth after 1973 in many sectors.

Certainly, something bad began happening in the 1970s, but the data do not prove that it was widespread technological failure. Other problems might well have caused slow growth, and slow growth might have affected the usual measures of productivity. The case that something other than technological failure caused the slowdown is particularly strong for Western Europe and Japan. By the end of the 1960s, their absolute productivity levels were still less than half those of the United States, according to conventional data.[7] That is, American workers were still producing two to three times more than European and Japanese workers. Existing technology therefore should have allowed Europe and Japan vast room for improvement. Yet productivity growth in those countries declined even more than in the United States. What went wrong?

The Golden Age is one of the deepest puzzles in the history of capitalism. We are expending great effort trying to understand the various financial crises that have struck since 2008—and we should—but in some sense, they are not such a puzzle. Crises have occurred repeatedly. The two decades of the Golden Age, out of the two centuries since the industrial revolution, are the period when things seemed to work best. Why on earth did they go so well? And what pulled apart an apparently functional system?

Classical and Keynesian Stories

Both Keynesian and classical views, or at least approximations of them, have suggested ideas about the Golden Age. The Treaty of Detroit, the bargain between capital and labor that governed wages in the 1950s and 1960s, embodied a cooperative Keynesian view. "Pattern bargaining" between unionized firms and unions set wages to rise at the same rate as productivity growth (plus an adjustment for inflation); major non-unionized firms such as IBM accepted comparable raises so as not to give their workers a motive to organize; and the labor lobby pressed the U.S. Congress to pass comparable increases in the minimum wage. Moreover, government, business, and labor broadly accepted this framework *because* they agreed that wages are not just deduction from profits but also a source of demand for goods.[8] One firm might benefit from driving down the wages of its employees, cooperative Keynesianism held, but all firms together could not.

In the troubled 1970s, "supply-side" economics turned cooperative Keynesianism upside down. Supply-side theory argued for tax cuts on the grounds that they would stimulate saving, investment, and growth.[9] *Wall Street Journal* editorialist Jude Wanniski, who coined the term "supply-sider," particularly emphasized eliminating taxes on capital gains.[10] Capital gains provide the incentive to invest, the "payoff for success" in a business venture, he said.[11] Encouraged by that incentive, entrepreneurs bet on new enterprises and hire new workers, including the unemployed. In the end, the argument goes, even total tax collection rises. Supply-siders dismissed concerns about sustaining demand by appealing to Say's law: firms' profits and workers' wages provide all the demand needed to buy the goods that are produced. Wanniski had been given a copy of Marx's *Capital* by his grandfather, a Communist coal miner, and proclaimed that he saw supply-side economics as reviving classical theory from Smith through Marx, particularly in its emphasis on production rather than demand.[12]

Supply-side economics didn't quite reflect Ricardo, let alone Marx. Ricardo simply assumed that savings are invested, and never stressed a need for incentives to invest. And cooperative Keynesianism didn't quite reflect Keynes. In fact, as a concession to neoclassicals, in *The General Theory* Keynes accepted the J. B. Clark production function, which says that as employment rises, wages must fall. When the economists John Dunlop and Lorie Tarshis pointed out that as employment rises over the course of a business cycle, wages usually rise along with it, Keynes said he was happy to drop the production function.[13] His theory works more clearly without it—and in that form does possibly allow higher real wages to raise output and employment. But he did not recommend them, and his *General Theory* model would not have seen them as working.

In any case, both cooperative Keynesianism and supply-side economics capture insights about capitalism. Investors have two distinct motives to commit their savings to production. One is the assurance of ample and stable demand, hence an expectation that they can sell all the goods they may produce. The other is the assurance of a high profit share, hence the possibility of claiming a high portion of sales as their reward.

There is inherent conflict, though not outright contradiction, between these insights, the one calling for adequate wages as a share of output to sustain demand, the other calling for adequate profits as a share of output to reward investment. But just because the insights may conflict with each other does not mean that one is right and the other wrong. The conflicts reflect capitalism itself. Opposing arguments may each capture aspects of an economy that, at times, may be torn in opposite ways.

Both insights, along with others, are incorporated in a family of models picturing a possibly torn economy. They have been named by attaching various prefixes such as "neo-" and "post-" to terms such as "Keynesian," "Ricardian," "Marxian," and "Kaleckian."[14] A few years before Keynes wrote his *General Theory*, the Polish economist Michal Kalecki (pronounced Ka-LET-ski) developed the first models along these lines. Since I am not a fan of "neo" or "post," and since Kalecki had a difficult name and, besides, developed only a particular strain of these models, I prefer Lance Taylor's term "structuralist."[15]

Structuralist models offer important insights that neoclassical theory does not. Structuralists agree with Keynes that demand affects investment and growth in the long run; they are long-run Keynesians. They also agree with the classical view that the division of income among classes—capital and labor at a first cut, but more narrowly defined groups in some models—affects investment and growth in the long run. The models are "structuralist" in that they allow different economies to have essentially different structures, shaped by social convention outside of markets. They do not envision any single ideal economy from which actual economies are mere imperfect deviations.

Although political scientists and sociologists often loosely assume something along structuralist lines, structuralist models lie outside the mainstream of economics. Structuralists have not adopted the DSGE approach to modeling, and most economists do not engage with them. This lack of engagement is a loss all around, especially to those of us who simply hope to understand a little better how economies work. The structuralist approach deserves far more attention. Among other things, the most plausible accounts I know of the Golden Age are based explicitly or implicitly on it.

The Generation of 1968 Diaspora

It cannot be quite an accident that, at least in the United States, a group of economists who were studying for their Ph.D.'s and beginning their teaching careers in the late 1960s and early 1970s—that turbulent moment when the labor-friendly Treaty of Detroit was being transformed into the business-friendly Reagan revolution—should have played the central role in this structuralist project. Many came to know one another in the Harvard Economics Department. Along with others from the University of Michigan, some founded the Union for Radical Political Economics (URPE) in the weeks before protests filled the Chicago streets at the 1968 Democratic Convention.[16] Structuralist macroeconomics hadn't yet been developed, but URPE espoused a range of economic thinking outside the mainstream. Many members considered themselves Marxist, though no orthodoxy was required, and many later moved toward Keynesian thinking.

As these economists dispersed geographically, they discussed and disputed ideas with one another. Stephen Marglin, one of the youngest professors to receive tenure at Harvard, would later write an important theoretical book comparing Marxian, Keynesian, and neoclassical models. After teaching at Harvard for a decade, Samuel Bowles faced a notorious tenure battle in 1974. Several prominent economists, among them three former presidents of the American Economics Association, including the Nobel laureate Kenneth Arrow, voted for Bowles, but he lost, and left Harvard to found the Economics Department at the University of Massachusetts, Amherst. It has since become a center of structuralist macroeconomics. Herbert Gintis followed Bowles to U. Mass.

David Gordon moved to the New School, which would become another center of structuralist macroeconomics. Gordon, Bowles, and Thomas E. Weisskopf, who had all taught at Harvard, wrote a major structuralist account of the troubled 1970s and 1980s, *After the Waste Land: A Democratic Economics for the Year 2000.* Trained at Harvard, Michael Piore became a professor of economics at MIT. At a conference in 2007 organized in tribute to David Gordon, who had died a few years earlier, speakers were admonished to explain their macroeconomics models. Piore protested he didn't have one. He had proposed a model a couple of decades earlier, when, with Charles F. Sabel, he wrote a seminal work, *The Second Industrial Divide*, tracing capitalist development across decades and nations. As a member of my own thesis committee in the early 2000s, Michael Piore provided both generous intellectual support and rigorous criticism.

Skipping over other economists to avoid listing too many names, I mention Lance Taylor, whom I also studied with at MIT. Having focused on the challenges that face developing nations, he came to know the important Polish-born theorist Paul Rosenstein-Rodan, then at the Center for International Studies at MIT. The center in those days was partially funded by the CIA, and Rosenstein-Rodan appears to have been a CIA agent. Taylor recalls, "There was this amiable old guard who would let you in, but he had a gun under his desk." Rosenstein-Rodan helped Taylor get a job working for the Christian Democratic administration of Eduardo Frei in Chile. Though Marxism was approaching its zenith in Chile at the time—Frei would be succeeded by the Marxist

Salvador Allende—Taylor never was a Marxist. His views were Keynesian, but he would incorporate insights from colleagues who at one time or another considered themselves Marxist, such as David Gordon and Stephen Marglin. Taylor returned to MIT and was on the faculty until the mid-1990s, when he joined Gordon at the New School. With many colleagues and former graduate students in Latin America, he was perhaps the most important progressive economist for the region in the late twentieth century.[17]

The Unemployed

Neoclassical models allow only the possibility of "frictional" unemployment in the long run, as people enter the labor market for the first time, take time to search for better jobs, move from declining to expanding industries, or undertake additional training. Except in these situations, long-run neoclassical models assume full employment. If any others don't have a job, it's supposed to be because the going wage is too low to induce them to work, so they choose leisure over employment.

Classical models, in which social custom or class struggle outside markets determine the division of income between wages and profits, can assume full employment in the neoclassical sense or can assume almost any level of unemployment. Ricardo supposed that long-term unemployment could and did exist, including subsistence farmers essentially outside the capitalist economy, others on "outdoor" relief doing make-work jobs, or the swelling ranks of the poorhouse. But the Ricardian model can also assume full employment. Neither the existence of pools of workers who can be drawn into the formal economy nor the lack of such workers affects the customary wage, established at a level that allows a family to live in a manner that society considers decent. After the customary wages of the workforce are deducted from total output, the remainder is profit. Profits are saved and invested, determining growth.

Keynesian models, assuming that entrepreneurs' animal spirits drive growth, can also formally (if somewhat oddly, given the spirit of Keynes's own concerns) assume neoclassical full employment.[18] A full-employment Keynesian model works as follows: Animal spirits—or some institutional environment that shapes animal spirits—determine the propensity of entrepreneurs to invest: that is, how much they desire to invest out of profits. This propensity, together with their desire to save, determines the total volume of investment, output, and profits. Workers are paid what is left. If animal spirits rise, causing investment and profits to increase, inflation may simply erode real wages. This model is thus in some sense the opposite of Ricardo's. In that model, capitalists receive whatever is left after customary wages are paid. In this model, workers receive whatever is left after capitalists make their profits.

However, you cannot build a structuralist model—a model that sees wages determined by social custom (per Ricardo) and, at the same time, investment determined by animal spirits (per Keynes)—unless you assume that permanent unemployment exists, in some sense.[19] There must be a pool of surplus labor—Southern field hands moving to the American North in the 1950s and 1960s, women leaving the kitchen in the 1970s, Mexicans crossing the border by the millions, or other groups that can be incorporated into the capitalist workforce. What happens in the model if workers are fully employed and no such pool of labor can be tapped? Either the socially determined wage or animal spirits must give way. Buoyant animal spirits can raise investment and profits, triggering inflation to erode the purchasing power of workers' earnings. The real wage ceases to be determined by social custom. Alternatively, if social custom raises the real wage, it cuts into saving and investment, so animal spirits cannot operate.

Does long-term unemployment exist, in the sense that new pools of labor can more or less always be pulled into the economy? At one extreme, official U.S. unemployment exceeds 9 percent as I write this chapter; counting discouraged and underemployed workers, unemployment is around 16 percent. Pools of workers with essential skills certainly could be tapped if jobs existed. At the other extreme, in the late 1990s, after many families who had been on welfare rolls entered the workforce, official unemployment fell to a mere 4 percent. The economy was near, if not at, full employment in the neoclassical sense. But both of these unemployment rates are short-run, business cycle data. They don't answer the question of whether new pools of labor are more or less always available to be pulled into an economy.

Historically, the U.S. economy has seemingly always tapped new labor. Leaving nations from Ireland to China, immigrants poured into the country during its rapid industrialization in the late nineteenth and early twentieth centuries. Beginning in 1940, as the nation geared up production for World War II, and continuing through the rapid expansion of the 1950s and 1960s, the U.S. economy needed millions of factory workers. In the Great Migration that began in the 1940s, some five million African Americans—many of them rural subsistence workers who had been outside the reach of minimum-wage legislation and effectively outside the modern economy—flocked to the North to find better lives and fill the available jobs.[20] As this migration tapered off around 1970, the baby-boom generation swelled the workforce, and women leaving the kitchen by the millions provided a huge new pool of labor. Then came immigration, legal and illegal, from countries across Latin America. Between 1980 and 2007, nearly 10 million Mexicans alone moved across the border to the United States seeking work.[21]

These are large numbers relative to the size of the U.S. workforce, suggesting that capital can find new labor when it needs to—perhaps not immediately (there can be labor shortages in particular industries or at particular moments), but within a reasonable time. Another means of effectively enlarging the labor pool is automation, which Marx saw as allowing capitalism to generate a reserve army of the unemployed. How many telephone operators are no longer required because of computerized switching? How many gas-station attendants have been made redundant by self-service pumps?

Once you step outside advanced economies such as the United States, it's nearly impossible to miss the seas of reserve labor. Mexican official data typically show low unemployment rates—3 percent in good times, 6 percent in bad—but all they really say is that everybody has a *chambita*, some little job to help them get by. Even outside the ranks of impoverished peasants and migrant farmworkers, about half the labor force is classified as belonging to the informal sector.[22] It is a nebulous category. Some workers pay no taxes and receive no benefits; others pay some taxes and receive some benefits. They range from children selling Chiclets on the street to profitable small-time entrepreneurs. But most would leap at jobs in the modern capitalist economy, where even in Mexico they would have job security, receive medical care, and get retirement benefits.

The surplus unemployed in developing nations—and Mexico is a middle-income, not a low-income, nation—affect the U.S. economy, as well as their own. If you can't bring Mohammad to the mountain, bring the mountain to Mohammad. If the United States should succeed in shutting down its borders—if labor could no longer be sent to this country—then this country could send capital to Mexico or China or India, and the goods could be sent back. This is an equally effective means to tap pools of labor. One way or another—through immigration, labor-saving technology, outsourcing, overseas investment, and other devices—in the long run, the economy will find pools of labor.

Structuralist Pictures of Economies

Structuralist models ask how the structure of economies, determined in good part by social convention or political decisions outside of markets, affects economic trajectories. One element of the structuralist picture depends on a socially determined division of output. What percent of total output goes to wages (the *wage share*) and what percent goes to profits (the *profit share*)?[23] Does a high wage share strengthen growth, providing demand and sustaining investment and employment? Or does it weaken growth, cutting into profits and undermining investment and employment? Structuralist models see the answer as depending on circumstances. Economies can be *wage-led*, in which case a higher wage share increases production and employment, or they can be *profit-led*, in which case a higher profit share increases production and employment.

Why would one economy be wage-led and another profit-led?[24] One factor is openness to trade. A more open economy is more likely to be profit-led. For example, U.S. unions saw the economy as wage-led in the 1950s and 1960s surely in part because it depended little on trade, so higher wages supported demand for domestic producers. By contrast, labor unions in small European countries highly dependent on trade (such as Sweden, Norway, and Denmark) explicitly understood the need to control wages in order to sustain exports.[25] In effect, they saw the economy as profit-led. As the average level of imports around the world rose from 14 percent in 1970 to 29 percent in 2008, many economies may have moved toward being profit-led.[26] Another, no less important factor in determining whether an economy is wage-led or profit-led is the difference between the saving rates of capitalists (essentially businesses' retained profits) and workers. If savings out of profits are substantially higher than savings out of wages, the economy is more likely to be wage-led.[27] If the saving rates are similar, the economy is more likely to be profit-led. You can see why this relationship might hold by thinking of what would happen if workers saved a large portion of their earnings. In this case, higher wages would largely flow into bank accounts or other financial instruments, rather than generating demand for goods.

Profit-led and wage-led economies behave differently on a number of dimensions. One dimension is the effect of higher productivity growth from technological innovation. In a strongly profit-led economy, it will raise both growth and employment; in a weakly profit-led economy— a category that may include many advanced economies—it will raise growth but *reduce* employment.[28] Another dimension is the effect of a currency crash. As the value of the currency falls in a wage-led economy, real wages and growth decrease. Mexico appears to have been wage-led from the 1970s through the early 1990s, when it suffered repeated currency crashes, which sometimes devastated the economy. As the value of the currency falls in a profit-led economy, wages also decline, but growth increases. Britain was probably profit-led when the pound crashed in 1992, and the economy proceeded to do splendidly. However, the difference between the two countries surely also stemmed from the fact that Mexico owed debts in U.S. dollars and could not print dollars, while Britain owed debts in pounds and could print pounds.

What happens in a structuralist model if an economy or a sector reaches absolute capacity and cannot produce more? Perhaps agriculture in a developing country cannot grow enough food. Effective demand clearly cannot determine real output: no matter what the demand may be, output will not rise. If demand is strong, inflation will set in. A likely scenario is that inflation will erode wages, and (as in the situation mentioned above of full employment) wages will cease to be socially determined.[29] Indeed, if the government tried to redistribute income—say, by taxing profits and using the revenue to make social-security payments to workers—the effort would backfire. The real wage could fall even further.[30] Populist regimes in Latin American have run into this problem.

Structuralist models consider a second distinction that helps to illuminate the disagreements between supply-siders, who seem to favor profit-led models, and cooperative Keynesians, who seem to favor wage-led models. The profit *share*, as already mentioned, is the percentage of total income that firms receive as profits. The profit *rate* is firms' return on their investment—the profits they receive as a percentage of the value of their capital stock. A firm can increase its profit rate either by securing a higher profit share or by increasing sales. For example, suppose an automaker has plant and machinery worth $10 billion. It earns $1,000 in profit per car (after paying labor and other input costs) and sells 10 million cars, for a total of $1 billion in profits. Its profit rate is 10 percent. Now suppose it cuts wage costs by $500 per car, earning $1,500 per car while still selling 10 million cars. It makes $1.5 billion in profits, for a profit rate of 15 percent. Alternatively, suppose higher demand allows it to sell 15 million cars, but without cutting wage costs, so it still earns $1,000 per car. Again, it makes a total of $1.5 billion in profits, and again its profit rate is 15 percent.

In principle, firms should care about the profit rate, and future investment should depend on the profit rate—or rather, the expected profit rate. A supply-sider underlines the effect of the profit share: other things being equal (demand and sales), a higher share increases the profit rate and supports investment. A cooperative Keynesian underlines the role of demand and sales: other things being equal (namely, the profit share), higher demand and sales increase the profit rate and support investment. Structuralist models can depict either view as correct, depending on the circumstances.

The End of the Golden Age

Models are one thing, history another, as Joan Robinson insisted. Even relatively open-ended structuralist models are satisfyingly tidy, compared with history. Economic history is compounded of models that may or may not be identifiable, policy decisions that could have gone any one of several ways, and plenty of sheer accidents. An economic model provides a good start if it can at least help us to understand history.

Explanations of the Golden Age have been based on various structuralist models. In *The Second Industrial Divide,* Michael Piore and Charles Sabel tell the story—in fact, an epic story—of capitalism since the Industrial Revolution, based on what I interpret as a wage-led structuralist model, or, in other words, a cooperative Keynesian model. Since formal structuralist models were developed after they wrote the book, I may be reading the model into their words. But Piore spells it out quite clearly in an MIT working paper. Capitalism inherently drives industry to pursue technical and managerial innovation, expanding its productive potential.[31] But capitalism is not inherently capable of sustaining demand to absorb all the goods that that productive potential could make. Unless some institutional framework supports consumer demand and reduces uncertainty so that firms are confident they can sell goods they produce, the economy falters. *"The central growth problem in a capitalist economy,"* Piore writes in italics, *"becomes that of how to organize demand so that the required expansion is assured."*[32] In *The Second Industrial Divide*, Piore and Sabel argue that "an economy in which decisions about saving and investment are made privately can fall into an underconsumption trap: demand will not absorb the output of aggregate productive capacity; output will fall; and no automatic mechanism will restore economic activity to its previous level."[33]

Diverse political arrangements across nations came to support a similar wage-led structuralist growth model, Piore and Sabel argue. In the United States, a set of customs and regulations emerged from initiatives and counter-initiatives during the Depression, World War II, and labor struggles of the late 1940s.[34] The policy of raising wages in line with productivity (plus inflation) in order to sustain demand came to be supported by unions, promoted in Congress to justify minimum-wage increases, and ratified in guidelines issued by the President's Council of Economic Advisors.[35] Keynesian fiscal and monetary management did not wait for President John F. Kennedy's high-powered academic advisors in the 1960s; it began in 1954, when the Eisenhower administration lowered interest rates and cut taxes to counter a recession.[36]

Piore and Sabel explain the crisis of the 1970s in two ways. They explain it, first, as resulting from a breakdown in the structure of the 1950s and 1960s economy; second, as resulting from a series of accidents, such as oil crises and the policy errors made in response to them.[37] They agree that both explanations could well have some element of truth.

The structure of the economy undermined its own prosperity, Piore and Sabel argue, partly because it depended on mass consumption of mass-produced goods, and consumer markets became saturated.[38] At a certain point, consumers had enough cars, televisions, and telephones, so demand faltered. This idea seems questionable; indeed, Piore and Sabel themselves raise questions about it after proposing it. If consumers have one car (or television) and money to spare, they will buy a fancier model or a second car (or TV). If nobody needs more plain old telephones, manufacturers will develop—and consumers will buy, if they have money—cordless phones, cell phones, and smart phones, all equally mass-manufactured. More plausibly, to my mind, Piore and Sabel also argue that steady trade expansion, integral to the 1950s and 1960s economic structure, undermined demand management. U.S.-manufactured imports increased from 5 percent of GDP in 1965 to 13 percent in 1980; French imports, from 12 percent of GDP in 1965 to 20 percent. And the pattern elsewhere was similar.[39] A rising share of these imports came from developing nations, where wages were inadequate for workers to buy the goods they made. "Sooner or later, therefore, a shortfall in demand would occur," Piore and Sable argue.[40]

Piore and Sabel also point to accidents and policy errors that undermined demand. First came the protests of the late 1960s and early 1970s—not only demonstrations that shook cities from Paris to Chicago, but also labor unrest, from a wave of European plant-level strikes to the "Industrial Woodstock" wildcat strike at GM's Lordstown plant. As firms raised salaries and extended benefits, inflation increased. Worse, uncertainty increased, undermining business confidence. But capital brought in new sources of workers—immigrants, guest-workers, women—and labor relations settled down.

Next, in 1971 President Richard M. Nixon abandoned the Bretton Woods exchange-rate system that had served well for two decades, fixing the parities of currencies against the dollar but allowing orderly realignment if a nation became uncompetitive. No doubt Bretton Woods ran into inevitable problems. As nations recovering from the war became more competitive and exported more goods to the United States, gold flowed out of Fort Knox to pay for U.S. imports. However, Piore and Sabel argue, the stabilizing Bretton Woods order could have been reformed. Instead, it was jettisoned and replaced with the disorder of floating exchange rates. Far from aligning currencies to nations' real productivity, gyrating exchange rates held nations hostage to currency speculation. In a world increasingly open to trade, firms lost their ability to predict the prices of inputs that they imported or the sales that they exported. Investor confidence eroded.

The two energy crises not only raised input costs, a problem that could have been managed in time, but aggravated uncertainty and undermined animal spirits. Everybody knew oil was running out, or else it wasn't. Automakers started making high-mileage cars, then reverted to making gas guzzlers as oil prices fell, then were hit by another oil shock.

Despite everything, Keynesian responses persisted—as Nixon famously said, "We are all Keynesians now"—and seemed to be working by the late 1970s, Piore and Sabel argue. But the 1979 oil crisis was more shock than policymakers or the public could take. As inflation rose and the dollar slid, the Federal Reserve tripled interest rates, jacking up the prime rate from 6.8 percent in 1979 to 18.9 percent in 1981, and the real interest rate (discounting inflation) from near zero to almost 10 percent.[41] Margaret Thatcher and Ronald Reagan took power, choked off inflation at the cost of precipitating the worst unemployment since the 1930s, broke unions, and ended the Keynesian order.

Did the Keynesian order have to end? Piore and Sabel aren't so sure. "Is it hopelessly farfetched to imagine," they ask, "that if the Iranian revolution and the second oil shock had occurred five years later than they did, [Keynesian] policies of the late 1970s could have produced a halfdecade of prosperity—and given world leaders the time, confidence, and resources to create international financial mechanisms for balancing supply and demand?"[42]

Aside from telling a fascinating and subtle economic history, this account is attractive. It makes the case that, at some essential level, capitalism need not be an arena of conflict. If only the economy is intelligently—or perhaps fortuitously—managed, responsible capital can collaborate with labor; workers can earn good wages while firms earn good profits. Moreover, the argument is convincing piece by piece—except, to my mind, the piece about the exhaustion of mass-consumption markets, but it is dispensable. The question is whether Piore and Sable start out with the right model.

Two essays in a 1990 volume, *The Golden Age of Capitalism*, propose a structuralist account that differs from Piore and Sabel's. If I may simplify an argument that I find too intricate, Stephen Marglin of Harvard and Amit Bhaduri of Jawaharlal Nehru University in New Delhi see the wage-led economy of the 1950s and 1960s as turning profit-led in about 1970.[43] An empirical chapter by the late Andrew Glyn of Oxford and several co-authors does not lay out an explicit model but broadly concurs.[44]

The *Golden Age* essays start their account in the immediate aftermath of World War II, underlining the widespread suppression of militant labor unions—suppression that ensured high profit shares in the advanced nations.[45] In the United States, General Motors broke a 1947 strike in which the United Auto Workers (UAW) demanded a 30 percent raise, shorter hours, a freeze on car prices, and more control over work organization. Only in 1948 did the company sign the far milder Treaty of Detroit with a chastened union.[46] This pattern was emblematic of U.S. labor relations at the time: before later reaching accords, firms crushed grassroots strikes, often using anti-Communism as a weapon. Individuals on the Hollywood blacklist, accused of being Communist and denied jobs, gained more fame, but many labor leaders met similar fates. The Marshall Plan helped to rebuild Europe but, except in the United Kingdom and Scandinavia, it also supported conservative governments and waged anti-Communist campaigns, defeating militant unions, blocking wage increases, and quashing inflation.[47] These events ensured profit shares of 24 percent in the United States and 25 percent on average across the advanced nations.[48]

The *Golden Age* essays underline the role of these events in their economic model. By 1950, Marglin and Bhaduri argue, firms no longer needed to worry about raising profit shares, since these were already so high, but memories of the Depression gave firms every reason to worry about selling output. The United States therefore appeared to be a cooperative Keynesian, or wage-led, economy. A stable real wage, rising in line with productivity growth, along with government spending and interest-rate policies to mitigate recessions, was more than acceptable to business.[49] But as the prosperous 1950s and 1960s continued, and firms felt confident in their ability to sell goods, they may well have begun to turn their attention to the additional profits they could make if they could push up profit shares. At this point, in capitalists' expectations—and expectations count just as much in structuralist models as in Keynes's model—prospects of a higher profit share might well have done more than prospects of stronger sales to support investment. The wage-led regime may have turned profit-led.[50]

This story about shifting regimes is rather speculative. Since wage and profit shares remained quite stable through the 1950s and 1960s, it seems impossible to tell from the data what might have happened had those shares changed. The regime could have been wage-led, in that if the wage share had risen, output would have risen along with it. Or the regime could have been profit-led all along, in that if the profit share had risen, output would have risen.[51] Absent significant changes in the division of income—after all, the rules called for wages to rise in line with productivity, not faster, not slower—who knows what would have happened in some alternative world? In any case, the economy found a sweet spot, hardly budged from it, and did splendidly.

But if structuralist models have any validity, there is one regime that could *not* fit the advanced economies after the late 1960s: Piore and Sabel's wage-led, or cooperative Keynesian, model. The problem is that the profit *share* fell, and the profit *rate* fell along with it. Those two developments simply cannot occur together in a cooperative Keynesian model.[52] In this model, if the profit share falls—or the wage share rises—no serious problem results: the profit rate must still rise. But it did not. Thus, either a wage-led regime must have turned profit-led, or the regime was profit-led all along.

One of these possibilities outlined in the *Golden Age* essays must be the case if the data are even approximately right. In the United States, the profit share of national income barely moved during the Golden Age, from 24 percent of GDP in 1951 to 23 percent of GDP in 1965. Given how crude macro data are, that is no evident change at all. But by the early 1970s, the profit share distinctly fell to 16 or 17 percent of GDP, and by the early 1980s it had fallen to about 15 percent of GDP.[53] Meanwhile, the profit rate slid drastically. It declined from 18 or 20 percent in the mid-1960s to 12 or 13 percent in the early 1970s, and plummeted to 9 or 10 percent in the early 1980s.[54] These are significant numbers. Even if they are somewhat off, as macroeconomic data often are, the pattern seems definitive.

The story was essentially the same across the advanced nations, and more drastic in the emblematic manufacturing sector. Across the advanced nations, the profit share sank from 23 percent of GDP in the late 1960s to barely 12 percent in the 1973–1975 recession, then clawed its way back up to 15 percent of GDP in the recovery of 1975–1979.[55] The profit rate plummeted from 22 percent in late 1960s to only 9 percent in 1973–1975, then merely inched back to 11 percent in 1975–1979.

Why did the profit share fall? Profits were squeezed by the obvious culprit of high energy prices and the less obvious culprit of poor productivity growth. I've expended enough words arguing that it's difficult to know what productivity data mean and whether poor economic growth causes poor productivity growth (as Piore and Sabel tend to argue and as I tend to believe), or vice versa. But there was something to the pervasive slowdown seen in standard productivity data. Perhaps part of the problem lay in the management of production, as Glyn and his co-authors argue. Workers resented and fought Fordist methods attempting to control the pace of work. Harvard Business School professor Richard Walton ratified this argument in the *Harvard Business Review:* "Especially in a high-wage country like the United States, market success depends on a superior level of performance, a level that, in return, requires the deep commitment, not merely the obedience—if you could obtain it—of workers. And as painful experience shows, this commitment cannot flourish in a workplace dominated by the familiar model of control."[56] The fact that workers will register protest by "working to rule"—which invariably slows rather than raises production—shows how much productivity depends on their informal effort.[57]

Despite these problems, the profit share could fall only if labor had more leverage to raise wages than firms had to raise prices. After all, the profit share depends only on the portion of production that firms can claim as profits. On the one hand, Glyn and his co-authors argue, labor militancy in the late 1960s and early 1970s won workers contracts that explicitly indexed wages to the cost of living. On the other hand, as trade shares and competitive pressures increased, firms lost some of the market power that had allowed them to raise prices in parallel with wages.[58]

Using a cooperative wage-led model, Piore and Sabel argue that there was at least the possibility of rescuing the international Keynesian regime until 1980, when the politics of Thatcherism and Reaganomics, emboldened by the second oil shock, decisively ended it. Based on a profit-led model, the *Golden Age* essays tell a darker account of how things started unraveling by about 1970. The decline in the profit share had already started eroding output, employment, and growth in the late 1960s.[59]

Reagan and Thatcher's policies, in Piore and Sabel's account, were essentially an error provoked by the second oil shock and by ideology. These policies gain some logic in the *Golden Age* account, as conservative leaders responded to business constituencies that had seen the profit share erode. Moreover, unless the data are grossly wrong, the model had to be profit-led in the 1970s, so eroding profit shares undermined investment and growth.[60] You don't want to bet on there being much economic logic behind any political regime change, but compromise in a capitalist economy seems tougher than a cooperative Keynesian model would have it.

What Now?

One lesson from these stories of the Golden Age is that today's cooperative Keynesians—such as former labor secretary Robert Reich—who propose raising wages to strengthen the economy, have probably way overstated their case. My caution is not about short-term stimulus. I agree that the federal government should support demand during a recession by building infrastructure, by sharing funds with states to employ teachers and police officers, and perhaps by cutting taxes for the middle class. (I would rather see investment in infrastructure or sustainable energy, since it supports long-run growth. Also, tax cuts may be saved rather than spent.) A structuralist model concurs with a short-run Keynesian model that such support for aggregate demand in a recession can boost output and employment.[61] But a profit-led structuralist model urges caution about raising the wage share.

Reich doesn't see any need for such caution. "The real problem has to do with the structure of the economy, not the business cycle," he declares, calling for higher wages and other measures to "spur the economy":

> This crisis began decades ago when a new wave of technology—things like satellite communications, container ships, computers and eventually the Internet—made it cheaper for American employers to use low-wage labor abroad or labor-replacing software here at home than to continue paying the typical worker at a middle-class wage. Even

though the American economy kept growing, hourly wages flattened. The median male worker earns less today, adjusted for inflation, than he did 30 years ago. . . . [C]onsumers no longer have the purchasing power to buy the goods and services they produce as workers; for some time now, their means haven't kept up with what the growing economy could and should have been able to provide them.[62]

The story sounds good. But Reich must be thinking of a long-run structuralist model—a neoclassical long-run model says that higher real wages reduce employment—and he doesn't even seem aware that such a model might be profit-led. The U.S. economy has certainly seemed profit-led since the 1970s, when the Golden Age ended. Things might have changed. But it behooves pundits to consider what the economy actually looks like before they push advice. The kind of economy Reich himself describes, where employers can readily offshore jobs, is rather likely to be profit-led. He should not be so confident that higher wages will increase employment or growth. At the same time, structuralist models do not suggest that perpetuating extremes of income inequality—the vast disparity in wages between top corporate officials and other workers—does any good.

FOURTEEN

Economies in Crisis

When Truman Bewley of Yale was doing interviews during the 1990s to try to learn why wages don't fall during recessions—a "stickiness" blamed for causing unemployment—several colleagues asked him why he was even bothering, since there wouldn't be another recession.[1] By the late 1990s, many economists began to think the economy had entered what would they would dub the "Great Moderation," a pronounced softening of business cycles.[2] In January 2000, three months before the technology-weighted NASDAQ index began its precipitous plunge, the President's Council of Economics Advisors declared not only that the economy still appeared "young and vibrant," but that it saw no real reason—other than unfortunate accidents—why expansions might not continue indefinitely:

> Studies find no compelling evidence that postwar expansions possess an inherent tendency to die of old age. Instead, they appear to fall victim to specific events related to economic disturbances or government policies. For instance, the Iraqi invasion of Kuwait, which led to a doubling of oil prices in the fall of 1990, contributed to the decline

in economic activity during the recession of 1990–91. American consumers, having suffered through the tripling of oil prices in 1973–74 and their subsequent doubling in 1979, anticipated negative repercussions on the U.S. economy, and consumer confidence declined sharply and consumption fell.[3]

The fact that the council proved to be wrong—since many people are wrong about economies much of the time—is less interesting than the *way* it was wrong. Its misguided prediction shows how the council, and the economic mainstream it represented, was *thinking* about the economy. Shocks might hit an economy from outside markets, but markets shape an inherently stable economy. This picture could hardly have been further off the mark. In fact, the bursting of a bubble driven by financial markets themselves caused the next recession. The NASDAQ index plunged from 5,049 on March 10, 2000, to 1,695 on September 10, 2001, a day before the external shock of the September 11 terrorist attacks.[4] It continued to fall after 9/11, but not by a much smaller percentage, to a nadir of 1,114 on October 9, 2002.

Economists did not learn their lesson. Their belief in the Great Moderation swelled into a whole subfield of macroeconomics. Both DSGE macroeconomic models used by central banks to manage interest rates and standard financial models rested on the implausible assumption that market economies are led as if by an invisible hand to equilibrium. As discussed, this is pure assumption. No model of decentralized market trading by diverse utility-maximizing individuals and of production by different profit-maximizing firms has shown how an economy would be led toward equilibrium. It gets worse. Stripped of external shocks, DSGE models reduce to the so-called Ramsey model, proposed as a curiosity by Keynes's friend Frank Ramsey in 1928. It has so-called "saddle-path" stability, which really means no stability at all.[5] A saddle provides an analogy to the economy's stability problem. Imagine distorting the saddle so that the line connecting front to back is sinuous. Roll a marble along that line. If it veers off on one side, consumption explodes, capital sinks to zero, and the representative agent presumably starves. If the marble veers off on the other side, capital explodes, consumption sinks to zero, and the representative agent presumably starves. So-called stability depends on the assumption that the representative agent is so far-sighted and his or her calculations so infallible, that no such catastrophe occurs. Admittedly, if you make that incredible assumption, the mathematics guiding the economy for all eternity is fascinating.

The problem with DSGE and financial models isn't just that they failed to predict the 2008 crisis. It is that, by depicting an economy as always snapping back to equilibrium, they provided false confidence that no crisis would occur. The Federal Reserve focused nearly all its efforts on targeting inflation at around 2 percent a year. Regulatory laws could be relaxed, since we had entered a period of Great Moderation. The U.S. foreign deficit, incurred as the country borrowed half a trillion dollars a year from abroad, was just a solution to the global savings glut. Of course, if the models were good representations of the economy, why hadn't they indicated the Great Moderation earlier? Why had periodic crises shaken economies since the dawn of capitalism? Was the cause really, as Milton Friedman argued, just wrongheaded central-bank policies? Was it just bad luck—the fact that larger external shocks had hit economies in the past? Or was it, to quote a canonical article on the question, that a formerly antiquated financial sector had failed to "facilitate intertemporal smoothing of consumption and investment"?[6] Seriously, economists asked this question. Few asked whether the models might have been flawed.

Some economists, paying little attention to the usual models, did fear that the U.S. economy was headed toward serious trouble in the 2000s. Wynne Godley argued for a decade, in a series of articles for the Levy Economics Institute of Bard College, that the rising trend of household borrowing was unsustainable.[7] The closest thing to a forecast of the U.S.

housing and financial bubble I have seen is the "Fact Sheet" that Dean Baker of the Center for Economic and Policy Research wrote in July 2005.[8] Nevertheless, I don't know of a model that can predict crises—what will happen and when. Anyone who had such a model prior to 2008 should be rich by now. Asset prices rise slowly but plunge fast. Shorting an asset is a quick and legal way to make money, *if* you are right.

For an example of what I mean when I say that models can't predict a crisis, take Nouriel Roubini of New York University, who is often said to have predicted the financial crisis. To his credit, he did warn that bad things would happen, but he seems less prescient if you ask what bad things he predicted and when. In 2005, surveying the massive U.S. foreign deficit, he said that within a year or two we might see "a sharp fall in the value of the US dollar, a rapid increase in US long-term interest rates, and a sharp fall in the price of a range of risk assets, including equities and housing."[9] He emphasized the fall in the dollar and the rise in interest rates. Those things did not happen. (True confession: I thought they might happen, too.) He included the fall in housing prices almost as an afterthought. Of course, housing prices drove the crash. As they did, the dollar rose against most currencies rather than falling, and interest rates on U.S. Treasury bonds fell almost to zero. The story is not over. The dollar could still plunge, and Roubini could turn out to be right, but it would be a decade late. You don't make money by shorting an asset ten years too early.

As long as you don't expect models to play Merlin, some can illuminate recurring stories of business cycles and economic crises. Good models need to start from the premise that these are not mere epiphenomena, not just accidents impinging on inherently stable economies. Rather, business and asset-price cycles are driven by destabilizing forces inherent in markets. "Cycles" is, of course, too tame a word for what occurs, but yet again I bow to convention and use it. Good models should show how markets themselves can generate these cycles.

An Insightful Contradiction

The Arrow-Debreu and Fisher general-equilibrium models discussed earlier certainly point to the generic problem of market instability, but in 1983 Douglas Diamond of the University of Chicago and Philip Dybvig of Yale published what is perhaps the canonical mainstream model describing how a banking crisis might occur.[10] It is skeletal—it misses numerous elements of the 2008 banking crisis—but provides important insights.

Diamond and Dybvig developed the first model incorporating a bank. What is a bank? It performs what they call "asset transformation." It takes in short-term funds through checking or saving accounts, and uses them to make long-term loans that firms can use for investment. This valuable service, on the one hand, provides customers with access to cash, and, on the other hand, provides firms with stable financing.

The model makes some wildly optimistic assumptions. First, it is a rational-expectations model: actors in the model understand it and use that understanding to maximize utility. The model assumes that bank loans are invested in a completely riskless technology, guaranteed to pay a high return after, say, two years. It assumes that the portion of customers who on average will need their funds back early to meet unexpected contingencies is known—say, a third. The bank maintains more-than-adequate reserves, so these customers can withdraw funds early and still earn a modest return, while those who leave funds in their accounts for two full years earn a large return.

Despite these rosy assumptions, the bank is vulnerable. This rational-expectations model does *not* assume that the economy gravitates toward a unique equilibrium. There is a good equilibrium, in which the bank returns funds to customers who need them early but retains adequate deposits to finance its investment for the full two years. There is a bad equilibrium, in which so many depositors demand their funds early that the bank is depleted of adequate deposits to finance its investment for the full two years. Since it can recover its principal and interest only after the two years are up, it fails.

If the bank has adequate reserves, over and above needed deposits, to return funds to the third of its customers who have an emergency and need them early, how can it fail? Although the rational-expectations approach assumes that depositors understand the model, they cannot read one another's minds. They have "asymmetric" information—that is, I don't know what you're thinking, and vice versa. If I see you going to the bank to withdraw funds, I don't know if you're among the third of depositors who need their money for unexpected contingencies or if you suddenly suspect a run and want to get your money out before the bank is depleted. Fearing the worst, when I see you going to the bank, I withdraw my money even though I have no emergency requiring it. In this situation, mere fear that the bank may fail—fear itself, not fundamental problems with the bank's loans—can impel rational depositors to withdraw funds and cause the bank to fail.[11] Asset transformation, the very function that defines a bank, itself makes the bank vulnerable.

If the government insures the bank, it prevents a run by quelling fear. It therefore improves on the best outcome private markets could achieve.[12] Diamond and Dybvig show that even *if* rational expectations are assumed, and even *if* investments are riskless, a bank run can occur. The danger would simply be worse in the absence of those assumptions. Diamond and Dybvig make a powerful argument for federal deposit insurance.

However, their argument raises questions. Another rational-expectations model notices that Wall Street doesn't always invest in riskless technologies; sometimes, to couch it in a technical phrase, Wall Street invests in toxic assets. John Kareken of the University of Minnesota and Neil Wallace of the Federal Reserve Bank of Minneapolis published a model in 1978 capturing this problem.[13] In their model, banks don't perform asset transformation; the funds they borrow and the loans they make have the same maturity. The only justification I see for this unrealistic assumption is that in 1978 no one had yet figured out how to model asset transformation; but regardless, their model has something to it. Very like real banks, Kareken and Wallace's banks make a portfolio of risky investments that on average produce a high expected return but can end in bankruptcy. In this context, government insurance creates "moral hazard." If the government does *not* insure banks in the model, the depositors insist that the banks hold adequate reserves to cover potential losses, and banks don't fail. If the government does insure the banks, lenders don't bother to monitor them, since they know they will get their money back in any case, and the banks do fail.

From one angle, the models seem contradictory. In Diamond and Dybvig, providing government deposit insurance prevents bank failures, while in Kareken and Wallace, eliminating government insurance prevents bank failures. Different conclusions result from different assumptions. Since Kareken and Wallace's banks don't do asset transformation, there is no essential need for deposit insurance—and sure enough, it turns out to be a bad idea. Since Diamond and Dybvig's banks always make riskless investments, there's no potential for moral hazard—and sure enough, it doesn't arise.

From another angle, you can see both models at work in 2008. On September 15, with something like Kareken and Wallace in mind, Treasury and the Fed let Lehman Brothers fail, in order to warn markets that moral hazard may have its consequences: if you lend to financial institutions, you had better police them or you can lose your money.[14] On September 16, the Diamond and Dybvig model asserted itself. If creditors merely fear a run on a bank—or on a financial institution such as AIG—they may withdraw funds, causing a run. Financial markets froze up around the world. Now Treasury and the Fed had to provide government insurance to allay fear and avert systemic disaster. They spent $170 billion just bailing out AIG and its creditors.

Put the two models together and you get a picture of a contradiction at the heart of capitalism. It is politely called the Bagehot problem, after

Walter Bagehot, the nineteenth-century editor of the London *Economist* who articulated it. Regulators want major financial institutions to believe they will be allowed to fail if they get into trouble—but when they do get into trouble, regulators must bail them out, in order to stop self-reinforcing panic. Saving capitalism from itself depends on finessing a grand contradiction.

A Minsky Moment?

Since the press dubbed the 2008 financial crisis a "Minsky moment," a look at Hyman Minsky's financial-instability hypothesis seems in order. He was a Keynesian who taught at Washington University in St. Louis during the 1970s and 1980s, sat on a bank board, and had a fine knowledge of financial markets. His hypothesis shows how markets themselves produce bubbles and crises, booms and busts. I see two problems with his model in this context. One is that I can't quite figure it out. Reading Minsky, I find fascinating ideas that are sometimes spelled out in equations but don't seem to add up to a model. Though sympathetic to him, I share this criticism with economists who are unsympathetic to him. This criticism can be answered: Lance Taylor developed a model that captures the essence of what Minsky seems to say. When I reread Minsky with this model in mind, his story falls into place. Another problem—not Minsky's fault—is that his model describes economic forces that could well come into play but that did not actually come into play in the 2008 crisis.[15] The press was so delighted to discover the idea that markets themselves could drive crises, that it forgot to consider what Minsky actually said.

Minsky divides firms into three categories: "hedge" firms, "speculative" firms, and "Ponzi" firms. Back in the day when "hedging" meant reducing financial risk—before it became a euphemism for making financial bets—Minsky referred to hedge firms as those that can always expect positive cash flows in the following sense: if the broader economy continues more or less on track, within each month or quarter they can project that their gross profits will exceed their financial commitments to pay principal and interest on loans.[16] Speculative firms expect negative cash flows in this sense for several months or quarters, as gross profits fall short of financial commitments and they depend on loans; but soon they can expect the situation to reverse so that they receive positive cash flows. Ponzi firms, named after the infamous swindler Charles Ponzi, who started a financial chain letter and ended up in jail, expect negative cash flows in this sense for a long period but hope for positive cash flow in some distant future. Minsky argues that, as a boom gets underway, firms at first voluntarily move from hedge toward speculative toward Ponzi, increasing their leverage in order to boost profits, and then later are pushed further in that direction by developments in the financial sector. Minsky draws on Keynes to describe enthusiasms within the financial sector that sustain this process far longer than one might ever expect, until it brings the economy down.

Although Minsky applies financial metaphors in naming hedge, speculative, and Ponzi firms, he is talking about firms in the real economy, such as manufacturing or software development, not primarily financial firms. Ponzi financial relations, Minsky agrees, "are much more widespread than the label I give them. . . . Ponzi finance characterizes any investment program with a significant gestation period."[17] In short, when Boeing bet on a new airliner, knowing it wouldn't break even for a dozen years, it was a Ponzi firm in Minsky's sense, even if the connotation seems wrong.

I don't mind Minsky's applying the term "Ponzi" broadly, but his argument doesn't explain the 2008 crisis. It describes interactions between the financial sector and the real economy that push firms in the real economy—like Boeing—toward "Ponzi" finance and bring the economy down. Before the crisis, few firms in the real sector did seem to be pushed toward Ponzi finance. There was no obvious proliferation of MCI WorldComs piling up debt. Rather, the crisis erupted within the financial sector. Only after the sector crashed did it bring the real economy down. Indeed, long after finance turned fragile, the Fed made the bad mistake of continuing to doubt that it would affect the real economy.[18]

Predator and Prey

A model from ecology describing how predator and prey species proliferate and subside provides a basis for several structuralist models depicting how inherent interactions among markets can cause booms and busts, bubbles and crises.[19] In the ecology model, there are predators, such as wildcats, and prey, such as hares. Sometimes these models predict fluctuations of these populations rather well—as well as other interactions such as those between consumers and resources, or between parasites and hosts—and sometimes they predict rather badly.[20] In one experiment, carnivorous predator mites were housed in a container where they could prey on vegetarian mites.[21] In the first trial, the vegetarian mites multiplied as they fed on oranges, but the carnivores fed on them until both populations just went extinct. In another trial, the same types of mites were housed in a more complex environment with barriers and hiding places. The populations rose and fell in ongoing cycles, as the model predicts. The environment outside a formal model can really matter.

The predator-prey model requires distinguishing among three things: the population *level* (the number of hares), the population *growth* (the increase in the *number* of hares per year), and the population growth *rate* (the *percentage* increase in the hare population per year). Populations are assumed to grow at a steady percentage growth *rate* if they have adequate food and are affected by no other factors such as predators. For example, microbes in a Petri dish of nutrients grow more or less at a steady rate—until they exhaust the nutrients and die.

If a population grows at a steady percentage rate, its level will increase exponentially. For example, if each family has several children who survive to adulthood, as is often the case during eras of rapid industrialization, the human population might grow at a steady rate of 3 percent a year. At that rate, the population doubles in about twenty-three years. Malthus's great concern was that that the English population would grow at such a steady rate, exhausting food supplies.

The relationship between population level and population growth per year is key to the predator-prey model. Given a steady growth rate, the higher the population *level* at the beginning of the year, the higher the numerical population *growth* per year. For example, suppose the growth rate of the hare population would be 50 percent per year if there were inexhaustible food supplies (hares reproduce a lot faster than humans). If the population level is 100 hares the first year, population growth will be 50 hares per year. When the population level reaches 150 hares the second year, population growth will be 75 hares per year. When the population level reaches about 760 hares the sixth year, population growth will be about 380 hares per year.

Now back to the predator-prey model—and remember, it's just a model. Sometimes it describes actual dynamics well, and sometimes badly, so follow the logic of the model and don't be distracted by elements that may seem unrealistic. The model describes relationships between, on the one hand, the *level* of the hare and wildcat populations (the number of hares or wildcats at the beginning of the year), and, on the other hand, the *growth* of the hare and wildcat populations (the increase or decrease in the number of hares or wildcats during the year). These relationships are specified in equations, but can be stated perfectly well in words. The key point is to consider distinct relationships one at a time. How would the hares be doing if, at some moment, they were the only thing in the picture? How would the wildcats be doing if, at some moment, they had a given hare population to prey on? The model combines these distinct relationships into an overall picture of population dynamics.

Start with the hares. They are assumed to have enough food to enable them to grow at a steady rate, so that their numbers increase exponentially. Obviously, if they continued at this rate for very long, they would exhaust their food supply. However, in the model, they never do continue long enough to exhaust their food, because the wildcats reduce the hare population first. Thus, in the model, at any moment, the hare population is always small enough so the food supply does not limit its growth. If the wildcats temporarily disappeared from the scene, hares would have enough food to grow at a steady rate for a time. Thus, the larger the population *level* of hares, the faster the hare population *growth* per year.

Now consider the effect of the population level of hares on wildcat population growth. Obviously, the more hares there are, the more food the wildcats will have available to prey on, so the faster the wildcat population will grow per year. What about the other way around? What is the effect of the wildcat population level on the hares' population growth? Since wildcats prey on the hares, the more wildcats there are at the beginning of the year, the more slowly the hare population will increase per year. Indeed, if there are enough wildcats, they will cause the hare population to decline; population growth will turn negative. Finally, how does the level of the wildcat population affect its own growth per year? The larger the population of wildcats, the harder they must compete to catch hares and the more slowly the wildcat population will grow. If the wildcat population level is large enough, some wildcats will not catch enough hares to survive, so the population growth per year will turn negative.

We have spelled out four relationships:

- Given an environment large enough that the hares' food supply is not limited, the larger the hare population, the more rapid its growth.
- Since hares provide food for wildcats, the larger the hare population, the faster the number of wildcats will grow.
- Since wildcats feed on hares, the larger the wildcat population, the slower the hare population will grow (or the faster it will decline).

• As the population of wildcats increases, they must compete harder to catch hares, and thus their population will grow more slowly (or decline more rapidly).

The model shows that unless the populations die out (extinction is one possible solution to the equations), there will be cycles. At the beginning of a cycle, hares start proliferating. As they proliferate, wildcats feed on them, and, following along behind the hares, they likewise proliferate. But at a certain point, as a large wildcat population overconsumes its food supply of hares, the hare population starts to decline. For a time, the wildcat population continues to rise even as the hare population starts declining—it "overshoots"—but then the wildcat population starts declining, too. At some point, as wildcats die off, hares start proliferating again. And on the cycles go.

Finance and the Real Economy

When hauled into economics, the predator-prey model can suggest how tensions arising within markets can affect an economy. A model developed by Lance Taylor suggests something like what actually happened in 2008: how the financial sector can drive the real economy.[22] Rising financial assets first strengthen and then undermine business investment and economic growth. The model assumes that the assets are stocks, because housing would complicate matters. This is a crude model, like the ones devised by Diamond and Dybvig and by Kareken and Wallace, intended merely to sharpen an intuition. It could not be used to make a confident economic prediction, but it can provide insight into how financial booms and crashes may affect the real, goods-producing economy. Too bad the economics frontier hasn't progressed further since Adam Smith, but this is where it lies.

Taylor starts from a standard equation for the return to equity developed in 1962 by Myron Gordon, then a professor at MIT. The crucial assumption is that the short-term change in stock prices that the average investor expects will occur. Keynes argued much the same thing: the prices of financial assets are determined by a "beauty contest" of the sort that English newspapers used to run. You won not by picking the woman who was truly the most beautiful (if it could ever be determined), but by picking the woman whom average opinion considered the most beautiful. In other words, the aim was to second-guess average opinion. Similarly, Keynes argued that speculators succeed, at least over the short term, not by guessing the "fundamental" value of an asset (if it could ever be determined), but by guessing the value that average opinion expects the asset will have.

Keynes knew a thing or to about trading: he (mostly) made money right through the Depression when placing trades for his own account and that of King's College, but it seems useful to place his notion in modern context. The whole aim of so-called technical trading is to use indicators—the overall direction of prices, the way they pull back, the volume of trades, and other patterns—to second-guess average opinion. Peter Reznicek, strategist for Shadow Trader, a service that provides trading advice and makes its backlog of advice available online, captured the idea in a transmission on February 24, 2008. "There's a trucking company called Conway," he noted, and outlined why stock chart indicators suggested that shares in Conway might be a good buy. Then, as an afterthought, he added: "You know, crude's $100 a barrel. Go figure. I mean, I don't even pay attention to the why because it doesn't make any sense to me, so who cares, you know? Just go by the charts."[23] In other words, go by the indicators of average opinion—if you can. In some sense, average opinion is never wrong in the short run, because it's what drives the market. If average opinion, weighted by buying power—one dollar, one vote—expects an asset to rise in price, it will rise in price. If you buy it, you will gain.

The Gordon equation assumes that average opinion drives asset prices to whatever level average opinion expects. Other than average opinion, what might drive short-term asset prices? Fundamentals could. If a company finds itself in fundamental trouble—falling profits, rising debt, a major product recall—the stock will go down. But most changes in broad market prices do not appear to be determined by identifiable events. Ray Fair, of Yale, tracked market changes during the period 1982–1999 that were both rapid (one to five minutes) and large (0.75 percent or more).[24] Of 220 such changes in those years, only 69 appeared to have been caused by identifiable events such as Fed interest-rate announcements. Moreover, many similar announcements had little or no effect on markets. It's hard to see what, other than average expectations, drives *most* price changes. So let's grant Gordon his big assumption.

The next step brings in "Tobin's q," a financial concept applied by the Nobel laureate James Tobin. His analytic acuity was not to be underestimated. I knew his daughter in high school and once played chess with him. After half a dozen moves, he pronounced, "Checkmate." I had no idea what he meant. A few moves later, I was in checkmate. In any event, his q compares the stock market value of firms with the actual value of their installed capital. In some theoretical world, q should be close to 1, so that a firm's financial equity is in line with the actual equity invested to create the firm. In practice, q can depart significantly from 1, but when it gets too far out of line, a firm can get into trouble. For example, if q is substantially below 1, so that its stock market value looks cheap compared with the real value of its capital, it is ripe for a takeover bid.

Taylor's model is driven by relationships between the average economy-wide equity premium, q, and real investment, g—that is, the rate at which firms are building up their real capital stock. First, the Gordon equation implies a relationship between the level of q and the growth of q. Specifically, the higher the level of q, the faster q grows. In other words, the higher the equity premium, the faster it grows. This relationship builds a potential bubble into the model. It takes a little math to get from the Gordon equation to this relationship, but the important assumption, as mentioned, is that *average opinion* about the stock market drives *actual prices* in the market, over the short term. It isn't hard to see that, if everyone thinks along the lines of Peter Reznicek or John Maynard Keynes, trying to second-guess average opinion, the equity premium, q, would build on itself.

How does the level of q affect the growth of g? It is widely thought that the higher q is, the faster g will grow. There are two reasons, a carrot and a stick. The carrot is that a high q indicates optimism about profits—otherwise equity prices wouldn't be high in relation to the value of installed capital—and thus indicates robust animal spirits that support investment. The stick is that if q is high and firms fail to invest robustly, investors might think the stock price isn't justified by real value, and the stock price might fall.

Now, how does the level of real investment, g, affect its own growth? If a higher level of investment increased investment growth, and a lower level decreased investment growth, the real economy could be very unstable, as investment soared ever upward or plummeted ever downward. The economies of advanced nations are not so unstable in practice.[25] A high level of investment tends to wear itself out. When investment is high, its own growth tends to slow; when it is low, its own growth tends to pick up again. Investment, g, is therefore something of a stabilizing factor.

Finally, how does the level of g affect the growth of q? It follows almost from accounting that the higher the level of investment, g, the slower the equity premium, q, will grow.[26] Recall that q measures not the level of equity prices, but rather their level in relation to the volume of capital stock. More capital investment—a more rapid buildup of capital stock—will reduce the growth of q. This is essentially a Red Queen story: as g rises, q would have to run even faster just to stay where it is.

This is not quite a predator-prey model. The relationships differ, and in any case an economy is not literally composed of hares and wildcats;

the same mathematical relationship can describe entirely different phenomena. But we have specified a model in terms of relationships between the growth of variables and their levels. To sum up:

- The higher the level of the equity premium, q, the faster q grows.
- The higher the level of the equity premium, q, the faster real investment, g, grows.
- The higher the level of real investment, g, the slower g grows.
- The higher the level of real investment, g, the slower the equity premium, q, grows.

Thus, the asset price, q, drives instability as it rises, pushing up its own growth and the growth of real investment, g. Real investment, g, is sluggish and stabilizing. As its level rises, it tends to cut off its own growth—investment in the real economy cannot quite keep up with asset prices—and also tends to lower the growth of q.

The model puts these relationships together. As a boom gets under way, the equity premium, q, starts to rise and, via financial traders' average opinion, drives up the growth of q itself. If financial traders' expectations should grow more buoyant, they could sustain this process quite a while. Any such subjective change would have to be taken as occurring outside the model—whether it does occur helps to explain why some bubbles are bigger than others. (The role of subjective change outside the model is a principal reason why this is just a framework for thinking about bubbles, not a literal model that could produce a confident prediction.) However far the process goes, the rising level of the equity premium, q, inspires optimism in the real economy and makes it easier for firms to raise funds, thus driving the growth of real investment, g. But at some point, as the level of real investment, g, rises, the tortoise-like behavior of the real economy comes into play, putting downward pressure on its own growth rate. Moreover, as the level of g rises, it erodes the growth of q, since in the Red Queen story q would have to grow ever faster just keep up. At some point, q levels off, and stock prices turn downward. However, in a notable conclusion of the model, there is over-shooting, much as in the predator-prey model. Even after the asset valu-ation, q, starts falling, real investment, g, keeps rising for a while—before it, too, starts to fall. This pattern is regularly observed in financial bub-bles and crashes.

Such overshooting occurred in 2008. When Casey Mulligan of the University of Chicago noted that the real economy still looked strong as late as October 2008, well over a year after the financial crisis had begun to break, he was not wrong about the data. "It turns out that John Mc-Cain, who was widely mocked for saying that 'the fundamentals of our economy are strong,' was actually right," he said.[27] But he was mistaken in that he missed the pattern the model suggests. Because of overshoot-ing, as in the predator-prey models, the real economy can keep moving along for a while after financial prices start crashing, but can still be brought down later.

Structural Change in the American Economy

The long-run structuralist models discussed in the previous chapter ig-nore business cycles. This is a limitation because key factors that those models consider—the distribution of income between profits and wages and the level of effective demand—fluctuate over business cycles. It seems useful to develop a structuralist model that incorporates these fluctuations. Nelson Barbosa, secretary of economic policy at the Brazil-ian Finance Ministry and professor at the Federal University of Rio de Janeiro, developed such a model in his Ph.D. thesis at the New School, with Lance Taylor as his advisor.[28]

This model ignores finance, a critical factor in causing the 2008 bank-ing crisis and the Great Recession that followed. It doesn't pretend to be a complete explanation of these events. Maybe someday someone will invent an all-encompassing model, though I doubt it. But the Barbosa-

Taylor model does reveal some of the economic wreckage that may have helped to cause the crisis and that in any case loomed large as it began to subside.

There can well be external shocks to the economy, but market tensions, not external shocks, drive booms and busts in the model. It focuses on the "wage share" and on "capacity utilization." (It has things to say about other variables, but let's leave them aside to focus on these two principal ones.) The wage share, designated ψ, is just the opposite of the profit share. If the profit share is 30 percent of total income, the wage share is 70 percent.[29] The Federal Reserve usually gauges capacity utilization by comparing current output with some assumed maximum possible output. By this usual measure, capacity utilization might reach 90 percent in a boom and sink to 70 percent in a recession.[30] The Barbosa-Taylor model uses a simpler measure: it just takes capacity utilization, designated u, as the ratio of current GDP to its long-run average trend. Capacity utilization thus fluctuates up in booms and down in recessions.

The model is based on relationships between the level and growth of capacity utilization, u, and the level and growth of the wage share, ψ, along predator-prey lines. But while the logic of predator-prey interactions dictates relationships between variables in that model, no economic logic inherently dictates relationships between variables in the economic model. Notably, as in other structuralist models, economies can be wage-led or profit-led. In a wage-led economy, the higher the level of the wage share, ψ, the faster capacity utilization, u, will grow. A profit-led economy works the other way around. Likewise, relationships among other variables in the model can go either way. But some combinations apparently never occur: they would lead an economy to soar Icarus-like to the Sun, burn its wings, and plunge to its death in the sea. Since even the most ebullient booms rarely exceed a 10 percent annual growth rate, and even the deepest recessions rarely sink below some comparable floor, these combinations do not appear in real economies.[31]

Looking at the U.S. economy (other economies may well differ), first consider the relationship between the capacity utilization and the wage share over the business cycle.[32] When capacity utilization, u, is *low* in a recession, firms have cut output and revenues are squeezed. Firms have also reduced their workforce, but more slowly than output, in part because they are reluctant to lay off core employees such as managers and engineers, who would be costly to replace later. With revenues sharply squeezed but the workforce relatively stable, the *level* of the wage share, ψ, is high. In the data, it is typically near its peak. Now what about *growth* of the wage share? As the economy starts to recover, firms increase output rapidly but initially don't add employees. They already have a larger workforce than they initially need, and they don't want to hire until they're sure recovery is under way. With labor markets slack, wages don't rise much. Thus, with the workforce and wages stagnant but output and revenue rising, the wage share, ψ, is *falling*.

Now jump to the top of the cycle, when capacity utilization, u, is *high*. Firms have pushed output per worker to a peak (you can see this pattern in the data) and are claiming a large portion of revenue as profit. The *level* of the wage share, ψ, is low. However, with labor markets tight and profits high, workers find it relatively easy to secure raises. As workers claim a higher portion of revenue, the wage share *rises*.

In short, when capacity utilization is low (in a recession), the wage share is high but falling; when capacity utilization is high (in a boom), the wage share is low but growing.

Suppose this economy were wage-led. In a boom, with capacity utilization high and a growing wage share pushing it even higher, the economy would soar Icarus-like toward the Sun. In a recession, it would plunge to its death in the sea. This scenario must be wrong. The economy must be profit-led. When the profit share is high, capacity utilization is growing. A different structuralist account in the previous chapter reached the same conclusion about the U.S. economy.

Two other relationships remain to be discussed—and in order to spare the reader a tedious run-through of two more equations, I'll just state them. The higher the level of capacity utilization, u, the slower u grows. In other words, a boom eventually wears itself out. Likewise, the higher the level of the wage share, ψ, the slower it grows. When the wage share gets high enough, workers become content and firms get truculent, so raises get smaller. Thus, a rise in the wage share also wears itself out. These two relationships make for a more stable economy than one that is wage-led. "More stable" does not mean even-keeled. It just means that the worst extremes are more likely to peter out, since there is no factor that, even in isolation, would produce exponential growth or collapse.

A statistical estimation of the model—fitted to actual U.S. data—adds some confidence to the relationships I have just discussed. A statistical estimation assumes the model is right and, on that assumption, assigns actual numbers to key relationships. If various confidence tests on these numbers turn out very badly, they should raise warning flags—but the mere fact that they turn out well doesn't prove the model is right.

To do a statistical estimation, you feed quarterly data (or annual data, if more frequent data are not available) into the model. Variables—in this case, the wage share, ψ, and the capacity utilization, u—as well as changes in them, will depend not only on the current quarter but also on previous quarters. To put it another way, models are said to exhibit "lags." And well they should: changes in economies are driven not only by the momentary situation, but also by the earlier historical record. A statistical estimation of the Barbosa-Taylor model confirms that the U.S. economy is profit-led.[33]

The estimated model can be used, in effect, to average across business cycles. If you run an estimate on the U.S. economy through the year 2002, a 3 percentage point decline in the wage share—or a 3 percentage point increase in the profit share—would raise capacity utilization 1 percent. If you run an estimate through mid-2008, a larger, 6 percentage point decline in the wage share—or comparable increase in the profit share—would be required to raise capacity utilization 1 percent.[34] The economy seems to have remained profit-led, but to have turned less strongly so.

Again, So What?

I wouldn't bet much on these specific numbers. But so long as the economy is profit-led (and on this score the evidence is strong), a distressing picture emerges. It is not the picture I would like to see—but the point is to describe the picture you see, like it or not.

On the one hand, the fact that the wage share declined by a stunning 10 percent of GDP from 1980 through 2009—this decline is not conjectural, but evident in the data—produced benefits in a profit-led economy.[35] A large decline in the wage share should boost output, growth, and employment substantially—and not just at the top of the business cycle, but on average across business cycles. It would go partway toward explaining the ability of the U.S. economy to generate jobs before the crisis.

On the other hand, the declining wage share had costs. Americans kept consuming as if the wage share had not shrunk. Only part of the problem lay in our conspicuous consumption and our obedience to advertisers. The other part was the growing cost of medical care, education, and (until the crash) housing. The cost of these important needs was not easy to limit. In fact, if a family is paying $1,000 a month for medical insurance, why not buy the latest smart phone? It's almost an afterthought in the budget. The clamor for tax cuts, even if whipped up by politicians, did somehow reflect Americans' almost desperate sense that our income was falling behind the conventional wage—the wage that the "rules of decency," in Adam Smith's phrase, demanded that any credible worker should receive. The macroeconomic counterpart of the declining U.S. wage share was rising debt. First we began saving less, and then we began borrowing more. Over the quarter-century that preceded the crisis, household debt doubled to 130 percent of GDP.[36]

Misplaced belief in an invisible hand—economists' so-called Great Moderation—as well as the consequent reckless financial deregulation, surely contributed to the global financial crisis; and the sovereign debt crises that Europe is now struggling to avert are not unrelated. At least as far as financial markets go, we should disabuse ourselves of the invisible-hand metaphor and re-regulate. So far, governments have not adopted anything remotely like the Glass-Steagall Act and other reforms passed during the Depression. Such reforms contributed importantly to preventing financial crises for a good half-century, and there's little evidence that they undermined growth of the real economy. Real growth, after the world emerged from the Depression, was rapid and sustained.

Unfortunately, the Barbosa-Taylor model suggests that there were other structural problems in the U.S. economy and, perhaps, other advanced economies. A falling wage share supported a profit-led economy but helped to provoke unsustainable borrowing. If this unhappy diagnosis is correct, what is to be done? Even though policy advice should be based on a coherent model, it always rests on judgments outside of models.

The financial crisis and the long-running aftermath were such powerful events, that they might have changed the structure of the economy. In this case, descriptions of it based on earlier data would no longer apply. Unfortunately, a great deal depends on conjecture. Among other things, the fact that trade accounts for more than a quarter of GDP tends to make the economy profit-led, since a lower wage boosts the competitiveness of exports and also boosts the competitiveness of homemade goods vis-à-vis imports. On the other hand, the fact that the profit share is near an all-time high and the economy seems to have entered a long-running slump might tip the economic balance away from being profit-led. Firms might start worrying more about the volume of their sales and thus consumer demand than about the portion of sales that they claim as profits. At most, the economy is probably only weakly profit-led. Indeed, the statistical picture of the U.S. economy based on the Barbosa-Taylor model through mid-2008 already shows it as more weakly profit-led than the does picture based on data running through 2002. A large additional increase in the profit share might be required to eke out a small average increase in output. Certainly, no such gambit is worth trying.

Nor does the model make a case for extreme income inequality—which is different from a high profit share. A high profit share boosts output and employment in the model because it lifts animal spirits and investment demand. If profits are distributed in megasalaries to top executives, they might lift animal spirits somewhat, but they would surely do so more if they were retained by firms. Growth was higher in the 1950s and 1960s, when profit shares were also high but top executives' salaries were far lower than they are now. Furthermore, to the extent that profits are not paid to executives in megasalaries or distributed in dividends, they constitute corporate saving that can be plowed back into investment. Reducing taxes on corporate profits plowed back into investment might be sensible. But retaining low taxes on the highest salaries only aggravates income inequality and the sense that most workers are not being paid in accordance with the rules of social decency.

Health-care reform could reduce the pressure on Americans to borrow. If there is one single cost we cannot now control, it's the cost of medical care. Insurance costs erode the family budget, whether these are paid directly or deducted by employers from wages; or else lack of insurance causes not only a frightening medical vulnerability, but a sense of being unable to afford what the rules of decency demand. The government needs to control costs, rather than merely transfer them to itself. Since Americans pay far more than other nations for medical care, yet do not live longer or enjoy better health, this seems a possible goal.

Finally, industrial policies aimed at increasing investment work in a structuralist model. Whether the economy is profit-led or wage-led does not matter. For a start, U.S. infrastructure has been eroding for years, weakening the productivity of domestic firms.[37] An important reason many U.S. firms do not move to Mexico is that, despite much cheaper labor, the infrastructure—roads, communications, security—is considerably poorer. But the United States should not congratulate itself for doing better than Mexico. It has no high-speed trains comparable to those of Europe, Japan, or China. Even Amtrak's showcase Acela, running on a far more limited network, averages only half their speed.[38] The United

States is only twenty-fifth in the world in broadband coverage, and its air-traffic control systems are famously antiquated.[39] In the 2008 election, Barack Obama pledged to repair infrastructure and promote green technology—a goal actually shared by his opponent, John McCain—but the results have fallen far short of the promises.[40] The optimal amount to invest in infrastructure could probably never be determined, but it is much more than we do invest.

Neoclassical economists warn against industrial policies beyond those affecting infrastructure, saying that it's difficult to tell what the sunrise industries might be, and that even if the answer were known, politicians might reward the wrong ones. They have a point, but the most important need isn't a big secret: renewable and low-carbon energy. Of course, some approaches will succeed, and some will fail. But a certain amount of waste is in the nature of things. As I write, the U.S. government has been attacking China for subsidizing energy programs, apparently believing that China can make good enough guesses to pose a danger. Why not promote U.S. industries instead of attacking China?

FIFTEEN

Thinking about Economies

Logos was, for Plato, the perfect truth lighting our imperfect existence, the luminous utopia standing above this shadow world. *Logos* meant "reason"—the English term "logic" derives from it—but had powerful spiritual dimensions, too. What the King James Bible translates as "the word" was *logos* in the original Greek. John echoes Plato when he says, "In the beginning was *logos*, and *logos* was God, and God was *logos*." *Logos* was the absolute underlying our uncertain world.

However scientific many economists may profess to be, at some level the neoclassical ideal holds sway as an unerring reality comparable to Plato's *logos*. This world's troubled economies are mere deviations from an imagined utopia. The good fight strives to eliminate market imperfections and bring humans closer to that imagined utopia. It's a fundamentalist economics. Alas, utopia is either inaccessible or corrupt.

My harsher criticisms of neoclassical theory have actually been directed at supposedly practical bastardizations of it. Gary Becker's insistence that individuals "maximize welfare *as they conceive it*, whether they be selfish, altruistic, loyal, spiteful, or masochistic," is only a colorful way of stating accepted theory. The problem comes in the next step, when supposedly practical economists turn around and impose their own conception of utility on the agents in their models. Complaining about this sleight of hand is not just a theoretical quibble. The sleight of hand affects important conclusions.

In *Why Wages Don't Fall*, Truman Bewley of Yale underlines problems that have arisen in widely known macroeconomic models when modelers attribute concepts of utility to workers and base those concepts on unrealistic psychology. Bewley asks why wages don't fall, or why they fall little, during recessions. This is an important question, since the J. B. Clark production parable used in most macroeconomic models says that if only wages did fall, firms would not lay off workers. Keynesians and neoclassicals develop models about why wages don't fall and why unemployment rises, based on their own assumptions about workers' conceptions of utility. They then use these models to argue for their own policy views. But nearly all these modelers' assumptions about workers' conceptions of utility are far from the mark—and for that reason undermine their models—according to some three hundred interviews Bewley conducted with businesspeople, personnel managers, labor leaders, employment counselors, and others who had direct knowledge of the matter.

For example, one well-known model by Robert Lucas and Leonard Rapping argues that wages would fall during recessions, except for the fact that workers refuse to take pay cuts, since they prefer instead to enjoy more leisure time.[1] Workers voluntarily decide not to be employed. The resulting decrease in the workforce prevents wages from falling, as they otherwise would. This theory ran into trouble, since the data show that few workers quit during recessions, but the economist Kenneth J. McLaughlin invented a variant to rescue it: firms let workers choose between pay cuts and layoffs, and when they refuse pay cuts, they are laid off.[2] There is just a little problem here. Bewley asked sixty-two managers whose firms had laid off workers whether they had offered their employees the choice between pay cuts and layoffs—and guess what? "None of the companies offered this choice."[3] On the contrary, "respondents indicated that workers who were laid off were told to leave, often with no warning."[4]

A more Keynesian model by Carl Shapiro of the University of California, Berkeley, and Joseph Stiglitz, a Nobel Prize winner, also runs into problems when the authors attribute their conception of utility to workers. Their "efficiency" wage hypothesis assumes that workers are prone to "shirking."[5] To limit shirking, firms monitor their employees and fire those who slack off. Neoclassical theory says that if workers were paid market wages, dismissal would have no sting, since the theory fancifully assumes they can readily find work elsewhere at the market wage. Firms therefore pay above-market wages to give dismissal some sting. The economistic fantasy underlying this theory supposes that managers "order subordinates around and control them through threats," Bewley notes.[6] Managers told Bewley that it is a good description of bad management. They said that holding the threat of dismissal over workers would undermine morale rather than elicit hard work. They use dismissal to get rid of bad workers, not to threaten good ones.[7] One human-resources official quipped, "The theory is bassackwards. It assumes that people don't want to work hard. Most people want to work hard. They want to be successful and to please their boss, and they usually do work hard."[8]

Bewley discovered various reasons why firms don't cut wages in recessions—life is messy—but the principal one was that they depend on employees' good "morale." Morale has two principal dimensions: employees' positive mood and their identification with the firm's objectives, at least as they see them. "Workers have so many opportunities to take advantage of employers that it is not wise to depend on coercion and financial incentives alone as motivators," notes Bewley, summarizing what he heard. "Employers want workers to operate autonomously, show initiative, use their imagination, and take on extra tasks not required by management; workers who are scared or dejected do not do these things."[9] Firms need such efforts even from low-level employees. For example, receptionists have contact with customers, affect their firm's image, and provide critical information. Pay cuts would undermine morale, disrupting employees' lives and, at least as important, delivering an insult. Employees see pay as reflecting their "self-worth and recognition of their value to the company."[10]

Notice that workers are motivated in part by altruism. "They may expect no reward," says Bewley, "but help the company simply because doing so gives them pleasure or is felt to be a duty." This motivation is entirely consistent with the coherent definition of utility. Contemporary neoclassical theory drops the idea that people behave like the nineteenth-century *homo economicus*. It does not specify the psychological dimensions of preferences, but only requires that people be consistent: "Rationality has to do with acting so as to achieve given goals," Bewley points out. "So that there is nothing irrational about adopting and furthering someone else's objectives."[11]

Misconceptions about how workers define utility are built right into the equations of the macro models purporting to explain why wages don't fall. For example, the neat trick of figuring out how to insinuate "shirking" into equations surely contributed to the wide recognition that was accorded Shapiro and Stiglitz's model. But the equations were bogus: they describe an economistic fantasy that does not generally capture employer-employee relations. The models appear to explain macroeconomic relationships between wage and employment data because they were invented to explain those relationships. But they are then illegitimately used to make arguments about whether unemployment is voluntary or involuntary and what policies should or shouldn't be adopted toward it.[12] Theoretical errors about the meaning of utility translate into practical defects in the models' claims and policy implications.

If macroeconomics worked better, you could see how a schism between practical models and coherent theory might persist. But illegitimate revisions of theory often lead to doubtful policies, not pragmatic answers. Macroeconomic models failed in guiding policy before the 2008 financial crisis. And they didn't fail by being correct in theory but wrong in practical terms. They failed in part *because* they got neoclassical theory wrong, ignoring the instability problems of Arrow-Debreu general equilibrium. They just assumed that economic problems are caused by shocks impinging on stable markets—that problems cannot emerge within markets and tear the economy apart. This misconception collapsed for a moment or two after global financial markets froze, and regulators bailed out the financial system as if no one had ever believed the assumption. Doubts linger about whether the old misconception will revive. Where economic theory will lead remains to be seen.

Modeling Complexity

I have suggested it is legitimate to impose informed assumptions on macro data—profits, wages, consumption, investment, and the rest—in order to build rough macroeconomic models of cause and effect. The role of models is to be sure that assumptions are consistent, to understand their implications as well as possible, and to frame a coherent view that you can compare with historical experience. Economists from Ricardo to Keynes to Solow generally took this approach, until they began yielding to the fad for basing models on so-called microfoundations by imposing a conception of utility on a "representative agent."

What might justify the traditional modeling approach I suggested? Societies, and therefore economies, are extraordinarily complex organisms. We really have no detailed idea how they function or develop. The justification for this approach must be that we can sometimes identify cause and effect at the macro level without understanding anything like every micro-level interaction. The predator-prey model describes a macro-level cause-and-effect mechanism. It certainly does not capture the entire ecology of actual predator and prey populations, but it may capture an important element of that ecology. Having posited the model, you can observe predator and prey populations, or other phenomena such as parasites and hosts, to better understand how important a role the model may play, why it may or may not be applicable, and what other factors may enter.

A so-called "complexity" approach to economics, attempting to investigate the organisms of economies at intertwined levels from micro to macro, was launched by economists, physicists, biologists, and computer scientists, largely at the Santa Fe Institute in the 1980s. The institute received substantial funding from John Reed, chief executive of Citicorp, who felt that conventional economics—and in particular his own bank's economists—were not seeing economies clearly.[13] Pioneers of this approach hardly made the discovery that economies are complex; that was known all along. But borrowing mathematical and computing techniques from fields such as artificial intelligence and statistical mechanics, they hope to actually model more of that complexity than was previously possible. I have no idea how far the project may eventually lead, but some of the models capture interesting pictures of economies.

No one seems to have found it useful to officially define the complexity approach, and models lumped under this rubric may be quite unlike one another, indeed may contradict one another. But they do share several loose assumptions.[14] No central controller organizes the economy; no auctioneer tallies up supply and demand to declare prices. Agents are heterogeneous. No representative or average individual can summarize them, though broad categories of individuals, which you might call "classes," can emerge. Agents' actions may be affected by their different understandings of the economy, the influences of other agents' preferences, or their geographic locations specified in the model. The economy does not necessarily gravitate toward equilibrium. Rather, an aggregate economy emerges—and may never stop changing—as agents continually adapt, on the basis of their experiences interacting with other agents, or changing rules of thumb positing where the economy is headed, or other developments within the model.

A fascinating model of a stock market along these lines was conceived by W. Brian Arthur, originally an operations researcher who became professor of economics at Stanford and at the Santa Fe Institute, in collaboration with another economist, a physicist, and two computer scientists.[15] The model is populated by agents who can buy either a risk-free bond or a risky stock that pays dividends. They do not have rational expectations; they are not wired with an understanding of how the economy works. Rather, each of them reasons inductively, based on his or her past experience, to try to understand where the market is headed. Each agent then buys the bond or the stock, hoping for the best return. Agents' understandings of the market shape its movements, and its movements shape their understandings.

A computer program sets this process up and runs through a history of trades, capturing descriptions of how agents behave and how stock prices evolve. It is useful to describe how this program works. The first step that agents take in developing hypotheses about the market is to recognize present and past market conditions. For example, "technical" indicators might tell whether the price of the stock is higher than its five-day, ten-day, or hundred-day moving average.[16] Technical traders in real markets use such indicators to ascertain market "sentiment," or (in Keynes's phrase) what average opinion holds. Standard finance theory says these indicators are useless noise. "Fundamental" indicators tell, for example, whether the return on bonds is more than 87.5 percent, 100 percent, or 112.5 percent of the current stock dividend. Fundamental investors in real markets use such indicators to try to discover the underlying value of stock. Standard finance theory sees these as the only valid types of indicators. The agent keeps "condition arrays"—sequences of digits, with 1 specifying that a corresponding technical or fundamental indicator was met on the most recent day, and 0 specifying that it was not. The arrays also contain meaningless marks that convey no information as to whether the indicator was met. The meaningless marks allow agents to ignore the corresponding indicator.

The agent develops theories about the market, using "predictors" to hypothesize what will happen based on condition arrays recording which indicators have been met. For example, the agent might predict that if the stock price is above its five-day moving average today and the stock dividend is less than 87.5 percent of the return on the bond, the price of the stock plus its dividend tomorrow will be less than 95 percent of what it is today.

Each agent is initially seeded with completely random condition arrays and predictors. Many agents obviously do a bad job, at least at first. Each agent keeps track of how predictors have performed. Each day, the agent statistically combines the forecasts of predictors that have worked best to calculate how much stock he or she desires to buy or sell, and to generate bid and offer prices. The agent ignores predictors that have not performed well. In time, badly performing predictors are "genetically" altered via "mutation" (some digits in the array are randomly switched) or "combination" (some elements of one array are joined to some of another). The agent tracks results from the newly created predictors and uses them only if experience shows that they have been working better than others.

Unknown to the agents, the underlying stock market model is actually neoclassical. If all agents understood how it works—if rational expectations were bestowed upon them—they would drive it to an equilibrium value and thereby optimize their returns. If the program is run to let agents explore new predictors at only a very low rate, they do converge to the rational-expectations equilibrium, with some random fluctuations. Key predictions of standard finance theory—*not* borne out in real financial markets—appear. Trading volume is low, since all agents share almost the same understanding of the market and thus have little reason to trade. The stock price is not volatile, departing little from its fundamental value determined by the equilibrium return. The market does not exhibit volatile periods with large price swings, followed by tranquil periods with small price swings. Moreover, all agents become fundamental traders, since, for the most part, they come to ignore technical indicators.

However, if agents are allowed to explore new predictors at a more normal rate, the usual patterns observed in actual financial markets suddenly break out.[17] This somewhat higher rate of exploration still seems moderate to me, compared with how fast professional traders in real markets respond to errors and explore new predictors. Technical trading emerges, can be profitable, and settles in for good. Apparently, once agents observe something akin to market sentiment, their predictors validate technical indicators, and they continue to use them. Bubbles and crashes erupt. Trading volume is three times higher than in the rational-expectations regime. Periods of high-volume trading and periods of low-volume trading alternate; likewise, periods of high price volatility and periods of low volatility. Keynes's beauty contest is played and replayed: agents form expectations about the market by forecasting other agents' expectations.

Thomas Sargent, a Nobel Prize winner, helped pioneer the rational-expectations revolution in the 1970s but subsequently moved away from consistently accepting its assumptions. He is known for his work as an econometrician, statistically testing models and identifying the actual numbers that fit a generic model to a particular economy. One model he developed has commonalities with the "complexity" approach as it explores conflicting views about an economy. In fact, it explores how one powerful organization, the Federal Reserve Board, may itself entertain conflicting views of the economy, learn about those conflicting views, and weigh them in setting policy.

First, some background. Sargent has taken to calling rational expectations "intelligent design."[18] This surely deliberate phrase captures a quasi-religious undertone. In rational expectations, he writes, "All agents inside the model, the econometrician, and God share the same model."[19] God, or intelligent design, is first supposed to have created the true universe of the economy. God then grants everyone in the model knowledge of the truth. The econometrician external to the model is actually the odd one out, uninformed about numerical details such as agents' preference for work versus leisure, or how much capital can be traded for how much labor in production. But knowing the basic structure of God's model and using statistical methods, the econometrician is able to uncover these numbers. The big question, Sargent concedes, is whether "God's model" exists.[20]

"Learning-theory" models explore departures from rational expectations, in that agents (not so unlike those in the stock market model) do not know how the economy works and try to learn. The most interesting models, to my mind, turn rational expectations on its head. How would people learn how an economy works if God doesn't create a true model—if no definitive model exists?[21] In trying to balance the ills of unemployment against those of inflation from the 1960s through the 1990s, the Federal Reserve weighed three relevant theories, Sargent posits. The first—call it Keynesian theory number one—says that allowing higher inflation (say, 5 percent instead of 2 percent) permanently lowers unemployment (say, from 6 percent to 4 percent). The second—call it Keynesian theory number two—says that allowing higher inflation lowers unemployment in the short run, notably during a recession, but in the end unemployment returns to its "natural" level. The third, a rational-expectations theory, says that allowing higher inflation has no effect on unemployment at all. A rational-expectations economist might argue that inflation data from the 1970s should have settled the dispute, "driving a stake" through the Keynesian models. But, Sargent notes, "No one has the authority to drive stakes."[22] Models that worked about the same way as the Keynesian theories still survived in 2007, when he published his model. They have not yet vanished as I write this book.

In the model, the Fed starts in 1960 heavily crediting Keynesian theory number one, since the other two theories had not yet been formally modeled. But we don't necessarily need models to believe theories, so the

Fed also gives some weight to the other two. The Fed revises the level of confidence it places in the three theories, based on past data. As inflation rises in the 1970s, it increasingly credits the rational-expectations model, which asserts that limiting the money supply to control inflation should have no effect on unemployment. However, the Fed does not fully adopt the model it credits most heavily based on the data, or reject the others. Aware that models can be wrong, it always weighs the costs the nation would incur if, in fact, one of the models it deems less likely turned out to be right. Thus, in Sargent's model, the Fed is reluctant to clamp down tightly on the money supply during most of the 1970s for fear that it could send unemployment soaring. Apparently, by 1979 the Fed becomes convinced that inflationary costs are so severe as to outweigh the Keynesian models' warnings that tight monetary policy could cause high unemployment. It clamps down on the money supply. But it never fully gives up on the other two theories; they can revive and reassert themselves, to affect belief and policy. The model allowing the Fed to hold the three conflicting and shifting theories does a much better job of capturing the actual evolution of inflation and unemployment than any model simply assuming that any one of the theories is the true model.

As Sargent himself points out, no one knows for sure that Fed policy was the principal force driving inflation and unemployment throughout those years. Other factors—oil shocks, the collapse of Bretton Woods, budget deficits, and who knows what else—might have overwhelmed anything the Fed did.[23] Nevertheless, his is an intriguing model that allows shifting and conflicting ideas about how the economy works— about what the economic model is—to affect the economy itself.

What Makes a Not-Too-Bad Model?

How are we to tell good assumptions and models from bad? Even graduate texts are appallingly mute about this question: David Romer comments on the plausibility of many models as he presents them in *Ad-*

vanced Macroeconomics, but spends barely a paragraph discussing his criteria. He starts out by arguing that "the purpose of a model is not to be realistic. After all, we already possess a model that is completely realistic—the world itself. The problem with that 'model' is that it is too complicated to understand." He then sets out his notion of a good assumption:

> If a simplifying assumption causes a model to give incorrect answers *to the questions it is being used to address,* then that lack of realism may be a defect. (Even then, the simplification—by showing clearly the consequences of those features of the world in an idealized setting— may be a useful reference point.) If the simplification does not cause the model to provide incorrect answers to the questions it is being used to address, however, then the lack of realism is a virtue; by isolating the effect of interest more clearly, the simplification makes it easier to understand.[24]

How convenient! If we already know the correct answers, we can tell good assumptions because they give correct answers. This isn't a criterion but a tautology.

Milton Friedman, in "The Methodology of Positive Economics," made the canonical argument flogging the view that assumptions should be realistic:

> Truly important and significant hypotheses will be found to have "assumptions" that are wildly inaccurate descriptive representations of reality, and, in general, the more significant the theory, the more unrealistic the assumptions (in this sense). The reason is simple. A hypothesis is important if it "explains" much by little, that is, if it abstracts the common and crucial elements from the mass of complex and detailed circumstances surrounding the phenomena to be explained and permits valid predictions on the basis of them alone. . . . [T]he relevant question to ask about "assumptions" of a theory is not whether they are descriptively "realistic," for they never are, but whether they are sufficiently good approximations for the purpose in

hand. And this question can be answered only by seeing whether the theory works, which means whether it yields sufficiently accurate predictions.[25]

Friedman was far too optimistic that models (his term, "theories," unfortunately blurs the distinction between models and reality) can be definitively tested. John Stuart Mill long ago pointed out that to test a theory, you need to vary one factor—say, whether a nation adopts protectionism or allows free trade—while keeping everything else about the economy the same. In fact, you need to carry out a number of such tests, not just one. Of course, no such test is possible. Economic history cannot be rerun; other things about an economy are never equal. Statistical tests attempt to hold other things equal, but how well they do so depends on the validity of more models. Aris Spanos writes in *Statistical Foundations of Econometric Modeling*, "No economic theory was ever abandoned because it was rejected by some empirical econometric test, nor was a clear-cut decision between competing theories made in light of the evidence of such a test."[26]

Worse, as Hyman Minsky points out, when economic models do appear to fail a test, the relevance of the test fades over time.[27] An experiment that invalidates a model in physics can be reproduced by any competent researcher, anytime, anywhere. The falsification is always present. Not so in economics. In time, an apparent historical failure of a model is forgotten. The experience fades into the past and cannot be rerun until the right circumstances again erupt.

Despite the obstacles to using statistics or historical events to test an economic model—and despite the fact that Friedman was wildly overoptimistic about how decisive tests can be—such tests are not useless. In fact, I would argue that the 2008 financial crisis put Friedman's *Monetary History of the United States* to the test, and it failed. He claims that inept monetary policies, not unregulated financial markets, caused financial crises throughout the course of American history. Bernanke espoused his theory, so presumably he tried to manage monetary policy in accordance with it. He is a distinguished macroeconomist; if he egregiously failed to follow Friedman's advice, it would be impossible to write a job description for anyone who could follow it. Moreover, if Bernanke or Alan Greenspan failed to follow Friedman's advice, why didn't Friedman himself, as sharp as ever until his death in 2006, mention it? I conclude that Friedman's theory was put to a historical test and proved terribly wrong. The instability of private financial markets largely drove the crisis. I would not dismiss statistical tests, either. Done fairly and transparently, they can be useful. Let me set down as a criterion, then: *models should not prove clearly inconsistent with historical or statistical experience.*

Still, given how tentative tests of models can be—if Friedman were still alive, he might discover some argument that would show why his model didn't fail—we need more criteria. In "A Contribution to the Theory of Economic Growth," Robert Solow poses some: "All theory depends on assumptions which are not quite true. That is what makes it theory. The art of successful theorizing is to make the inevitable simplifying assumptions in such a way that the final results are not very sensitive."[28] In other words, Solow is not just saying that you can accept a simplification if it gives "correct" answers; he's saying that you can accept it if it does not significantly affect the answers you get. This is an actual criterion: you might well be able to tell whether incorporating or omitting an aspect of reality in a model will change the answers it gives, without knowing the right answer a priori. Solow continues: "A 'crucial' assumption is one on which the conclusions do depend sensitively." Change a "crucial" assumption, and you will indeed affect the answer you get. In this case, Solow maintains that realism matters: "It is important that crucial assumptions be reasonably realistic. When the results of a theory seem to flow specifically from a special crucial assumption, then if the assumption is dubious, the results are suspect." Any assumption that crucially affects answers should be realistic.

Solow's view that crucial assumptions should be realistic has a long ancestry, Friedman notwithstanding. Knut Wicksell, the clearest of the neoclassical pioneers, said the same thing. The extent to which conclusions "accord with reality" depends on two criteria, he says: "First and foremost, [it depends on] whether our assumptions are themselves founded on reality, i.e., contain at least some elements of reality—which we must always demand, for otherwise all reasoning about them would be sterile. . . . Further, the conditions from which we abstract"—that is, the conditions we ignore in a simplified model—"must be relatively unessential, at least as regards the question under discussion.[29] Economists ranging from the general-equilibrium theorist Michael Mandler to the Cambridge Keynesian economist Geoffrey Harcourt concur about this criterion, even if they might disagree about which assumptions meet it.[30] Robert Lucas, who studied with Friedman, heartily agrees: "If we are serious about obtaining a theory of unemployment, we want a theory of unemployed *people*, not unemployed 'hours of labor services'; about people who look for jobs, hold them, lose them, people with all the attendant feelings that go along with these events."[31] If that isn't a call for realism, I don't know what is.

A qualification is in order here. It is too much to ask that realistic assumptions be corroborated by every shred of evidence. Take the dispute between neoclassicals and Keynesians about whether saving or investment is the economic engine. Neither assumption is patently right all of the time. On the one hand, saving can be the limiting factor. Keynes's job at the British Treasury during World War I was to allocate scarce savings—and debt—among alternative uses: the quintessential neoclassical economic problem. Britain was taking out loans as fast as it could beg or borrow dollars from New York, sending to the front every scrap of food and every bullet it could make or buy on credit. On the other hand, investment can be the limiting factor. In June 2010, U.S. banks held more than a trillion dollars of "excess reserves"—cash over and above the legal requirement—at the Federal Reserve.[32] If those trillion dollars had been lent out for investment, think of the economic activity they could have generated, especially since investors would have used them to buy goods, recipients would have deposited them in their banks, banks would have lent them out again, and so on. The problem was either banks' fear of lending the funds, or firms' fear of investing.

Simply asserting that one assumption is more realistic than another does not get you far. You need a sound argument for why your assumption is generally realistic. I hope I have supplied such an argument for investment as the principal economic engine, but you should never forget that its realism may depend on circumstances. I slightly rephrase Solow's criterion: *a critical assumption should capture essential features of our economic world.*[33]

Economists are often accused of a foolish consistency, but their worse sin is a devious inconsistency. Like Ptolemaic astronomers, they add epicycles to epicycles, contriving new twists on models to explain awkward situations without questioning their basic paradigm. Consider free trade. In 1993, at Boston University, I took part in a panel discussion about the North American Free Trade Agreement (NAFTA); the panel included economists and other social scientists. Of course, I expected that the economists would be most insistent about the virtues of free trade, but I was truly startled by their emotional vehemence. It sounded as if they were defending freedom against tyranny. Yet if you actually use neoclassical theory to estimate the benefits of free trade, the benefits turn out to be remarkably small. The University of Chicago economist Arnold Harberger, a friend of free markets if there ever was one, calculated in a 1959 paper that if Chile eliminated 50 percent tariffs across the board, the result would be a one-time gain of only 2.5 percent of GDP.[34] He did *not* say that Chile's annual growth rate would increase by 2.5 percentage points (neoclassical theory implies no such thing), but claimed only that over several years its GDP would achieve a level 2.5 percent higher than it otherwise would have, and that would be that. In other words, slashing 50 percent tariffs—truly a high level—gains a developing country half of a year's healthy growth; it would be more like a quarter of a year for China. Subsequent efforts to estimate the effects of trade liberalization have come up with similarly paltry effects.[35] Why? Though high tariffs cost consumers dearly, they raise producers' profits. Consumers lose more than producers gain, in the neoclassical model, but the net difference is small.

Somehow, neoclassical economists in general (not just the economists on the panel) find it hard to give up their free-trade convictions, so to make protectionism look worse, they invented epicycles: models of lobbying, bribery, and other "directly unproductive profit-seeking" that supposedly flower under trade protection.[36] Aside from doubts about whether such problems are worse under protectionist regimes—both free-trade Mexico under Carlos Salinas and free-trade Chile under Augusto Pinochet turned out to be stunningly corrupt—this is a sloppy way to do economics. If your core model challenges your convictions, change your convictions or your model. In this case, I think the model is wrong (trade *can* make a big difference for better or worse, among other things by affecting investment demand), so maybe economists were right to take their convictions seriously. But strong convictions plus an inconsistent model make for bad advice.

Thus, I add a criterion for models along the lines of Occam's Razor—the idea, attributed to a medieval scholastic, that "plurality should not be posited without necessity."[37] *Good models should consistently reflect the underlying paradigm; they should add as few ad hoc assumptions as possible.* Using models that closely reflect your paradigm forces you to weigh your commitment to it. If too many conclusions conflict too sharply with experience, something is wrong. If you heap epicycle on top of epicycle, you can explain almost anything you want using some model or other, but you're really only proving your own cleverness.

And one more thing: *a good model should illuminate something you otherwise would have understood less clearly.* I like Fisher's general-equilibrium model better than the Arrow-Debreu model (though admittedly Fisher published his decades later) because it shows how the very process that might move markets toward equilibrium—the ability of those rational agents posited by economic theory to perceive that the economy is out of equilibrium and act on their perceptions—might go awry.

These criteria obviously do not constitute a cookbook recipe for judging assumptions and models. Indeed, if such a recipe existed, you could use it to concoct one great meta-model that would tell you everything you need to know about all economies. And you could also find the Holy Grail. But even if these criteria don't constitute a cookbook, neither are they mere words that can be twisted however you want. Crucial assumptions should be realistic; models should be consistent with experience, and they should reflect the underlying paradigm, not a proliferation of epicycles.

Formulating a not-too-bad model is the first step. The next step is applying it. Given how complex an economy is and how simple models are (even those that fall under the "complexity" rubric), a healthy dose of conservatism is in order. The conservative political writer Edmund Burke saw society as enormously complex and, as a result, feared any program that relied too heavily on abstract principles. As he wrote in *Reflections on the Revolution in France,* utopian ideals like *liberté, égalité,* and *fraternité* might sound very fine in the abstract, but when abruptly imposed on a complex society, they could well (as he foresaw correctly) degenerate into "massacre, torture, hanging." More uncertain benefits imagined in perfect models for some distant future, whether neoclassical, Marxian, or even Keynesian, should be discounted if they involve more certain and immediate dangers. And whatever the model, because it is a model it inherently ignores important aspects of reality. Those aspects matter, as Burke insists: "Circumstances are what render every civil and political scheme beneficial or noxious to mankind."

For better or worse, like Burke, I tend to snap at theories I find deeply problematic but try to be more cautious about positive recommendations. Let me nevertheless set down a few positive recommendations:

- Economists should transparently describe critical assumptions. These assumptions should be realistic and pertinent to the situations that a particular model seeks to explain.

- Economists should explain the structure of their models. The structure of a model constitutes the perspective it sheds on some crucial aspects of an economy. Thoughtful individuals should not believe, and policymakers should not use, an unexplained model.
- However realistic its assumptions, a model stands an excellent chance of ignoring crucial aspects of an economy because, among other things, incorporating them might well make the model too complex to handle. Think what factors it might miss.
- There are always conflicting models to explain any given aspects of an economy. In looking for practical conclusions, weigh conflicting models.
- Macroeconomies are incredibly complex. One of the most useful things economists can do is explain publicly what they do not know.

Notes

1. The Metaphor of the Invisible Hand

1. Smith 1976, 1:379.
2. Smith 1976, 1:344–345.
3. Eichengreen 2010.
4. Constantinides et al. 2003, ix.
5. John Kemp, "Inside the Markets: Limits on Commodity Traders Sought," *New York Times*, Nov. 8, 2009; "Mr. Obama's Economic Advisors," editorial, *New York Times*, Nov. 25, 2008; Eric Lipton and Stephen Labaton, "The Reckoning: Deregulator Looks Back, Unswayed," *New York Times*, Nov. 17, 2008.
6. On Summers's young tenure: "Spotlight: Lawrence Summers," *Belfer Center Newsletter*, Kennedy School of Government, Harvard University, summer 2008, belfercenter.ksg.harvard.edu/publication/18299/spotlight.html (accessed Nov. 15, 2009).
7. Gretchen Morgenson and Don Van Natta Jr., "Back to Business: In Crisis, Banks Dig in for Fight against Rules," *New York Times*, Jun. 1, 2009.
8. Keynes 1953, 383.
9. Samuelson and Nordhaus 1989, 289; ibid., 706–713, on unions' causing unemployment; ibid., 439–441, especially Fig. 18–12, on minimum wages' causing unemployment.

10. Levy and Temin 2007.

11. "FMC Program Segments 1960–2000: The Changing Economy: Inflation, Stagflation, and Deregulation: Alfred Kahn and Paul Volcker," Public Broadcasting System (PBS), www.pbs.org/fmc/segments/progseg14. htm (accessed Jul. 13, 2009).

12. Samuelson and Nordhaus 1989, 440.

13. Ellis 1998.

14. The law was the Depository Institution Deregulation and Monetary Control Act of 1980.

15. Not all had studied at the University of Chicago, but all shared its free-market ideology. Chilean finance minister Sergio de Castro had studied with Milton Friedman (Everett G. Martin, "The Chicago Boys in Chile," *Wall Street Journal,* Oct. 5, 1979). Arnold Harberger, a University of Chicago economist, closely advised the Chilean economists (Normal Gall, "How the 'Chicago Boys' Fought 1,000% Inflation," *Forbes,* Mar. 31, 1980).

16. Taylor 1988, 14. "Goodbye Chicago?" *The Banker,* Feb. 1983, 69, notes that the banks "quickly became the lynch-pins of each group servicing the needs of other companies in the conglomerate."

17. Quote from "Chile, Peru: Virtue Unrewarded," *The Economist,* Apr. 30, 1983. "Temps Only Need Apply," *The Economist,* Feb. 19, 1982; and "Goodbye Chicago?" *The Banker,* Feb. 1983, 69, report that the government initially said it would not guarantee debt owed to foreigners but that it later recanted.

18. On Chile's debt in 1982, see "Chile: Recession Has a Firm Grip on the Economy; Efforts to Cope with Debt Problem Make Importers Wary," *Business America,* May 30, 1983; and "Chile, Peru: Virtue Unrewarded," *The Economist,* Apr. 30, 1983. Concerning its debt in 1973, see Martin, "The Chicago Boys in Chile."

19. On the dismissals: "Chile, Peru: Virtue Unrewarded," *The Economist,* Apr. 30, 1983.

20. Toye 2008 notes that the IMF and the World Bank adopted financial liberalization as a component of "structural adjustment" programs in the 1980s and 1990s. Chang 2002, 83, quotes Joseph Stiglitz as calling IMF economists "third-rate students from first-rate universities."

21. Williamson and Mahar 1998, 29–30.

22. Williamson and Mahar 1998, 2. Toye 2008 concurs that "financial liberalization led to increasingly frequent financial crises." Williamson and Mahar 1998, 1, say there had been no previous comprehensive study of liberalization.

23. Williamson did not include financial liberalization as an essential component of the Washington Consensus, but most who adopted it did—for example, Córdoba 1994, 233. Córdoba was a high-level advisor to Mexican president Carlos Salinas.

24. World Bank 2005, 220.

25. Stephen Labaton, "Accord Reached on Lifting of Depression-Era Barriers among Financial Industries," *New York Times*, Oct. 23, 1999.

26. Kathleen Day, "Reinventing the Bank: With Depression-Era Law About To Be Rewritten, the Future Remains Unclear," *Washington Post*, Oct. 31, 1999.

27. Day, "Reinventing the Bank"; and Stephen Labaton, "Congress Passes Wide-Ranging Bill Easing Bank Laws," *New York Times*, Nov. 5, 1999.

28. For a succinct summary of his view, see Friedman 1968, 3.

29. Mankiw 2006, 33, confirms that the consensus accepted the Friedman argument.

30. Bernanke 2002.

31. Hahn 1984, 11.

32. Hahn 1984, 125.

33. Walras 1984, 256, makes clear that he saw actual markets as imperfect.

34. Colander et al. 2004, 298.

35. Geanakoplos 1989, 43–61, provides a sophisticated, concise treatment. There are a few typographical errors, which the online *New Palgrave* unfortunately only aggravates.

36. Hahn 1984, 114, emphasizes this point.

37. Fisher 1983, 26, notes that several theorists in the 1950s explicitly conjectured that the *tâtonnement* process, which I have called the auctioneer process, was stable.

38. Scarf 1960.

39. Fisher 1983, 27. Fisher discusses the instability results in his second chapter and categorizes the conditions that would ensure convergence to equilibrium as "wildly restrictive."

40. Blaug 2001, 160.

41. Ackerman 2002, 122.
42. Fisher 1983, 23–24, including footnote 7.
43. Interview with Franklin Fisher, Cambridge, MA, November 28, 2007.
44. Interview with James Galbraith, San Francisco, January 6, 2008.
45. For a typical DSGE model that assumes the economy is always in equilibrium but has market imperfections, see Clarida et al. 1999.
46. Writing before the crisis, Woodford (1999, 11–12) noted that macroeconomists came to express increasing "skepticism about the benefits of activist stabilization policy, while being correspondingly more optimistic . . . about the self-regulating capacities of the market system."
47. Lucas 2003, 1.
48. Greenspan 2008.
49. Interview with Duncan Foley, New York, November 14, 2007.
50. Ackerman 2002, 124–125.
51. Fisher (1983, 4) provides this quote, attributing it to an "extremely prominent economist." When I interviewed him on November 28, 2007, he identified the economist as Friedman.
52. Greenspan 2000.
53. Fisher 1983, 11, and elsewhere: this is a central assumption in his model.

2. What Do Economists Do?

1. Samuelson and Nordhaus 1989, 10–11.
2. Nicholson 1989, 8.
3. Hannah Fairfield, "Metrics: Driving Shifts into Reverse," *New York Times*, May 2, 2010, BU 7 (print edition), gives a striking chart showing this relationship.
4. Elder 1993, 56.
5. Interview with David Colander, Middlebury, VT, June 21, 2008.
6. Lucas 2001, 4–5.
7. Kasper 2002, 131. Lucas 1987, 18, on "thought experiment."
8. Lucas 1987, 15.
9. Richard Parker, "Can Economists Save Economics?" *American Prospect*, Mar. 21, 1993.
10. Robert Kuttner, "Real-World Economist," *Washington Post*, Jan. 7, 1993.
11. Samuelson, cited in Kennedy 2008, 8.
12. Blanchard 2000, 1388.

13. Colander 2007, 230.
14. Blaug 2001, 145.

3. In Search of a Model

1. On Smith's job as customs inspector: Cannan 1976, xx.
2. Smith 1976, 1:273, on the use of the spinning wheel, a relatively recent invention.
3. Smith 1976, 1:8–9.
4. Smith 1976, 2:161, on spinners.
5. Smith 1976, 1:144.
6. Smith 1976, 1:133.
7. Smith 1976, 1:152–157. See Polanyi 1944, 87, on the meaning of "poor" through the nineteenth century.
8. Smith 1976, 1:493.
9. Dobb 1973, 56, concurs that Smith's principal argument was against mercantilism.
10. Smith 1976, 1:450.
11. Smith 1976, 1:456.
12. Smith 1976, 2:102.
13. Smith 1976, 2:54–58.
14. Smith considers this figure exaggerated but reports it.
15. Smith 1976, 2:161
16. Smith 1976, 2:161.
17. Smith 1976, 2:256–257.
18. Smith 1976, 2:146.
19. Smith 1976, 2:272.
20. Smith 1976, 2:277, on the way the East India Company exercised the right to make war or peace; 2:273 on its acquisition of Madras, Pondicherry, and Calcutta.
21. Smith 1976, 2:273–274. To reduce arithmetic in the text, I added up various categories of revenue.
22. Smith 1976, 2:274.
23. Smith 1976, 2:277.
24. Smith 1976, 2:276.
25. Smith 1976, 1:405.
26. Smith 1976, 1:387.

27. Smith 1976, 1:477.

28. Smith 1976, 1:32–33.

29. Smith 1976, 1:63. Meek 1967, 200–201, notes that the supply-and-demand story was already a conventional explanation of prices in Smith's day.

30. Smith 1976, 1:67.

31. Smith 1976, 1:65.

32. Smith 1976, 1:53.

33. Smith 1976, 1:34.

34. Smith 1976, 1:276; also (less elegantly) 1:58.

35. Smith 1976, 2:399–400.

36. Smith 1976, 1:112–117.

37. Smith 1976, 1:127.

38. Smith 1976, 1:124.

39. Smith 1976, 1:62.

40. Smith 1976, 1:161.

41. Heilbroner 1973 sees Smith's argument about growth and the steady state as Smith's central claim.

42. Smith 1976, 2:200.

43. Smith 1976, 1:88.

44. Smith 1976, 1:105

45. Smith 1976, 1:78.

46. Smith 1976, 1:98.

47. Smith 1976, 1:80.

48. Smith 1976, 1:107.

49. Smith 1976, 1:80–81.

50. Economists Intelligence Unit, CountryData, www.eiu.com (accessed Jun. 16, 2011). I compared wages in U.S. dollars at purchasing-power parity; the difference was twice as great ($2,006 for China versus $41,463 for the U.S.) if measured at the exchange rate.

51. Following Smith, I here implicitly assume Say's law, explained in the next chapter.

52. Chang 2002 discusses virtually all currently developed nations, and reaches this conclusion.

53. Smith 1976, 2:180.

54. Smith 1976, 2:165.

55. Smith 1976, 2:165.

56. Smith 1976, 2:177.
57. For more on U.S. industrial policies, see Chapter 11.
58. Smith 1976, 2:179.

4. Economics When Society Matters

1. Hilton 2006, 313–314.
2. Toynbee 1995, 33–34. Hilton 2006, 11, discusses the evidence showing that small-scale production remained extensive in the mid-nineteenth century.
3. Toynbee 1995, 33, says that from 1710 to 1760, 300,000 acres were enclosed, and from 1760 to 1843, nearly 7 million were enclosed.
4. Toynbee 1995, 33.
5. Hilton 2006, 3.
6. Hilton 2006, 576.
7. Hilton 2006, 574.
8. Toynbee 1995, 34.
9. Toynbee 1995, 35.
10. Ricardo 2005, 4:15.
11. I refer to the "Speenhamland" system. See Hilton 2006, 591–592; Polanyi 1944, 78.
12. Contemporary commentaries may have been based on grossly distorted data. See Blaug 1963; J. S. Taylor 1969.
13. Polanyi 1944, 79.
14. Polanyi 1944, 99, on the "promiscuity of the poorhouse"; 98 on "some terrible catastrophe."
15. Ricardo 2005, 1:106.
16. My notes about Ricardo's life are from the editors' introduction and the "Memoir of Ricardo" by his brother, in Ricardo 2005, vol. 10, *Biographical miscellany.*
17. Total reserves minus required reserves in June 2010 were $1,035,032,000. Federal Reserve, Board of Governors, "Table 1: Aggregate Reserves of Depository Institutions and the Monetary Base," online at www.federalreserve.gov/releases/h3/hist/h3hist1.txt (accessed Jul. 24, 2010).
18. In a modern version of Say's law, there can be a "general glut" in the short run.
19. Smith 1976, 1:301. Ricardo 2005, 1:290, explains the law, citing Say.

20. Marshall 1920, 421–422, recognizes that Ricardo saw wages as socially determined.

21. Ricardo 2005, 1:96–97. I added the italics to the phrase about the habits and customs of the people.

22. Senate Committee on Commerce, Science, and Transportation, hearing on S. 2467, GATT Implementing Legislation, October 4, 5, 13, 14, 17, and 18, and November 14 and 15, 1994. Dorgan made his during the November 15 hearing (page 483). Available online at www.archive.org/details/s2467gattimpleme00unit and from the U.S. Government Printing Office.

23. Louis Uchitelle, "Economic View: A Recovery for Profits, but Not for Workers," *New York Times*, Dec. 21, 2003.

24. Levy and Temin 2007.

25. Mandler 1999, 46–49, astutely points out that if neoclassical preferences are added to Sraffa's long-run Ricardian model, relative demand for goods can determine income distribution. However, he goes on to argue that, in a realistic Ricardian economy where prices may change from one period to the next, markets do not determine income distribution, just as Ricardo and Sraffa held.

26. Some mainstream macroeconomic models do allow for monopolistic industries.

27. Ricardo 2005, 1:12.

28. Ricardo 2005, vol. 1, ch. 4, "On Natural and Market Price." Neoclassical economists speak of the "interest rate," assumed to equal the return to capital in competitive markets; they use "profit" to mean a monopolistic return. I use "profit" in the classical economists' sense, as a normal return to capital in competitive markets.

29. Ricardo 2005, 1:46, explicitly includes mines.

30. I base my discussion of rent on Ricardo's chapter "On Rent." See Ricardo 2005, 1:69–70, for a brief statement.

31. Alternatively, Ricardo supposes that instead of exploiting, say, third-rate land, farmers develop more expensive techniques, such as using richer fertilizer, to exploit the same first- and second-rate land. As long as the difference between qualities of land persists, so do rents in an analogous fashion.

32. Ricardo 2005, 1:41.

33. Ricardo 2005, 1:21.
34. Marglin 1984, 112–113.
35. Taylor 2004, 45.
36. Ricardo 2005, 1:266.
37. Ricardo 2005, 1:71.
38. Nordhaus 1992, cited and summarized in Romer 2006, 38–42.
39. Nordhaus 1991, cited and summarized in Romer 2006, 44.
40. Ricardo 2005, 1:76.
41. Ricardo 2005, 1:40.
42. Hilton 2006, 8, notes that rents fell after the Napoleonic Wars, but less quickly than other prices. Thus, real rents rose.
43. Hilton 2006, 573–574, on real wages; Toynbee 1995, 35, on bread prices.
44. Ricardo 2005, 1:80. See also Dobb 1973, 259–260.
45. Ricardo 2005, 1:57.
46. On the topic of wages, Ricardo sometimes takes a contradictory tack that other classical economists often accepted. He proposes that high investment, hence high demand for labor, tends to raise real wages over a sustained period, but that workers do *not* become accustomed to increased wages. Rather, they have more children, until wages fall to their old level. Mandler 1999, 54, underlines serious problems with this argument.
47. Ricardo 2005, 1:95.

5. Chasing a Chimera

1. Dobb 1973, 138. Hodgskin 1825 repeatedly cites Ricardo.
2. All Hodgskin quotes from Hodgskin 1825. Hilton 2006, 345, identifies him as a former naval officer.
3. Hodgskin writes: "How much more labour a labourer must give to have a loaf of bread than that loaf costs, it is impossible for me to say. I should probably underrate it were I to state it at six times; or were I to say that the real cost of that loaf, for which the labourer must give sixpence, is one penny."
4. Hilton 2006, 20.
5. Hilton 2006, 616–617, on leaders' appeal to "workers" and the suggestion that they espoused a "proto-Marxian political economy" stressing the labor theory of value and economic exploitation.

6. Hilton 2006, 613.
7. Dobb 1973, 141, notes Marx's acknowledgment of the post-Ricardian socialists, particularly Hodgskin.
8. Dobb 1973, 152. Marx's discussion of his theory of value is spread across three volumes of *Capital,* the second and third of which he never even considered finished.
9. Many modern economists, such as Nicholson 1989, 10, say that Ricardo espoused a labor theory of value. As Stigler 1958 argues, not only did Ricardo not espouse the labor theory, but no one who believes he did can have even read his *Principles.*
10. Dobb 1973, 149.
11. Dobb 1973, 151.
12. Stigler 1958. The essay is actually about Ricardo.
13. For example, Marx 1909, 1:64, notes "the recent scientific discovery, that the products of labour, so far as they are values, are but material expressions of the human labour spent in their production." For the quotes about his critics, see Marx 1909, 1:153, note 32.
14. I have simplified the arithmetic from an example given in Ricardo 2005, 1:37.
15. Sraffa 1960 demonstrates this point generally.
16. Blaug 1985, 231–232, does the well-known algebra.
17. Meek 1967, 175.
18. I am also not persuaded by arguments for the labor theory of value in Foley 2006, which I otherwise consider important and largely persuasive book. Foley (2008) focuses on the issue in an article and also fails to persuade me.
19. There are special cases in which the labor theory works: for example, if the profit rate is 0 percent, or if capital intensity in all industries is the same—that is, if the ratio of capital to labor is the same in an oil refinery as in a garment sweatshop. These special cases do not apply to any plausible economy.

6. Utopia

1. Dobb 1973, 111–112, says that the group associated with Senior and Longfield opposed, above all, the Ricardian "stress on the antagonistic

relationship between wages and profit and between profit and rent . . .
which they regarded as socially dangerous and hence untenable."
 2. Cited by Dobb 1973, 98, unnumbered footnote.
 3. Blaug 1985, 304, counts nine economists in several countries, going back
    to 1834, who seized essentially on the same notions that Jevons, Walras,
    and Menger formalized in the 1870s.
 4. Quote from Meek 1967, 71. On Scrope's pamphlet writing and his seat
    in Parliament: Encyclopædia Britannica Online, "Scrope, George Julius
    Poulett (2010)," search.eb.com/eb/article-9066399 (accessed Jan. 30,
    2010). On his nickname: Peerage.org, "Scrope, George Poulett (1797–
    1876)," www.peerage.org/genealogy/george_poulett_scrope.htm (ac-
    cessed Jan. 30, 2010).
 5. On Longfield's positions: Encyclopædia Britannica Online, "Longfield,
    Mountifort (2010)," search.eb.com/eb/article-9104518 (accessed Jan. 30,
    2010). Quote about the wages of the laborer, as well as the quote about
    legislation or unions ("combination") causing only mischief, from Dobb
    1973, 108; see also his discussion on 107.
 6. Cited by Meek 1967, 69.
 7. For the quotation about value arising from the "pleasure" derived from a
    good: Jevons 1888b, 54.
 8. For the quotation about abstinence deserving remuneration: Jevons
    1988b, 233. Dobb 1973, 104, quotes Senior as saying, "Profit is the re-
    muneration of abstinence."
 9. Concerning Senior's notorious opposition to trade unionism: Dobb 1973,
    103. On his writing the Poor Law Reform of 1834: Encyclopædia
    Britannica Online, "Senior, Nassau William (2010)," search.eb.com/eb/
    article-9066765 (accessed Jan. 30, 2010). Polanyi (1944, 82) says of the
    Poor Law Reform, "Never perhaps in all modern history has a more ruth-
    less act of social reform been perpetrated."
10. Cited in Campus 1987, 320.
11. Wicksell 1977, 28.
12. Jevons 1888a, xiii.
13. Jevons 1888a, xiv.
14. Jevons 1888a, xv.
15. Jevons 1888b, 18.
16. Jevons 1888b, 18–19.

17. Jevons 1888a, xliii.
18. Jevons 1888a, xvi–xvii.
19. Stigler 1994, 1.
20. Stigler 1994, 11, Table 1.
21. Blaug 1985, 307.
22. Lionel Robbins 1977, x, wrote that "the system [Wicksell] constructed was not specifically his own but the system common to the best works of the past hundred years of economic theory. . . . There is no work in the whole range of modern economic literature which presents a clearer general view of the main significance and interrelations of the central propositions of economic analysis than these lectures."
23. Alan Ehrenhalt, "Keepers of the Dismal Faith," *New York Times*, Feb. 23, 1997.
24. Jevons 1888b, 14.
25. Becker 1993, 386.
26. See Mandler 1999, 79, for a statement along these lines. But this is not at all a controversial point.
27. Jevons 1888b, 44.
28. Wicksell 1977, 31.
29. Jevons 1888b, 14.
30. Wicksell 1977, 43ff., extends this example to markets with given prices.
31. Jevons 1888b, 11.
32. The early neoclassicals were ambivalent, sometimes seeming to reject the idea that utility is cardinal and other times adopting it in their calculations. Mandler 1999, 115, concludes that Alfred Marshall and William Jevons seem to have "believed in cardinality but not cardinal measurability"—that there exist cardinal units of utility but they cannot be measured—a hypothesis that is not a logical fallacy (111).
33. Blaug 1985, ch. 9, "Marshallian Economics: Utility and Demand," explains the matter well.
34. Blaug 1985, 308, confirms that Jevons never drew a demand curve. He mentions that supply-and-demand curves were drawn before Marshall, but Marshall derived them from utility theory in the form that economists have widely adopted.
35. Robbins 1977, x, makes this point.
36. Wicksell 1977, 55–57. He refers to commodities A and B, instead of to corn and chickens, but my treatment follows his in essentials.

37. Wicksell 1977, 52ff. Likewise Varian 1992, 152.
38. Wicksell 1977, 49–51.
39. Wicksell 1977, 65–67, lays out the mathematics defining an equilibrium, which, he realizes, need not be unique and can be unstable.
40. This result is well known, but, for example, see Nicholson 1989, 90, footnote 10.
41. Varian 1992, 153.
42. Stigler 1950b, 395–396.
43. Marshall 1920, 351.
44. Nicholson 1989, 197.
45. Romer 2006.
46. Jevons 1888b, 141.
47. Walras 1984, 256–257. Quote is from 256, qualifications from 257.
48. Ruskin 1885, 163.
49. Heilbroner 1980, 116.
50. Marx 1978b, 197 (the brackets are in the edition cited).
51. Walras 1984, 61.

7. This Imperfect World

1. Robert Kuttner, "Real-World Economist," *Washington Post,* Jan. 7, 1993.
2. "Unemployment" is not quite the right word to use in Lucas's case. His models suggest that voluntary decisions (even if possibly misinformed) cause situations in which a large portion of the labor force lacks employment.
3. Blanchard 2000, 1385, footnote 9.
4. Paul Krugman, "Driller Instinct," *New York Times,* Jun. 20, 2008, on Cheney's argument. U.S. Senate, "Senate Fact Sheet," Jun. 26, 2002, on the 670 percent price increase. Fact sheet on McCullough Research website, www.mresearch.com/pdfs/18.pdf (accessed Feb. 25, 2010).
5. Joskow and Kahn 2001. Joskow and Kahn wrote a series of similar reports, the first (see footnote 1 in the version cited) on November 22, 2000.
6. Taylor 2004, 67.
7. Polanyi 1944, 147.
8. Krugman 1990, particularly section 14.4.
9. Krugman 1990, 257.

10. Thomas Palley, June 4, 2007, "Challenging Orthodoxy, Part II: Rigor vs. Neo-classical Economics." Online at bookclub.tpmcafe .com/blog/bookclub/2007/jun/04/challenging_orthodoxy_part_ii_rigor _vs_neo_classical_economics (accessed Oct. 15, 2007).
11. Taylor 2004, 67–68.
12. Heilbroner 1980, 153.

8. Entering the Realm of Production

1. This account of the American strikes draws on Brecher 1972, 37–47.
2. On establishing Workers' Day to commemorate the Haymarket Riot and on Cleveland's response: "Workers' Day (2010)," Encyclopædia Britannica Online, search.eb.com/eb/article-9438716 (accessed May 12, 2010).
3. Stigler 1994, 297, on Clark's Christian socialist leanings in his early writings.
4. Clark 1899, 4.
5. Clark 1899, 4.
6. Clark 1899, 3.
7. Stigler 1994, 3.
8. The Arrow-Debreu model can assume Ricardian technologies and determine factor prices. But it determines them only if one assumes a truly long-run model, in which prices are set once and forever at the beginning of time. If prices are re-negotiated after production gets underway, factor prices are indeterminate. See Mandler 1999, 42, and much of ch. 2.
9. Stigler 1994, 3–4, noting that Walras also originally followed Ricardian distribution theory.
10. Stigler 1994, 39, footnote 1.
11. Actually, modern microeconomic theory rejects diminishing marginal utility and adopts alternative assumptions. But diminishing marginal productivity still reigns supreme in aggregate macroeconomic models.
12. Derrick Z. Jackson, "Income Gap Mentality," *Boston Globe*, Apr. 19, 2006.
13. Samuelson and Nordhaus 1989, 440.
14. The production function is assumed to be differentiable, but I don't emphasize this point, since I see it as mainly a mathematical convenience. The fundamental assumption is that there is a wide menu of choices.

15. Clark 1899, viii.
16. Thomas Palley, "Marginal Productivity Theory and the Mainstream," Jun. 7, 2007, www.thomaspalley.com/?p=81#more-81 (accessed Dec. 6, 2007).
17. Stigler 1994, 4; Campus 1987, 321.
18. Campus 1987, 321.
19. Keith Bradsher, "Thanks to Detroit, China Is Poised to Lead," *New York Times,* Mar. 12, 2006.
20. See, for example, Keith Bradsher, "General Motors Plans to Build New, Efficient Assembly Plants," *New York Times,* Aug. 6, 1998.
21. Shaiken 1990, 36–37.
22. Interview with Alejandro Flores, Electronic Data Systems (EDS), Mexico City, February 1, 2006.
23. Gerschenkron 1962, 9–10.
24. Warren P. Seering, "Who Said Robots Should Work Like People?" *Technology Review,* Apr. 1985.
25. John F. Krafcik, "A New Diet for U.S. Manufacturers," *Technology Review,* Jan. 1989.
26. Krafcik, "A New Diet for U.S. Manufacturers."
27. Chenery 1949, 514.
28. Chenery 1949, 517.
29. Chenery 1949, 522.
30. Chenery 1949, 528.
31. Chenery 1949, 528.
32. If output is Y, capital is K, and the labor force is L, then Y/K, the output-capital ratio, has been about constant over the long term in the United States (Taylor 2010, 179). With Y/K roughly constant, the capital-labor ratio K/L has grown at about the same rate as labor productivity, Y/L. Labor productivity growth from Council of Economic Advisors, *Economic Report of the President: 2010 Report,* Table B-49, "Productivity and related data, business and nonfarm business sectors, 1960–2009," www.gpoaccess.gov/eop/tables10.html (accessed May 24, 2010).
33. I adapt this argument from Paul David 1975.
34. Nicholson 1989, 638.
35. Wicksteed's example is in Stigler 1994, 48.
36. Stigler 1994, 67.
37. Douglas 1948, 5.

38. Clark 1899, 101.
39. Clark 1899, 249, 251.
40. Clark 1899, 120.
41. Clark 1899, 118.
42. Clark 1899, 124.
43. Samuelson 1966. He treats capital as time, a concept introduced by Ricardo and accepted by Wicksell and the Austrian branch of neoclassical economists.
44. Felipe and Fisher 2003, 211.
45. The value of capital can also be determined by the discounted value of production, but this approach, too, requires a known interest or profit rate.
46. Cohen and Harcourt 2003, 201–202.
47. Samuelson 1966.
48. Cohen and Harcourt 2003, 202.
49. This paragraph summarizes results reported in Felipe and Fisher 2003.
50. Felipe and Fisher 2003, 218.
51. Cited in Cohen and Harcourt 2003, 205.
52. Cohen and Harcourt 2003, 209.

9. What Caused Income Inequality?

1. Johnson 1997, 41.
2. Data from Piketty and Saez 2003, updated at www.econ.berkeley .edu/~saez/TabFig2008.xls, Table B-4 (accessed June 22, 2011). The precise ratios are 39 to 1 in 1970 and 1,039 to 1 in 2000.
3. Two classic papers—Katz and Murphy 1992, and Bound and Johnson 1992—use this approach, as does Johnson's 1997 survey.
4. Johnson 1997, 43.
5. Katz and Murphy 1992, 47.
6. Katz and Murphy, 1992, 76. This problem is also mentioned in Bound and Johnson 1992.
7. Bound and Johnson 1992, 377, set out the algebra of their model.
8. Bound and Johnson 1993, 378, footnote 10, argue that taking this sort of average has little effect on overall results. I'm not convinced by the footnote, since income inequality varies within industries.
9. Bound and Johnson 1992, 385.

10. The institutional variable that they incorporate, μ_{ij} (375–377), identifies only "rents" for wages of particular workers in particular industries.
11. Levy and Temin 2007, 2, 27.
12. Levy and Temin 2007, 12.
13. Levy and Temin 2007, 37.
14. Howell 2002, 7.
15. Gary S. Becker, "Why Europe Is Drowning in Joblessness," *Business Week*, April 8, 1996, cited in Howell 2002, 5.
16. Howell 2002, 8, 51, on the relation between income inequality and unemployment.
17. World Bank, World Development Indicators, data.worldbank.org/indicator (accessed June 11, 2010).
18. Economist Intelligence Unit, CountryData, www.eiu.com (accessed June 11, 2010). Data on Denmark are available only for the years 2000–2009.
19. Howell 2002, 9, 53 (figure 3a).
20. Howell 2002, 25, 58 (Figure 7); likewise Dew-Becker and Gordon 2005, 115. The same sources note that the late 1990s saw some amelioration of income inequality. This pattern is not controversial.
21. Dew-Becker and Gordon 2005, 119.
22. Bound and Johnson 1992, 383.
23. Dew-Becker and Gordon 2005, 117–118.
24. Dew-Becker and Gordon 2005, 119, but this is not controversial.
25. Dew-Becker and Gordon 2005, 122; Howell 2002 makes the same point.
26. See, for example, "A Cozy Arrangement," editorial page, *New York Times*, April 13, 2006, A26.
27. Goldin and Katz 2008, 106, Table 3.3.
28. See especially Goldin and Katz 2008, 120.
29. Goldin and Katz 2008, 297, Table 8.1. I round all numbers to one decimal point.
30. U.S. Census Bureau, CPS Historical Time Series Tables, Table A-1, "Years of School Completed by People 25 Years and Over, by Age and Sex: Selected Years, 1940 to 2010," www.census.gov/hhes/socdemo/education/data/cps/historical/index.html (accessed Jul. 20, 2011). Both my calculation and Goldin and Katz's calculation distribute workers with some college evenly between "college-educated" and "high-school-educated" categories. I compared the years 1950–1980 with the years

37. Romer 2006, ch. 1 (on the Solow model) and ch. 3 (on new growth theories).
38. Keynes 1953, 162.
39. Keynes 1953, 150.
40. Keynes 1953, 215–216.
41. Keynes 1953, 174.
42. Keynes 1953, 167.
43. Keynes 1953, 216.
44. Greenspan 2004.
45. Federal Reserve, Board of Governors, Table 1: "Aggregate Reserves of Depository Institutions and the Monetary Base," www.federalreserve .gov/releases/h3/hist/h3hist1.txt (accessed Jul. 24, 2010).
46. Data in this paragraph are from Bureau of Economic Analysis, Table 1.1.6: "Real Gross Domestic Product, Chained Dollars"; and from Table 2.1: "Personal Income and Its Disposition," both last revised Jun. 25, 2010, www.bea.gov/ (accessed Jul. 28, 2010). Real personal saving is not available from the BEA. I estimated it two ways: by figuring in current dollars (inflation was extremely low during this period); and by taking current personal saving as a percentage of current disposable income, then applying that percentage to real disposable income. The results differed very little and are entirely adequate for illustrative purposes.

11. In the Long Run

1. Musacchio, Vietor, and García-Cuéllar 2010.
2. Musacchio, Vietor, and García-Cuéllar 2010, 10.
3. Musacchio, Vietor, and García-Cuéllar 2010, 9.
4. OECD 2011, Figure 7.7.
5. OECD 2011, Figure 7.10.
6. OECD 2011, Table 4.13, Figure 7.21.
7. Musacchio, Vietor, and García-Cuéllar 2010, 12.
8. Musacchio, Vietor, and García-Cuéllar 2010, 12.
9. Musacchio, Vietor, and García-Cuéllar 2010, Exhibits 8 and 9.
10. Data from OECD 2011, Annex Table 1, "Real GDP"; Annex Table 5, "Real total gross fixed capital formation"; and Annex Table 12, "Labour

productivity in the total economy." I omitted 2009 and 2010, when the crisis hit developing nations. Including those years does not change relative performance.

11. World Economic Forum 2009, Table 4.

12. I summarize the Kaldor model based on Taylor 2004, 188–199.

13. Dore 1983 makes the sociological arguments about Japanese versus British factories. I may be making the macroeconomic argument about how cultural norms can affect aggregate investment more sharply than he did, but in an email communication on July 13, 2011, Dore found the interpretation not wrong.

14. Felipe and Fisher 2003, 208.

15. Felipe and Fisher 2003, 251.

16. Felipe and Fisher 2003, 251.

17. Mandler 1999, ch. 2, especially sections 2.7–2.9, shows that you can append demand to Sraffa's model, and suggests—to me—that such an aggregation *might* be possible. Mandler does not carry it out.

18. Samuelson and Nordhaus 1989, 291.

19. Keynes accepted the neoclassical production function in *The General Theory*, but it is an unnecessary complication, arguably a concession he made to neoclassicals to show that his argument works despite that conventional assumption. When the labor economists John Dunlop and Lorie Tarshis pointed out that the neoclassical production function conflicts with business-cycle data, Keynes said he was happy to drop it. His theory works, indeed more clearly, without it.

20. Arrow 2004, 293.

21. Some models that might be called neoclassical—for example, positing that an economy can land in good or bad equilibria—are exceptions to this rule.

22. Felipe and Fisher 2003, 248.

23. Taylor 2004, ch. 1, advocates this approach to macroeconomic modeling, but it is essentially the approach that nearly all macroeconomists used until the 1970s.

24. Interview with Michael Mandel, New York, May 8, 2008.

25. Solow 1956, 91–94.

26. Herbert A. Simon, "Rational Decision-Making in Business Organizations," Nobel Memorial Lecture, December 8, 1978. nobelprize

.org/nobel_prizes/economics/laureates/1978/simon-lecture.pdf (accessed Aug. 23, 2010).

27. Taylor 2004, 58, derives the Solow model along these lines. He also derives the neoclassical production function as an accounting for growth *over time,* but without any implication that you can substitute capital for labor at a given time. Felipe and McCombie 2003 do the same in a slightly different way.

28. I took figures from Dornbusch, Fischer, and Startz 2004, 55, and rounded to simplify the arithmetic.

29. Abramovitz 1993, 237.

30. Calculated from Wright 2006, "Table Cb28–31: Indexes of industrial production, 1884–2003."

31. David Leonhardt, "The Depression: If Only Things Were That Good," *New York Times,* Oct. 8, 2011, quotes Alexander J. Field to this effect.

32. Richard W. Stevenson, "Fed Chief Says New-Age Economy Can Have Old Problems," *New York Times,* Jun. 15, 1999.

33. Baily et al. 2000, 80.

34. Baily et al. 2000, 77.

35. National Bureau of Economic Research, "Business Cycle Expansions and Contractions," wwwdev.nber.org/cycles/cyclesmain.html (accessed Dec. 17, 2008).

36. Fair 2004, ch. 6.

37. Fair 2004, 97, and Figure 6.16a.

38. Romer 2006, 26–27.

39. Romer 2006, 26, calculates that GDP would be 2.5 percent higher after 17 years; hence the growth rate.

40. Romer 2006, 126.

41. Romer 2006, 138.

42. Romer 2006, 140.

43. Romer 2006, 28, 120, 145, 151–152.

44. Chang 2002.

45. Michael Wines, "China Fortifies State Businesses to Fuel Growth," *New York Times,* Aug. 29, 2010.

46. Chang 2002, 25.

47. Chang 2002, 26.

48. Chang 2002, 28–29.

49. Chang 2002, 17; World Bank 1991, 97.
50. Chang 2002, 29.
51. Smith 1985.
52. Total land area from Morison et al., 1977, 418–419. Land areas of Texas and Massachusetts from U.S. Census Bureau, State and County Quick Facts, quickfacts.census.gov/qfd/index.html (accessed Aug. 27, 2010).
53. On the army and the transistor, Misa 1985. On the integrated circuit, Ceruzzi 1998. On DARPA and the Internet, DARPA's website: www .darpa.mil/history.html (accessed Aug. 27, 2010).
54. March 1990; and MIT Commission on Industrial Productivity 1989, on the aircraft industry.
55. Quoted, for example, by José Luis Calva (an economist at the National University, UNAM), "Competitividad industrial," *El Universal,* Dec. 8, 2006.
56. Not a single growth model in Romer 2006, out of dozens detailed, meets this criterion.
57. Federal News Service, Hearing of the Senate Finance Committee (chaired by Senator Max Baucus), June 21, 2001, Washington, D.C.
58. Taylor 2010, 22, notes that Robinson coined the phrase.

12. In the Short Run

1. Bryce 1996, 42.
2. Bryce 1996, 44–45.
3. Bryce 1996, 44–45.
4. Samuelson 1946, 187–188.
5. Mankiw 1991, 3.
6. Samuelson 1996, 159.
7. Colander and Landreth 1996, 15, on Knight; Samuelson 1996, 157, on Henry Simons and the University of Chicago group who favored deficit spending. Dimand 1990 shows that they were in a small minority of the profession.
8. Quote from Samuelson 1996, 159.
9. Samuelson 1996, 160.
10. Colander and Landreth 1996, 21.
11. Colander and Landreth 1996, 12.

12. Colander and Landreth 1996, 8–9.

13. Tarshis 1996, 64.

14. Tarshis 1996, 68. On Hart's opposition to child labor laws and support for Franco: "Merwin K. Hart of Birch Society: Controversial Lawyer Was Head of Chapter Here, Target of Ickes," *New York Times*, Dec. 2, 1962.

15. Tarshis 1996, 69–70. The ellipsis is included only because in its place the text contains the word "page" in a way that doesn't make sense.

16. Samuelson 1996, 171.

17. Samuelson 1996, 171–172.

18. Samuelson 1996, 172.

19. Samuelson 1996, 172.

20. Samuelson 1996, 172.

21. Samuelson 1955, 360. Nearly all American Keynesians in the 1930s accepted this assumption, according to Colander and Landreth 1996, 24. The neoclassical synthesis of the 1950s and 1960s, as well as contemporary accounts such as Woodford 1999 and Blanchard 2008, certainly do.

22. I omit here the short-run Keynesian model of money supply and demand—the "LM" curve. Absent the bells and whistles it simply says that the central bank affects output by setting the short-term interest rate.

23. U.S. Census Bureau, 2011 Statistical Abstract, Table HS-36: Consumer and Gross Domestic Price Indexes, 1913 to 2002," and Table HS-32: "Gross Domestic Product in Current and Real (1996) Dollars, 1929 to 2002," www.census.gov/compendia/statab/hist_stats.html (accessed Jul. 8, 2011).

24. Taylor 2010, 24.

25. The story often involves a fall in the interest rate, but the gist is the same.

26. I adapt this example from Taylor 2010, 158–159.

27. Romer 2006, 264–266, explains several studies and concludes that the real wage is pro-cyclical (i.e., rises in a business upswing). Dornbusch and Fischer 1990, 502, say that evidence isn't very clear, but "certainly does not show that the real wage is consistently lower when output is higher."

28. Friedman 1968, 8–9.

29. Lucas 1996, 663.
30. Colander 1996, 7.
31. I take this description of the model largely from Romer 2006, 272–280. Lucas 1972 used an overlapping-generations model. Explaining it would require unhelpful complications.
32. Lucas 1987, 99, puts the dilemma in these terms.
33. Interview with Thomas Sargent, San Francisco, January 5, 2009.
34. Lucas 1996, 667–668.
35. Romer and Romer 1989; Romer 2006, 263–264, reports on a stronger and more sophisticated test.
36. For example, Woodford 1999, 25, says economists widely accept "the fact that productivity measures are strongly procyclical."
37. Bewley 1999, 18.
38. Bewley 1999, 400.
39. Ormerod 2009, 7.
40. Lucas 1996, 668.
41. Kydland and Prescott 1996, 82.
42. Taylor 2010, 236.
43. My description of these models is something of a composite. Romer 2006, ch. 2, describes the underlying Ramsey model; ch. 8 incorporates investment; chs. 4 and 6 discuss real-business-cycle and Keynesian DSGE variants. McCandless 2008 explains concepts and math clearly, step by step. Kydland and Prescott 1996, especially 77–78, summarize their approach succinctly. Clarida et al. 1999 present a version of the DSGE models actually used by central banks.
44. Solow 2007, 236.
45. Solow 2007, 235.
46. Lucas 1987.
47. Actually, DSGE models, based on the Ramsey model, have only "saddle-path" stability: See Romer 2006, 56–63. Try rolling a marble from the front to the back of a twisted saddle. If it falls off one side, in the model, consumption explodes, capital sinks to zero, the economy grinds to a halt. If it falls off the other side, capital explodes, and consumption sinks to zero. This is not a stable model in any plausible sense.
48. Clarida et al. 1999, 1662.
49. Ormerod 2009, 13.

50. N. Gregory Mankiw, "Economic View: But Have We Learned Enough?" *New York Times,* Oct. 26, 2008.
51. Romer and Bernstein 2009, Table 1.
52. Barro 2009, 3. The "multiplier" associated with peacetime government purchases, he estimates, is "statistically insignificantly different from zero."
53. Barro 2009, 2.
54. Economist Intelligence Unit, CountryData, www.eiu.com (accessed Feb. 11, 2011), on all government debt figures. I did not use OECD data, because they overstate U.S. debt by including the social-security liabilities of the United States but not those of most other countries. See OECD 2011, note to Annex Table 32.
55. Roscini and Schlefer, 2011, 4.

13. The Puzzle of the Golden Age of Capitalism

1. Growth data are from Maddison 2006, taken from 1950 to 1973, the conventional end of the Golden Age.
2. Consejo Nacional de Población (of the Mexican government), México en Cifras, Migración Internacional, Series Sobre Migración, Población Residente en Estados Unidos, Table 3.5.1, "Población de origen mexicano residente en Estados Unidos, 1900–2007," www.conapo.gob.mx (accessed Jul. 11, 2011).
3. For one example, see Dornbusch and Fischer 1990, 719: "Table 19-5 spotlights the cause of the worsened growth performance: In the 1970s average growth rates of productivity declined throughout the industrialized world."
4. "Two Trillion Dollars Is Missing; Why Is U.S. Prosperity Eroding? It's No Mystery," editorial, *New York Times,* Jan. 8, 1989.
5. Peter Passell, "What Counts Is Productivity and Productivity," *New York Times,* Dec. 13, 1992.
6. Baily et al. 1988, 415, Table 23.
7. Glyn et al. 1990, 91–92.
8. Piore and Sabel 1984, 79–81.
9. Douglas Martin, "Jude Wanniski, 69, Journalist Who Coined the Term 'Supply-Side Economics,' Dies," *New York Times,* Aug. 31, 2005.

10. On Wanniski's adopting the term "supply-side" from an attack on him by Herbert Stein, see Alan Reynolds, 2007, "What Supply-Side Economics Means," Creators Syndicate, www.creators.com/opinion/alan-reynolds/what-supply-side-economics-means.html (accessed Sep. 7, 2010).

11. Quotes from Wanniski on capital gains from Jude Wanniski, "Capital Gains in a Supply-Side Model," Statement before the Committee on Finance, United States Senate, 104th Congress, First session, Feb. 15, 1995.

12. On Wanniski's grandfather giving him a copy of *Capital:* Martin, "Jude Wanniski, 69." On Wanniski's emphasis on reviving classical theory: Jude Wanniski, "Learning Supply-side," Polyconomics Institute, Nov. 27, 1996. www.polyconomics.com/ssu/ssu-961127.htm (accessed Sep. 7, 2010).

13. Taylor 2004, 134.

14. Taylor 2004, 1.

15. Taylor borrowed the term from Latin American economists of the 1960s and 1970s who called themselves "structuralist," although his use of the word is rather different from theirs.

16. URPE website, www.urpe.org/about/history.html (accessed Sep. 6, 2010).

17. Epstein 2004.

18. See Taylor 2004, 176–177. Kaldor's growth model also assumes full employment (Taylor 2004, 188–189).

19. See Taylor 2004, 173–178. If you assume full employment, the structuralist model is "overdetermined." You have to drop either social determination of the wage or the independent investment function.

20. Schomburg Center for Research in Black Culture, New York Public Library, 2010, "In Motion: African American Migration Experience, The Second Great Migration," www.inmotionaame.org/migrations/topic.cfm?migration=9&topic=1 (accessed Sep. 9, 2010).

21. Comisión Nacional de Población, www.conapo.gob.mx (accessed Jul. 11, 2011).

22. The U.N. International Labour Organization reported that 54 percent of Mexican nonagricultural workers are in the informal sector. "Women and Men in the Informal Economy: A Statistical Picture" (Geneva: ILO, 2002).

23. Distinguishing the wage share from the profit share is a very rough busi-

ness. The U.S. national income and product accounts (NIPA) do separate flows of income, including "corporate profits" and "wage and salary accruals." Unfortunately, the megasalaries of top CEOs, reported on W-2 forms, are lumped together with those of people one might more usually think of as workers. However, if some of these megasalaries were indeed moved into the profit share beginning in the 1970s, that fact would only strengthen the arguments in this chapter.

24. On wage-led versus profit-led models, see Taylor 2004, 125–129 and 173–176.
25. Katzenstein 1985.
26. World Bank, World Development Indicators, "Exports of goods and services (percent of GDP)," databank.worldbank.org (accessed Jul. 22, 2011).
27. Taylor 2004, 125–129 and 173–176.
28. Taylor 2010, 186.
29. Taylor 2004, 177.
30. Taylor 2004, 178.
31. Piore 1981, 7.
32. Piore 1981, 20.
33. Piore and Sabel 1984, 73. They preface this statement by stating that it was Keynes's argument, but they clearly accept it. They later say they have argued that "the crisis of the last decades is a crisis of underconsumption" (1984, 252).
34. Piore and Sabel 1984, 103.
35. The fact that the CEA set such benchmarks is from Dornbusch and Fischer 1990, 442.
36. Piore and Sabel 1984, 74.
37. Piore and Sabel 1984, 252, speak of "the saturation of core markets for consumer durables."
38. Piore and Sabel 1984, 184–189.
39. Piore and Sabel 1984, 187.
40. Piore and Sabel 1984, 184.
41. Piore and Sabel 1984, 178.
42. Piore and Sabel 1984, 193.
43. Marglin and Bhaduri 1990. I have simplified their model and used different terms. Marglin and Bhaduri call an economy "stagnationist" if a

higher wage share increases current output and employment, "exhilarationist" if a higher profit share increases current output and profits. They then make a further distinction. An economy is stagnationist and "cooperative" if a higher wage share not only increases current output and employment but also increases long-run growth. (I call this type of economy "wage-led" or "cooperative Keynesian.") They call an economy stagnationist and "conflictual" if a higher wage share increases current output and employment but reduces long-run growth. Analogously, an exhilarationist economy can be either cooperative or conflictual. I call all exhilarationist economies "profit-led."

44. It is possible that Glyn et al. 1990 saw the economy as profit-led throughout.

45. Piore and Sabel 1984 discuss these events but do not emphasize them as part of their model.

46. Piore and Sabel 1984, 101. They do not ignore the suppression of labor militancy in the late 1940s, but the *Golden Age* essays describe it as playing a more central role in shaping the economic regime.

47. Glyn et al. 1990, 54, 68; Marglin 1990, 5 (the introduction, consistent with Marglin and Bhaduri 1990).

48. Marglin and Bhaduri 1990, 182, Table 4.4.

49. Marglin and Bhaduri 1990, 174–175.

50. Marglin and Bhaduri 1990, 175–176, actually see the economy as initially turning stagnationist but conflictual, then turning exhilarationist, or (in my term) profit-led. I doubt that their fine distinctions, depending on curves that change shape and shift position, could ever really be identified.

51. Taylor 2004, 286–292, presents a statistical estimate concluding that the U.S. economy was profit-led in this era.

52. Marglin and Bhaduri 1990, 173.

53. Marglin and Bhaduri 1990, 182, Table 4.4.

54. Marglin and Bhaduri 1990, 178, Table 4.1.

55. Glyn et al. 1990, 78–79, Table 2.11. There are slightly different data for averages weighted by the size of the economy in Table 2.12, but they tell the same story.

56. Walton 1985, 77–78, cited in Glyn et al. 1990, 89.

57. Glyn et al. 1990, 89.

58. Glyn et al. 1990. 94–95.
59. If the model was wage-led but conflictual, output would rise but growth would still decline.
60. Marglin and Bhaduri 1990, 180. Reducing the profit share in a conflictual wage-led model, by lowering the profit rate, does lower growth.
61. For a short-run structuralist model, see Taylor 2004, chapter 4, particularly 124–129. On the way it translates into a long-run model, see Taylor 2004, ch. 5, esp. 173–182.
62. Robert B. Reich, "How to End the Great Recession," *New York Times,* Sept. 3, 2010, A-19.

14. Economies in Crisis

1. Interview with Truman Bewley, November 13, 2008.
2. Stock and Watson 2003. They originally gave their paper at a conference on April 5–6, 2002, and they refer to studies that were published in 1999 and 2000.
3. Baily et al. 2000, 77–78.
4. NASDAQ Composite Index, Global Financial Data, www.globalfinancialdata.com (accessed Jul. 24, 2011).
5. Romer 2006, 56–63, describes saddle-path instability. He does not say it is really no stability at all.
6. Stock and Watson 2003, 162.
7. See, for example, Wynne Godley, Dimitri B. Papadimitriou, Greg Hannsgen, and Gennario Zezza, "Strategic Analysis: The U.S. Economy: Is There a Way Out of the Woods?" Levy Economics Institute of Bard College (Annandale-on-Hudson, NY), November 2007; and Wynne Godley, "Imbalances Looking for a Policy," Policy Note 2005/4, Levy Economics Institute of Bard College.
8. Dean Baker, "The Housing Bubble Fact Sheet," *Issue Brief,* Washington: Center for Economic and Policy Research, July 2005.
9. Roubini and Setser 2005, 5.
10. Diamond and Dybvig 1983. Sargent described to me both the Diamond and Dybvig model and the Kareken and Wallace model discussed in this chapter; I borrow some analogies from him. My discussion is also based on a reading of their articles.
11. Diamond and Dybvig 1983, 410, 417.

12. Diamond and Dybvig 1983, 404.
13. Kareken and Wallace 1978.
14. Paulson claimed that a legal technicality prevented him from bailing out Lehman, but few outsiders took that claim seriously.
15. Taylor 2010, 198.
16. Minsky 1982.
17. Minsky 1982, 24.
18. For example, Edmund L. Andrews, "Fed Seeks a Delicate Balance as Investors Clamor for Action," *New York Times*, Aug. 22, 2007.
19. Taylor 2004, 281–283, describes the basic model, along with its initial application by Goodwin. See also Hoppensteadt 2006, and Chisholm et al. 2005.
20. On these applications: Hoppensteadt 2006.
21. Chisholm et al. 2005.
22. Taylor 2011, 14–17.
23. Shadow Trader, video weekly, Feb. 24, 2008, www.shadowtrader.net/videos/sunday022408st.html (accessed Oct. 19, 2010).
24. Fair 2002.
25. It still could be that, even though real investment is unstable in isolation, some other factor prevents it from soaring uncontrollably.
26. This relationship would not follow if U.S. firms were issuing large amounts of stock, but firms were buying back stock (Taylor 2011, 16).
27. Casey Mulligan, "An Economy You Can Bank On," *New York Times*. Oct. 10, 2008.
28. Barbosa's full name is Nelson Barbosa Filho ("Filho" meaning "Junior"). I omit "Filho" to avoid confusion.
29. "Proprietor's income"—the income of unincorporated businesses—is significant in the United States, but standard data allocate it, as accurately as possible, between profits and wages.
30. Federal Reserve, Statistical Release G.17, Industrial Production and Capacity Utilization, October 18, 2010, www.federalreserve.gov/releases/g17/Current/g17.pdf (accessed Nov. 4, 2010).
31. Taylor 2011, Table 1. Alternatively, other variables such as the interest rate might stabilize both capacity utilization and the wage share, in what would amount to a higher-dimensional predator-prey model.
32. This explanation is adapted from Taylor 2010, 189–190.
33. Taylor 2004, 286–292, reports results from 1948 through 2002. Barbosa

and Taylor 2006 report much the same results. Rezai and Taylor 2010 report results through the second quarter of 2008.

34. I am comparing results from Taylor 2004, 291, with those of Rezai and Taylor 2010, Table 1.
35. Taylor 2010, Figure 5.5, on the wage share. The argument in this paragraph and the next is based in good part on Taylor 2010, 208–212.
36. Taylor 2010, 201.
37. Ghilarducci et al. 2008.
38. Ghilarducci et al. 2008, 21, on the Acela.
39. On internet coverage: Internet World Stats, 2011, List of Countries Classified by Internet Penetration Rates. www.internetworldstats.com/list4.htm (accessed Jun. 28, 2011).
40. Milberg 2008, 11, on broadband coverage and on Obama's and McCain's support for infrastructure investment.

15. Thinking about Economies

1. I paraphrase Bewley's summary (1999, 3). The paper is Lucas and Rapping 1969. Rapping subsequently changed his mind about the approach to economics adopted in this article.
2. Bewley 1999, 3, 5.
3. Bewley 1999, 242.
4. Bewley 1999, 241.
5. Bewley 1999, 6. As Bewley notes, if the assumptions of the "shirking" theory were correct, it would explain why wages are set above market levels but would not explain why they don't fall. No matter; the theory is sometimes proposed to explain why wages don't fall.
6. Bewley 1999, 113.
7. Bewley 1999, 129.
8. Bewley 1999, 115.
9. Bewley 1999, 431.
10. Bewley 1999, 432.
11. Bewley 1999, 438.
12. Bewley 1999, 7.
13. Santa Fe Institute, 2011, History of the Santa Fe Institute (unclear when the history was most recently updated), www.santafe.edu/about/history (accessed Jul. 15, 2011).
14. Arthur, Durlauf, and Lane 1997, 3–4; and Kirman 2008.

15. My description of the model is taken entirely from Arthur, Holland, LeBaron, Palmer, and Tayler 1997.
16. The model has trading periods; I call them "days" just for concreteness.
17. Arthur, Holland, LeBaron, Palmer, and Tayler 1997, 28 and Appendix A.
18. Sargent 2007 repeatedly uses this phrase to describe rational expectations. (I have not cited a shorter version of the same paper from the *American Economic Review,* 2008, 98.1: 5–37, since it omits interesting points.)
19. Evans and Honkapohja 2005, 4.
20. Sargent raises this question in Evans and Honkapohja 2005, referring specifically to "God's model."
21. Sargent 2007, 28–31.
22. Sargent 2007, 30.
23. Sargent 2007, 31–32. Sargent does not name the specific factors I mentioned, but simply notes that shocks other than monetary policies could have caused inflation.
24. Romer 2006, 14. The italics are his.
25. Friedman 1953, 14–15.
26. Spanos 1986, cited in Kennedy 2008, 8.
27. Minsky 1975, 16.
28. Solow 1956, 65.
29. Wicksell 1977, 9.
30. Cohen and Harcourt 2003, 205. Mandler's argument (1999, 67 and elsewhere) weighing assumptions about the definition of "rationality" asks if the definition captures what we really mean by the term.
31. Lucas 1987, 53.
32. In June 2010, total reserves minus required reserves were $1,035,032,000. Federal Reserve, Board of Governors, Table 1: "Aggregate Reserves of Depository Institutions and the Monetary Base," www.federalreserve.gov/releases/h3/hist/h3hist1.txt (accessed Jul. 24, 2010).
33. I borrow the term "essential features" from Cohen and Harcourt 2003, 205.
34. Harberger 1959, 135.
35. Shapiro and Tayler 1990, 865.
36. Shapiro and Tayler 1990, 864.
37. Encyclopædia Britannica, 2010, "Ockham's Razor," www.search.eb.com/eb/article-9056716 (accessed Jul. 25, 2010).

of the president. Washington, DC: United States Government Printing Office.

Barbosa-Filho, Nelson H., and Lance Taylor. 2006. Distributive and demand cycles in the us economy—A structuralist Goodwin model. *Metroeconomica* 57.3: 389–411

Barnett, William A. 2004. An interview with Paul A. Samuelson. *Macroeconomic Dynamics* 8: 519–542.

Barro, Robert J. 2009. Demand side voodoo economics. *Economists' Voice* 6:2. Online at www.bepress.com/ev/vol6/iss2/art5 (accessed Nov. 25, 2009).

Becker, Gary S. 1976. *The economic approach to human behavior.* Chicago: University of Chicago Press.

Becker, Gary S. 1993. The economic way of looking at behavior. *Journal of Political Economy* 101.3: 385–409.

Bernanke, Ben S. 2002. On Milton Friedman's ninetieth birthday. Remarks at the conference to honor Milton Friedman, University of Chicago, Chicago, Illinois (Nov. 8). Online at www.federalreserve.gov/boarddocs/speeches/2002/20021108/default.htm (accessed Feb. 12, 2010).

Bewley, Truman F. 1999. *Why wages don't fall during a recession.* Cambridge, MA: Harvard University Press.

Blanchard, Olivier Jean. 2000. What do we know about macroeconomics that Fisher and Wicksell did not? *Quarterly Journal of Economics,* 115.4: 1375–1409.

Blanchard, Olivier Jean. 2008. Neoclassical synthesis. In *The new Palgrave dictionary of economics online,* ed. Steven N. Durlauf and Lawrence E. Blume, 2nd ed. Palgrave Macmillan. At www.dictionaryofeconomics.com/article?id=pde2008_N000041 (accessed Jul. 24, 2011).

Blaug, Mark. 1963. The myth of the old poor law and the making of the new. *Journal of Economic History* 23.2: 151–184.

Blaug, Mark. 1985. *Economic theory in retrospect,* 4th ed. Cambridge: Cambridge University Press.

Blaug, Mark. 2001. No history of ideas, please, we're economists. *Journal of Economic Perspectives* 15.1: 145–164.

Bound, John, and George Johnson. 1992. Changes in the structure of wages in the 1980s: An evaluation of alternative explanations. *American Economic Review* 82.3: 371–392.

Brecher, Jeremy. 1972. *Strike!* Boston: South End Press.

Bryce, Robert. 1996. Interview. In *The coming of Keynesianism to America:*

Conversations with the founders of Keynesian economics, ed. David C. Colander and Harry Landreth. Cheltenham, UK: Edward Elgar.

Calomiris, Charles W. 2008. Banking crises. In *The new Palgrave dictionary of economics online,* ed. Steven N. Durlauf and Lawrence E. Blume, 2nd ed. Palgrave Macmillan. At www.dictionaryofeconomics.com/article?id= pde2008_B000051 (accessed Jun. 14, 2009).

Campus, Antonietta. 1987. Marginalist economics. In *The new Palgrave: A dictionary of economics,* ed. John Eatwell, Murray Milgate, and Peter Newman, vol. 3. London: Macmillan.

Cannan, Edwin. 1976. Editor's introduction. In Adam Smith, *An inquiry into the nature and causes of the wealth of nations,* ed. Edwin Cannan. Chicago: University of Chicago Press.

Ceruzzi, Paul. 1998. *A history of modern computing.* Cambridge, MA: MIT Press.

Chang, Ha-Joon. 2002. The Stiglitz contribution. *Challenge* 45.2: 77–96.

Chenery, Hollis B. 1949. Engineering production functions. *Quarterly Journal of Economics.* 63.4: 507–531.

Chisholm, Penny, Graham Walker, Julia Khodor, and Michelle Mischke. 2005. 7.014 Introductory Biology, spring 2005. Massachusetts Institute of Technology: MIT OpenCourseWare. Online at ocw.mit.edu (accessed Aug. 20, 2010).

Clarida, Richard, Jordi Galí, and Mark Gertler. 1999. The science of monetary policy: A new Keynesian perspective. *Journal of Economic Literature* 37.4: 1661–1707.

Clark, John Bates. 1899. The Distribution of Wealth: A Theory of Wages, Interest and Profits. London: Macmillan. Online at books.google.com.

Cohen, Avi J., and G. C. Harcourt. 2003. Retrospectives: Whatever happened to the Cambridge capital theory controversies? *Journal of Economic Perspectives* 17.1: 199–214.

Colander, David. 1996. Overview. In *Beyond microfoundations: Post Walrasian macroeconomics,* ed. David Colander. Cambridge: Cambridge University Press.

Colander, David. 2006. *The stories economists tell: Essays on the art of teaching economics.* Boston: McGraw-Hill Irwin.

Colander, David. 2007. *The making of an economist, redux.* Princeton: Princeton University Press.

Colander, David, Richard P. F. Holt, and J. Barkley Rosser, Jr. 2004. *The changing face of economics: Conversations with cutting edge economists.* Ann Arbor: University of Michigan Press.

Colander, David, and Harry Landreth. 1996. Introduction. In *The coming of Keynesianism to America: Conversations with the founders of Keynesian economics,* ed. David C. Colander and Harry Landreth. Cheltenham, UK: Edward Elgar.

Constantinides, George M., Milton Harris, and René M. Stulz. 2003. Preface. In *Financial markets and asset pricing,* ed. George M. Constantinides, Milton Harris, and René M. Stulz. Vol. 1, part 2 of *Handbook of the economics of finance,* 1st ed. Amsterdam: Elsevier/North-Holland.

Córdoba, José. 1994. Mexico. In *The political economy of policy reform,* ed. John Williamson. Washington, DC: Institute for International Economics.

David, Paul A. 1975. Concepts and preconceptions. In *Technical choice, innovation and economic growth: Essays on American and British experience in the nineteenth century,* ed. Paul A. David, 19–91. Cambridge: Cambridge University Press.

Dew-Becker, Ian, and Robert J. Gordon. 2005. Where did the productivity growth go? Inflation dynamics and the distribution of income. NBER Working Paper 11842, National Bureau of Economic Research, Cambridge, MA.

Diamond, Douglas W., and Philip H. Dybvig. 1983. Bank runs, deposit insurance, and liquidity. *Journal of Political Economy* 91.3: 401–419.

Dimand, Robert W. 1990. The New Economics and American Economists in the 1930s Reconsidered. *Atlantic Economic Journal* 18.4: 42–47.

Dobb, Maurice. 1973. *Theories of value and distribution since Adam Smith: Ideology and economic theory.* Cambridge: Cambridge University Press.

Dore, Ronald. 1983. Goodwill and the spirit of market capitalism. *British Journal of Sociology* 34.4: 459–482.

Dornbusch, Rudiger, and Stanley Fischer. 1990. *Macroeconomics,* 5th ed. New York: McGraw Hill.

Dornbusch, Rudiger, Stanley Fischer, and Richard Startz. 2004. *Macroeconomics,* 9th ed. New Delhi: Tata McGraw Hill.

Douglas, Paul H. 1948. Are there laws of production? *American Economic Review* 38.1: 1–41.

Dutt, Amitava K. 1984. Stagnation, income distribution, and monopoly power. *Cambridge Journal of Economics* 8.1: 25–40.

Edlin, Aaron S., and Dwight M. Jaffee. 2009. Show me the money. *Economists'*

Voice 6.4: 1–5. Online at www.bepress.com/ev/vol6/iss4/art8 (accessed Jul. 19, 2010).

Eichengreen, Barry. 2010. The last temptation of risk. *The National Interest* (March). Online at nationalinterest.org/article/the-last-temptation-of-risk -3091 (accessed Nov. 14, 2010).

Elder, Alexander. 1993. *Trading for a living*. Hoboken, NJ: John Wiley and Sons.

Ellis, Diane. 1998. The effect of consumer interest-rate deregulation on credit-card volumes, charge-offs, and the personal bankruptcy rate. *Bank Trends* 98–05 (March). Washington, DC: Federal Deposit Insurance Corporation.

Epstein, Gerald. 2004. Review of *Reconstructing macroeconomics: Structuralist proposals and critiques of the mainstream. Challenge* 47.5: 116–122.

Evans, George W., and Seppo Honkapohja. 2005. An interview with Thomas J. Sargent. *Macroeconomic Dynamics* 9: 561–583.

Fair, Ray C. 2004. Estimating how the macroeconomy works. Cambridge, MA: Harvard University Press.

Fair, Ray C. 2002. Events that shook the market. *Journal of Business* 75.4: 713–731.

Felipe, Jesus, and Franklin M. Fisher. 2003. Aggregation in production functions: What applied economists should know. *Metroeconomica* 54.2&3: 208–262.

Felipe, Jesus, and J. S. L. McCombie. 2003. Cambridge capital controversies (response to Cohen and Harcourt 2003). *Journal of Political Perspectives* 17:4 (fall), 230.

Fisher, Franklin M. 1983. *Disequilibrium foundations of equilibrium economics*. Cambridge: Cambridge University Press.

Foley, Duncan K. 2006. *Adam's fallacy: A guide to economic theology*. Cambridge, MA: Harvard University Press.

Foley, Duncan K. 2008. The long-period method and Marx's theory of value. Department of Economics, New School for Social Research (June 25).

Friedman, Milton. 1953. The methodology of positive economics. In Milton Friedman, *Essays in positive economics*, 3–43. Chicago: University of Chicago Press.

Friedman, Milton. 1968. The role of monetary policy. *American Economic Review* 58.1: 1–17

Geanakoplos, John. 1989. Arrow-Debreu model of general equilibrium. In *The new Palgrave: General equilibrium,* ed. John Eatwell, Murray Milgate, and Peter Newman, 43–61. London: Macmillan.

Gerschenkron, Alexander. 1962. *Economic backwardness in historical perspective.* Cambridge, MA: Harvard University Press.

Ghilarducci, Teresa, Michelle Holder, Jeff Madrick, Nikolaos Papanikolaou, and Jonathan Schlefer. 2008. Infrastructure for America's economy: Evaluating the evidence. In Schwartz Center for Economic Policy Analysis, *The promise of public investment.* New York: The New School.

Glyn, Andrew, Alan Hughes, Alain Piepitz, and Ajit Singh. 1990. The rise and fall of the Golden Age. In *The golden age of capitalism,* ed. Stephen A. Marglin and Juliet B. Schor. Oxford: Clarendon Press.

Goldin, Claudia, and Lawrence F. Katz. 2008. The Race between Education and Technology. Cambridge, MA: Harvard University Press.

Gordon, Robert J., and Ian Dew-Becker. 2007. Unsettled issues in the rise of American inequality. PowerPoint from paper presented at Realistic Growth Policy for Our Times: A Conference in Memory of David Gordon, New School, New York City, April 13.

Greenspan, Alan. 2000. Technology and the economy. Remarks at the Economic Club of New York, New York (January 13). Online at www.federal reserve.gov/boarddocs/speeches/2000/200001132.htm (accessed Nov. 16, 2010).

Greenspan, Alan. 2004. Risk and uncertainty in monetary policy. Remarks at the Meetings of the American Economic Association, San Diego, Jan. 3. Online at www.federalreserve.gov/BoardDocs/Speeches/2004/20040103/ default.htm (accessed Apr. 4, 2008).

Greenspan, Alan. 2008. A response to my critics. *Economists' Forum,* FT.com (April 6). Online at blogs.ft.com/economistsforum/2008/04/alan-greenspan -a-response-to-my-critics (accessed Feb. 13, 2010).

Hahn, Frank. 1984. *Equilibrium and macroeconomics.* Oxford: Basil Blackwell.

Harberger, Arnold C. 1959. The fundamentals of economic progress in underdeveloped countries: Using the resources at hand more effectively. *American Economic Review, Papers and Proceedings* 49.2: 134–146.

Heilbroner, Robert L. 1973. The paradox of progress: Decline and decay in *The Wealth of Nations. Journal of the History of Ideas* 34.2: 243–262.

Heilbroner, Robert L. 1980. *The worldly philosophers: The lives, times, and ideas of the great economic thinkers.* New York: Simon and Schuster.

Hilton, Boyd. 2006. *A mad, bad, and dangerous people? England, 1783–1846.* Oxford: Oxford University Press.

Hodgskin, Thomas. 1825. Labour defended against the claims of capital: Or the unproductiveness of capital proved with reference to the present combinations amongst journeymen. Online version: New Haven: Yale Law School, The Avalon Project. Online at avalon.law.yale.edu/19th_century/labdef.asp (accessed May 18, 2009).

Hoppensteadt, Frank. 2006. Predator-prey model. *Scholarpedia* 1.10: 1563 (accepted: Oct. 16, 2006).

Howell, David R. 2002. Increasing earnings inequality and unemployment in developed countries: Markets, institutions and the "unified theory." Working Paper 2002–01, Schwartz Center for Economic Policy Analysis, The New School, New York.

Jevons, William Stanley. 1888a. Preface to the second edition (1879). In William Stanley Jevons, *The theory of political economy*, 3rd ed. London: Macmillan. Available online through Liberty Fund, Indianapolis, at files. libertyfund.org (accessed Jan. 14, 2010).

Jevons, William Stanley. 1888b. *The theory of political economy*, 3rd ed. London: Macmillan. Available online through Liberty Fund, Indianapolis, at files. libertyfund.org (accessed Jan. 14, 2010).

Johnson, George E. 1997. Changes in earnings inequality: The role of demand shifts. *Journal of Economic Perspectives* 11.2: 41–54.

Joskow, Paul, and Edward Kahn. 2001. Identifying the exercise of market power: Refining the estimates. Cambridge, MA: Harvard Electricity Policy Group, Harvard Kennedy School. Available at www.hks.harvard.edu/hepg/ Papers/kahn-joskow%20market%20power%207-5-01.PDF (accessed Feb. 25, 2010).

Kareken, John H., and Neil Wallace. 1978. Deposit insurance and bank regulation: A partial-equilibrium exposition. *Journal of Business* 51.3: 413–438.

Kasper, Sherryl Davis. 2002. *The revival of laissez-faire in American macroeconomic theory: A case study of the pioneers.* Northampton, MA: Edward Elgar.

Katz, Lawrence F., and Kevin M. Murphy. 1992. Changes in relative wages, 1963–1987: Supply and demand factors. *Quarterly Journal of Economics* 107.1: 35–78.

Katzenstein, Peter J. 1985. *Small states in world markets: Industrial policy in Europe.* Ithaca: Cornell University Press.

Kennedy, Peter. 2008. *A guide to econometrics,* 6th ed. Oxford: Blackwell.

Keynes, John Maynard. 1937. The general theory of employment. *Quarterly Journal of Economics* 51.2: 209–223.

Keynes, John Maynard. 1953. *The general theory of employment, interest, and money.* New York: Harcourt Brace Jovanovich.

Kindleberger, Charles P. 1989. *Manias, panics, and crashes: A history of financial crises.* New York: Basic Books.

Kirman, Alan. 2008. Economy as a complex system. In *The new Palgrave dictionary of economics online,* 2nd ed., ed. Steven N. Durlauf and Lawrence E. Blume. Palgrave Macmillan. Online at www.dictionaryofeconomics.com/article?id=pde2008_E000246 (accessed Jan. 23, 2011).

Krueger, Anne O. 1974. The political economy of the rentseeking society. *American Economic Review* 64.3: 291–303.

Krugman, Paul R. 1990. Industrial organization and international trade. In Paul Krugman, *Rethinking international trade.* Cambridge, MA: MIT Press.

Kydland, Finn E., and Edward C. Prescott. 1996. The computational experiment: An econometric tool. *Journal of Economic Perspectives* 10.1: 69–85.

Lequiller, François, and Derek Blades. 2006. *Understanding national accounts.* Paris: Organisation for Economic Co-Operation and Development. Online at www.oecd.org/dataoecd/37/12/38451313.pdf (accessed Jun. 17, 2010).

Levy, Frank, and Peter Temin. 2007. Inequality and institutions in 20th-century America. NBER Working Paper 13106, National Bureau of Economic Research, Cambridge, MA.

Lucas, Robert E., Jr. 1972. Expectations and the neutrality of money. *Journal of Economic Theory* 4.2: 103–124.

Lucas, Robert E., Jr. 1987. *Models of business cycles.* Oxford: Basil Blackwell.

Lucas, Robert E., Jr. 1996. Nobel lecture: Monetary neutrality. *Journal of Political Economy* 104.4: 661–682.

Lucas, Robert E., Jr. 2001. Professional memoir. Lecture given in the Nobel Economists Lecture Series at Trinity University, San Antonio, TX (April 5). Online at home.uchicago.edu/~sogrodow/homepage/memoir.pdf (accessed Nov. 24, 2008).

Lucas, Robert E., Jr. 2003. Macroeconomic priorities. *American Economic Review* 93.1: 1–14.

Lucas, Robert E., Jr., and Leonard A. Rapping. 1969. Real wages, employment, and inflation. *Journal of Political Economy* 77.5: 721–754.

Maddison, Angus. 2006. *A millennial perspective,* vol. 1 of *The world economy.* Paris: Development Centre of the Organisation for Economic Co-Operation and Development.

Mandler, Michael. 1999. *Dilemmas in economic theory: Persisting foundational problems of microeconomics.* Oxford: Oxford University Press.

Mankiw, N. Gregory. 1991. The reincarnation of Keynesian economics. NBER Working Paper 3885, National Bureau of Economic Research, Cambridge, MA.

Mankiw, N. Gregory. 2006. The macroeconomist as scientist and engineer. *Journal of Economic Perspectives* 20.4: 29–46.

March, Artemis. 1990. The future of the U.S. aircraft industry. *Technology Review* (Jan.), 26–36.

Marglin, Stephen A. 1984. *Growth, distribution, and prices.* Cambridge, MA: Harvard University Press.

Marglin, Stephen A. 1990. Lessons of the golden age: An overview. In *The Golden Age of Capitalism*, ed. Stephen A. Marglin and Juliet B. Schor. Oxford: Clarendon Press.

Marglin, Stephen A., and Amit Bhaduri. 1990. Profit squeeze and Keynesian theory. In *The Golden Age of Capitalism*, Stephen A. Marglin and Juliet B. Schor. Oxford: Clarendon Press.

Marshall, Alfred. 1920. *Principles of economics*, 8th ed. Philadelphia: Porcupine Press.

Marx, Karl. 1909. *Capital: A critique of political economy.* Chicago: Charles H. Kerr. Available online through Liberty Fund, Indianapolis, at oll.libertyfund .org (accessed Nov. 7, 2009).

Marx, Karl. 1978a. Capital, vol. 1. In *The Marx-Engels Reader*, 2nd ed., ed. Robert C. Tucker. New York: W. W. Norton.

Marx, Karl. 1978b. The German ideology. In *The Marx-Engels Reader*, 2nd ed., ed. Robert C. Tucker. New York: W. W. Norton.

McCandless, George. 2008. *The ABCs of RBCs: An introduction to dynamic macroeconomic models.* Cambridge, MA: Harvard University Press.

McCloskey, Deirdre. 2004. Interview. In *The changing face of economics: Conversations with cutting-edge economists*, ed. David Colander, Richard P. F. Holt, and J. Barkley Rosser. Ann Arbor: University of Michigan Press.

Meek, Ronald L. 1967. *Economics and ideology and other essays: Studies in the development of economic thought.* London: Chapman and Hall.

Milberg, William. 2008. It's not the budget deficit, stupid. In Schwartz Center for Economic Policy Analysis, *The promise of public investment.* New York: The New School.

Minsky, Hyman P. 1975. *John Maynard Keynes.* New York: Columbia University Press.

Minksy, Hyman P. 1982. The financial-instability hypothesis: Capitalist processes and the behavior of the economy. In *Financial crises: Theory, history, and policy,* ed. Charles P. Kindleberger and Jean-Pierre Laffargue. Cambridge: Cambridge University Press.

Misa, Thomas J. 1985. Military needs, commercial realities, and the development of the transistor, 1948–1958. In *Military enterprise and technological change,* ed. Merritt Roe Smith, 253–287. Cambridge, MA: MIT Press.

MIT Commission on Industrial Productivity. 1989. The US commercial aircraft industry and its foreign competitors. Paper prepared by Artemis March. In *Working papers of the MIT Commission on Industrial Productivity,* vol. 1. Cambridge, MA: MIT Press.

Morison, Samuel Eliot, Henry Steele Commager, and William E. Leuchtenburg. 1977. *A concise history of the American republic.* New York: Oxford University Press.

Musacchio, Aldo, and Jonathan Schlefer. 2010. Sherritt goes to Cuba (A): Political risk in unchartered territory. Harvard Business School case 711–001 (Sep. 17).

Musacchio, Aldo, Richard H. K. Vietor, and Regina García-Cuéllar. 2010. Mexico: Crisis and Competitiveness. Harvard Business School case 710–058 (revised June 30).

Nicholson, Walter. 1989. *Microeconomic theory: Basic principles and extensions,* 4th ed. Chicago: Dryden Press.

Nordhaus, William D. 1991. To slow or not to slow: The economics of the greenhouse effect. *Economic Journal* 101: 920–937.

Nordhaus, William D. 1992. Lethal model 2: The limits to growth revisited. *Brookings Papers on Economics Activity* 2: 1–43.

Organisation for Economic Co-operation and Development. 2011. *OECD Economic Outlook,* vol. 2011, issue 1, no. 89.

Ormerod, Paul. 2009. The current crisis and the culpability of macroeconomic theory. Paper presented to the Annual General Meeting of the British Academy of Social Sciences, London. Version cited is dated Oct. 2009. Online at www.paulormerod.com (accessed May 5, 2010).

Pasinetti, Luigi L. 1974. *Growth and income distribution: Essays in economic theory.* London: Cambridge University Press.

Piketty, Thomas, and Emanual Saez. 2003. Income inequality in the United States, 1913–1998. *Quarterly Journal of Economics* 118.1.

Piore, Michael J. 1981. The theory of macro-economic regulation and the current economic crisis in the United States. MIT Working Paper (July), MIT, Cambridge, MA.

Piore, Michael J., and Charles F. Sabel. 1984. *The second industrial divide: Possibilities for prosperity.* New York: Basic Books.

Polanyi, Karl. 1944. *The great transformation: The political and economic origins of our time.* Boston: Beacon Press.

Rezai, Armon, and Lance Taylor. 2010. Business cycles in real and monetary terms. Draft. Schwartz Center for Economic Policy Analysis, the New School, New York.

Ricardo, David. 2005. *The works and correspondence of David Ricardo,* ed. Piero Sraffa with the collaboration of M. H. Dobb. Available online (from the 1973 edition published by Cambridge University Press) through Liberty Fund, Indianapolis, at oll.libertyfund.org/title/265 (accessed Sep. 28, 2009).

Robbins, Lionel. 1936. The place of Jevons in the history of economic thought. *Manchester School* 7.1: 1–17.

Robbins, Lionel. 1977. Introduction. In *Lectures on Political Economy,* vol. 1: *General Theory,* ed. Knut Wicksell. Fairfield, NJ: Augustus M. Kelly.

Romer, Christina, and Jared Bernstein. The job impact of the American Recovery and Reinvestment Plan. Jan. 9, 2009. Online at otrans.3cdn.net/ 45593e8ecbd339d074_l3m6bt1te.pdf. (accessed Nov. 26, 2009).

Romer, Christina D., and David H. Romer. 1989. Does monetary policy matter? A new test in the spirit of Friedman and Schwartz. *NBER Macro-economics Annual* 4: 121–170.

Romer, David. 2006. *Advanced macroeconomics,* 3rd ed. Boston: McGraw-Hill/ Irwin.

Roubini, Nouriel, and Brad Setser. 2005. Will the Bretton Woods 2 regime unravel soon? The risk of a hard landing in 2005–2006. Paper presented at symposium on the Revived Bretton Woods System: A New Paradigm for Asian Development? organized by the Federal Reserve Bank of San Francisco and the University of California at Berkeley, San Francisco, Feb. 4.

Roscini, Dante, and Jonathan Schlefer. 2011. How government debt accumu-lates. Harvard Business School Note 711-087 (April).

Rowthorn, Robert E. 1982. Demand, real wages, and economic growth. *Studi Economici* 18: 2–53.

Ruskin, John. 1885. *The stones of Venice: The sea stories,* vol. 2. New York: John B. Alden.

Samuelson, Paul A. 1946. Lord Keynes and the General Theory. *Econometrica* 14.3: 187–200.

Samuelson, Paul A. 1955. *Economics: An introductory analysis*, 3rd ed. New York: McGraw-Hill.

Samuelson, Paul A. 1966. A summing up. *Quarterly Journal of Economics* 80.4: 568–583.

Samuelson, Paul A. 1996. Interview. In *The coming of Keynesianism to America: Conversations with the founders of Keynesian economics*, ed. David C. Colander and Harry Landreth. Cheltenham, UK: Edward Elgar.

Samuelson, Paul A., and William D. Nordhaus. 1989. *Economics*, 13th ed. New York: McGraw-Hill.

Sargent, Thomas J. 2007. Evolution and intelligent design. Presidential address delivered at the American Economic Association, January 5, 2008, New Orleans (version dated Sept. 21, 2007). Online at www.econ.northwestern .edu/seminars/Nemmers07/Sargent.pdf (accessed Sept. 3, 2010).

Scarf, Herbert. 1960. Some examples of global instability of the competitive equilibrium. *International Economic Review* 1.3: 157–172.

Schlefer, Jonathan. 2008. *Palace politics: How the ruling party brought crisis to Mexico*. Austin: University of Texas Press.

Shaiken, Harley. 1990. *Mexico in the global economy: High technology and work organization in export industries*. Monograph Series, 33. San Diego: Center for U.S.-Mexican Studies.

Shapiro, Helen, and Lance Taylor. 1990. The state and industrial strategy. *World Development* 18.6: 861–878.

Skidelsky, Robert. 1986. *John Maynard Keynes*, vol. 1: *Hopes betrayed, 1883–1920*. New York: Viking.

Skidelsky, Robert. 1992. *John Maynard Keynes*, vol. 2: *The economist as saviour, 1920–1937*. New York: Penguin.

Smith, Adam. 1976. *An inquiry into the nature and causes of the wealth of nations*, ed. Edwin Cannan. Chicago: University of Chicago Press.

Smith, Merritt Roe. 1985. Army ordnance and the "American System" of manufacturing, 1815–1861. In *Military enterprise and technological change*, ed. Merritt Roe Smith, 39–86. Cambridge, MA: MIT Press.

Solow, Robert M. 1956. A contribution to the theory of economic growth. *Quarterly Journal of Economics* 70.1: 65–94.

Solow, Robert M. 2000. Toward a macroeconomics of the medium run. *Journal of Economic Perspectives* 14.1: 151–158

Solow, Robert M. 2007. Reflections on the survey. In David Colander, *The making of an economist, redux*. Princeton: Princeton University Press.

Spanos, Aris. 1986. *Statistical foundations of econometric modelling.* Cambridge: Cambridge University Press.

Sraffa, Piero, 1960. *Production of commodities by means of commodities: Prelude to a critique of economic theory.* Cambridge: Cambridge University Press.

Stigler, George J. 1958. Ricardo and the 93% labor theory of value. *American Economic Review* 48.3: 357–367.

Stigler, George J. 1994. *Production and distribution theories.* New Brunswick, N.J.: Transaction.

Stock, James H., and Mark W. Watson. 2003. Has the business cycle changed and why? In *NBER Macroeconomics Annual 2002,* vol. 17, ed. Mark Gertler and Kenneth Rogoff. Cambridge, MA: MIT Press. Online at www.nber.org/chapters/c11075 (accessed July 12, 2011).

Tarshis, Lorie. 1996. Interview. In *The coming of Keynesianism to America: Conversations with the founders of Keynesian economics,* ed. David C. Colander and Harry Landreth. Cheltenham, UK: Edward Elgar.

Taylor, James Stephen. 1969. The mythology of the old poor law. *Journal of Economic History* 29.2: 292–297.

Taylor, Lance. 1988. *Varieties of stabilization experience.* Oxford: Clarendon Press.

Taylor, Lance. 2004. *Reconstructing macroeconomics: Structuralist proposals and critiques of the mainstream.* Cambridge, MA: Harvard University Press.

Taylor, Lance. 2010. *Maynard's revenge: The collapse of free market economics.* Cambridge, MA: Harvard University Press.

Taylor, Lance. 2011. Growth, cycles, asset prices and finance. *Metroeconomica.* Onlinelibrary.wiley.com/doi/10.1111/j.1467-999X.2010.04117.x/full. First published online March 7.

Toye, John. 2008. Financial structure and economic development. In *The new Palgrave dictionary of economics online,* 2nd ed., ed. Steven N. Durlauf and Lawrence E. Blume. Palgrave Macmillan. Online at www.dictionaryof economics.com/article?id=pde2008_F000104 (accessed June 14, 2009).

Toynbee, Arnold. 1995. The chief features of the industrial revolution. In *Classic readings in economics,* ed. David Colander and Harry Landreth, 31–35. New Haven, VT: MaxiPress.

Varian, Hal R. 1992. *Microeconomic analysis,* 3rd ed. New York: W. W. Norton.

Walras, Léon. 1984. *Elements of pure economics, or, the theory of social wealth,* trans. William Jaffé. Philadelphia: Orion Editions.

Walton, Richard E. 1985. From control to commitment in the workplace.

Harvard Business Review (March).Wicksell, Knut. 1977. *Lectures on political economy*, vol. 1: *General theory.* Fairfield, NJ: Augustus M. Kelly.

Williamson, John. 1994. In search of a manual for technopols. In *The political economy of policy reform*, ed. John Williamson, 9–48. Washington, DC: Institute for International Economics.

Williamson, John, and Molly Mahar. 1998. A survey of financial liberalization. Essays in International Finance, no. 211. Princeton: Princeton University Department of Economics.

Woodford, Michael. 1999. Revolution and evolution in twentieth-century macroeconomics. Paper presented at conference on Frontiers of the Mind in the Twenty-First Century, Library of Congress, Washington, DC, June 14–18. Online at www.columbia.edu/~mw2230/macro20C.pdf (accessed Feb. 6, 2010).

World Economic Forum. 2009. *The Global Competitiveness Report, 2009–2010.* Geneva.

World Bank. 1991. *The world development report 1991: The challenge of development.* Oxford: Oxford University Press.

World Bank. 2005. *Economic growth in the 1990s: Learning from a decade of reform.* Washington, DC: World Bank.

Wright, Gavin. 2006. Indexes of national productivity, by sector and type of input: 1929–1970. In *Historical statistics of the United States, earliest times to the present: Millennial edition*, ed. Susan B. Carter, Scott Sigmund Gartner, Michael R. Haines, Alan L. Olmstead, Richard Sutch, and Gavin Wright. New York: Cambridge University Press. Online at hsus.cambridge.org (accessed April 6, 2009).

Index

and unemployment, 157; Lehman
Brothers collapse, 162, 203, 244,
313n14; Federal Reserve during, 162,
244; as unpredicted, 240–241; and
Minsky, 245–247; and Barbosa-
Taylor model, 250, 255–258; and
Friedman's *Monetary History of the
United States*, 275–276
Fine tuning of economy, 15–16, 142,
189, 193, 214
Finland, 127
Fiscal expansion, 199
Fiscal stimulus, 174
Fischer, Stanley, 156, 157, 308n3
Fisher, Franklin, 174, 286n51; on model
stability, 14, 20–21, 285n37; on gross
substitutes, 15; *Disequilibrium Foun-
dations of Equilibrium Economics*, 21;
general-equilibrium model of, 21,
242, 279, 286n53; on aggregate quan-
tities, 118–119, 170, 171
Fixed point theorem, 12, 14
Foley, Duncan, 19, 292n18
Ford Motor Co.: Chongqing, China,
plant, 107; River Rouge plant, 107
France, 95, 139–140, 230; Revolution,
46, 280
Free trade, 48, 76, 188, 275; NAFTA,
110, 186, 278–279
Frei, Eduardo, 221
Friedman, Milton, 25, 198, 284n15,
286n51; on monetary policies, 8, 16,
20, 199, 240, 275–276; on Federal
Reserve and Great Depression, 8, 16,
20, 285n29; *Monetary History of the
United States*, 8, 204, 275–276; on
economic stability, 20; on markets as
self-regulating, 20; permanent-
income hypothesis, 156–158, 163;

on expansion of money supply, 199;
on Federal Reserve and inflation, 199;
on inflation, 199–200; on natural rate
of unemployment, 200; on assumptions as unrealistic, 274–275; "The
Methodology of Positive Economics,"
274–275; on predictions, 274–275
Full employment, 59–60, 136, 227,
309nn18,19; in neoclassical economics, 222, 223, 224
Fundamental value of financial assets,
251
Future, the: fear of, 52, 159, 161, 162,
199, 243, 244, 273, 278; as fundamentally uncertain, 98; probability estimates regarding, 152–153, 154, 159,
202, 203, 212. *See also* Uncertainty
about future

Galbraith, James, 16
Galí, Jordi, "The Science of Monetary
Policy," 210–211
Garn-St. Germain Act, 5
GDP (gross domestic product), 146,
163, 174, 180, 212, 256; profits as
percentage of, 53–54, 234; vs. net domestic product, 146; GDP deflator,
196; and sovereign debt, 213; imports
as percentage of, 230; household debt
as percentage of, 259; trade as percentage of, 260; and free trade, 278–279
Geanakoplos, John, 285n35
General equilibrium models, 17–21,
200; and invisible hand, 8–11, 13, 14,
15, 20, 21–22, 23, 239; Arrow-Debreu model, 9, 11–15, 17, 20–21, 89,
157, 170, 204, 242, 267, 279, 296n8;
auctioneer in, 12–14, 21, 285n37;
DSGE models, 17–18, 58, 89, 117,

38–39, 42–44, 55–56, 90, 288n29; on value, 38–41; on capitalism, 39; on land/natural resources, 39; on natural rents, 39, 40–41; on natural profits, 39, 40–42; on labor theory of value, 39, 68, 70–71; on natural wages, 39–42, 53, 259; on special privileges, 41; on China, 42–43; on investment, 42–44; on consumption vs. production, 45; on natural rights, 47
Smoot-Hawley tariffs, 184, 188
Snow, John, 104–105
Social capital, 168, 181
Social convention: relationship to wages, 32, 39–40, 53–54, 56, 58, 60, 61, 63, 64, 65, 73, 90, 132, 171–172, 222, 223, 259, 261, 290n20, 309n19; Smith on, 32, 41–42, 43, 53, 56, 259; Ricardo on, 32, 53–54, 58, 61, 73, 222, 223, 290n20; Keynes on, 155–156, 161–162, 173; in structuralist economics, 220, 225
Social determination of wages: by convention, 32, 39–40, 53–54, 60, 61, 63, 64, 65, 68, 73, 90, 132, 134, 171–172, 222, 223, 259, 290n20, 309n19; by class struggle, 32, 73, 222; role of markets in, 54; by bargaining, 114, 132
Solow, Robert, 119, 211, 214; on hospital wages, 135–136; on Keynes, 143; on Say's law, 175; on DSGE model, 209–210; "A Contribution to the Theory of Economic Growth," 276; on assumptions and reality, 276, 278
Solow growth model, 216, 304n27; accumulation of capital in, 119–120; labor in, 119–120, 168, 175–176; total-factor productivity in, 119–120,

168–169, 176, 177, 180–181, 182, 182–183, 206, 207; investment and saving in, 168, 175–176, 177, 180; technology in, 168–169, 175, 178, 180, 181, 182–183; as growth accounting framework, 175–176; pragmatic version of, 175–176, 182–183; Solow residual, 177, 180–181, 182–183, 206, 207; neoclassical version of, 177–181, 182
South Korea, 183
Spanish colonialism, 34–35
Spanos, Aris: on econometric tests, 275; *Statistical Foundations of Econometric Modeling,* 275
Speculation, 13, 22, 23, 26, 173, 208
Speculative firms, 245
Speenhamland system, 289n11
Spencer, Herbert, 75
Sraffa, Piero, 50, 58, 59, 290n25, 292n15, 303n17; on standard commodity, 171; on wages, 171–172
Stability, economic, 3, 8–9, 20, 90–91, 241, 253, 258, 285n37, 286n46; as saddle-path stability, 239–240, 307n47, 312n5
Stagnation, economic, 17, 310n43, 311n50
Standard commodity, Sraffa on, 171
Standard & Poor's, 153
State of nature, 11–12
Statistical mechanics, 268
Sticky prices. *See* Price rigidity
Sticky wages. *See* Wage rigidity
Stigler, George, 292n9, 296n9; "93 Percent Labor Theory of Value," 68–69; on neoclassical economics, 76, 77, 101–102, 103; on market demand curve, 88

United Kingdom *(continued)*
with Portugal, 35, 44; textile industry,
35, 44–45, 46–47, 62; trading companies established by, 35–36; British colonialism, 36, 41, 44, 287n20; Industrial Revolution in, 46–47; enclosures
in, 47, 49, 56, 289n3; Corn Laws, 48–
49, 50, 76; Reform Act of 1832, 67;
Cambridge (UK)–Cambridge (US)
debates, 116–118; income inequality
in, 126–129; relations with United
States, 139, 140; Bank of England,
140; investment in, 169–170, 303n13;
industrial policies, 183–184; currency
crash of 1992, 227; unemployment in,
231
United States: income inequality in, 4,
54, 126–133, 237, 299n20; financial
deregulation in, 6–8; housing market
in, 23, 154, 158, 163, 240–241, 259;
economic conditions in, 43–44, 45,
127–128, 177–178, 178–180, 215,
216, 223–224, 229–231, 233, 241,
256–260, 297n32; vs. China, 43–44,
261; railroads in, 45, 184; trade policies, 45, 184; cash reserves of banks
in, 51–52, 150, 161, 277, 301n17;
industrial policies, 96, 183–186;
Knights of Labor, 99; May 1, 1886,
strike, 99, 100; Haymarket Riot, 99–
100; Cambridge (UK)–Cambridge
(US) debates, 116–118; unions in,
124, 125–126, 133–135, 226, 231,
232; vs. Europe, 126–128, 135–136,
261; trade deficits, 127, 163; unemployment in, 127–128, 223–224, 231;
economic productivity in, 128; executive income in, 129, 261; education
in, 129–133, 136; New Deal, 133,

134; National Labor Relations Act,
133–134; Chamber of Commerce,
134, 136; wages in, 134–135, 136,
176, 217, 220, 232, 233, 259, 313n29;
relations with United Kingdom, 139,
140; saving in, 157–158, 162, 163,
180, 302n46; vs. Mexico, 165–167,
180, 181, 215, 216, 261; profits in,
176, 234, 311n51, 313n29; during
Great Depression, 177–178, 229, 233;
productivity in, 177–179, 206, 216–
217, 297n32; New Economy of late
1990s, 178–180; stock market in,
179–180; Civil War, 184; War of
1812, 184; tariff policies, 184, 188;
Postal Service, 185; relations with
China, 188; anti-Communism in,
191–192, 232; sovereign debt in, 213–
214, 308n54; economic growth in,
215; middle class in, 215, 216; migrants from Mexico in, 215, 216, 223,
224; foreign investment in, 216; poverty in, 216; Great Migration of African Americans, 224; trade expansion,
230, 235; Hollywood blacklist, 232;
Marshall Plan, 232; budget deficit,
240; Treasury Department, 244; business cycles in, 256–257; infrastructure
in, 261; national income and product
accounts (NIPA), 310n23; proprietor's income in, 313n29. *See also*
Federal Reserve
United Steel Workers, 126
University of Chicago economists, 6,
127, 152, 158, 278, 284n15, 305n7
University of Massachusetts, Economics
Department, 221
University of Michigan economists, 220
Utilitarianism, 78